OH SHIT!
I'M OVER 50 AND SINGLE

A Guide for Mature Men and the Women They Date

P A Brook

Oh Shit! I'm Over 50 and Single, A Guide for Mature Men and the Women They Date

Copyright © 2017 by P A Brook

All rights reserved. No part of this publication may be reproduced, distributed, or transmitted in any form or by any means, including photocopying, recording, or other electronic or mechanical methods, without the prior written permission of the publisher, except in the case of brief quotations embodied in critical reviews and certain other noncommercial uses permitted by copyright law.

For permission requests: https://pabrook.com/

Ordering Information: https://pabrook.com/

Editing by The Pro Book Editor

Design by Indie Author Publishing Services

ISBN: 978-0-9984304-1-6

    Main category—Family & Relationships>Dating
    Other category—Humor>Men, Women & Relationships

Printed in the United States of America

First Edition

CONTENTS

NOTE FROM THE AUTHOR 1

GETTING READY 7

    Chapter 1:
    Welcome to 50
    (Oh Shit) 9

    Chapter 2:
    Are You Ready to Date?
    (Don't Worry Too Much, Neither is She) 23

    Chapter 3:
    Dating in the 21st Century
    (AKA Online Dating) 39

    Chapter 4:
    Dating Ladies in Their 40s, 50s, or 60s?
    (Or Yikes! Their 30s) 57

    Chapter 5:
    Sprechen Sie Deutsch?
    (Meeting Foreign Women) 79

    Chapter 6
    The "Who" and the "What"
    (Things Are Not Always as They Appear) 101

ON THE DATE 111

    Chapter 7:
    Diary of a Serial Dater
    (Where the Ego Meets the Wallet...And Wins) 113

    Chapter 8:
    Dating...the Old Fashioned Way
    (Blind Dates, Church Socials, and Bars, Oh My!) 129

Chapter 9:
To V or Not to V
(Where Not Enough Men Have Gone Before) **149**

Chapter 10:
The Approach
*(How to Maximize Your Very Minimal Chance
to Get a Response)* **159**

Chapter 11:
After the First Date
*(Do I Really Have to Learn How to
Make Hospital Corners?)* **171**

THE NEXT LEVEL **183**

Chapter 12:
So Now You're Dating
*(Somewhere Between a Rock and a
Hard Place...and Heaven)* **185**

Chapter 13:
Toys
(Not Your Grandfather's Choo-Choo Train) **199**

Chapter 14:
Dating Tips for Women From a Man's Point of View
*(We Do Love You Ladies, Even If Your Profiles
Are Too Long)* **211**

Chapter 15:
You Can't Make This Shit Up
(Dating Stories from the Front Lines) **229**

Chapter 16:
It's an Uphill Battle
*(But It's Good Exercise and There's Light at
the Top of the Rabbit Hole)* **249**

Meet the Author **257**

NOTE FROM THE AUTHOR

When I broke up with the woman I thought was going to be my next wife, I had some time on my hands. Well, really, she broke up with me. I decided to take a break from dating and obsessing over women, so I had *lots* of free time. I wondered, if I had no prospects of ever having another woman in my life, what would I do to occupy my time and feel good about myself? As things evolved, I became engaged with online poker and trading stocks, and even fantasized about making a career out of one or the other. Fortunately, I realized that I sucked at both. So I took them up as hobbies instead and decided to try writing a book.

Let's see how this goes.

So this is a man's guide to dating in his 50s. Not a woman's guide. Or is it? What is good for the gander is often good for the goose, so much of the wisdom imparted on my male brethren will be helpful to women as well. And if you ladies want some insight into what makes a single 50-year-old male tick, reading this book will be well worth your time.

Warning: you may not like what you read.

We all share the same stories, just from different perspectives. Just like a woman's perspective has helped me, mine should help her. But, this is not a course in sensitivity training. I deal in truths and hate bullshit. I speak frankly and don't worry about being politically correct.

If you want PC, watch *Oprah* reruns.

I don't profess to have the final say on anything—just sharing my thoughts and experiences on suddenly being alone and then regrouping to hopefully save some of you undue trouble.

I know, what self-respecting man *or woman* is going to take advice about dating from someone who has no medical license attached to his name. But that is exactly the point. I write from personal experience and an openness that defies most men. I want to be happy, and I want you to be happy. I may not always be right, but I always will give you my thoughtful best. You too are 50+ and wondering what is next. Work on healing yourself, and understand that your potential mate is trying to do the same. There is a lot of subconscious shit going on that neither of you will be able to figure out right away. My objectiveness can help.

There was a lot of introspection in writing this book. I had to figure out why my two marriages didn't work and how to do it better next time. And there was a lot of dating. A lot. Sometimes it was frivolous, sometimes serious. There was a lot of laughter and fun, as well as some heartache. I took it all in and made progress. My shrink bills can attest to that. Hopefully, you will learn something here about yourself and the woman you are trying to find. And she, something about you. Maybe you'll even have some fun along the way.

I have put forth my perceptions of women and how men should deal with them. Men are as different at this age as women are. Yet, neither of us really recognizes that. Empathy breeds compassion, which breeds understanding. At the end of each chapter there is a section titled "The Other Side" where I share my thoughts on how that chapter applies for women, and how they should deal with men. The goal is to provide insight into how we tick to maybe make your dating journey a little easier.

I would like to thank each and every woman that I have ever dated, whether long or impressively short-term. Every single one was worthwhile. Even the "one-daters" were rewarding. Eye-opening to something about myself or something about women in general. I have found that I enjoy the company of women more than many men, even just as friends.

Why?

Because the affection of a woman, more so than anything else, has helped me deal with my significant insecurities. Unfortunately, I discovered this late in life, leaving a wake of busted relationships and women scratching their heads about who the fuck it was they just invested months (years) in.

In the early going, there was no such thing as a female friend. I was a teenaged nerd, and girls were there to dream about and maybe date. Maybe. I was far too nerdy to finish that sentence with "maybe screw." Then, in my junior year of college, all that changed.

My dorm at Rutgers was co-ed. I fantasized that every other room was occupied by two young, nubile, nymphomaniac women. And while they were young and nubile, they saw me as their nerdy little brother, not a potential fuck buddy.

Witness Phyllis and Brenda, who lived three doors down from me. One weekend I was in desperate need of a date because my best friend had a tough week and his girlfriend convinced me that we had to take him out. Knock, knock. Hoping for Phyllis, Brenda answered. (Why Phyllis? She looked like a librarian. I can handle librarian. Brenda was the hottest chick on the floor. I couldn't handle fire.) Staring tongue tied at Brenda's breasts, I went for it anyway. I explained the situation and asked her if she was free. I almost fainted when she was.

When I returned to pick her up for the double date, she opened her door wearing hot pants, spaghetti strap heels, and a purple silk shirt with cleavage to her navel. Holy shit. My friend lived an hour away. I had no idea what we were going to talk about on the drive, or how I was going to keep my eyes on the road. But guess what—she was just a normal 20-year-old dealing with life and college just like me. Except she was wrapped in an exceptional package. It turned out that we had fun talking on the way, and actually had things in common. I knew we'd never date, but I enjoyed the conversation.

What's this all about? We got to my friend's house and his father opened the door. Oops. He worked with my dad and I was supposed to be at school studying for an exam. This could turn ugly.

It did.

The four of us went out to a dance club and I was on the dance floor with my scantily-clad date when my best friend tapped me on the shoulder. "Don't turn around, but your dad is here."

My worst nightmare. I could never get away with shit with my dad. I was sure I was going to die from embarrassment when he lectured me in front of the hottest chick in New Jersey. But he didn't. He bought us a round. One of my better "father moments." One of my only "father moments."

Brenda and I had a good time, but the night ended without even a kiss. We didn't travel in the same social circles and this created the first entry in my Wow-I-Can-Be-Friends-With-A-Girl file.

I ended up best friends with the librarian.

I also wish to thank my sister who has provided me balance and perspective, and a kick in the ass when needed, especially during my most recent bachelorhood.

Finally, I would like to thank my wife. Well, my future wife that is. She doesn't know that yet. I'm not even sure I have met her. If I do get married again, it will be the painstaking result of working hard to figure out who I am and how to do it better, and she will have a significant role in that process. Of course, it being me and all, she may well be my ex-wife by the time you read this.

Please remember, that despite my teasing of the tender sex, I adore women and treat them very well. And most of what I say about them is with tongue firmly implanted in my cheek. But I do find that, at times, I end up with my foot firmly planted in my mouth and her foot firmly planted up my ass.

Everything I say comes from my opinions, experiences and bloated assessment of my ability to psychoanalyze everybody. But I have had years of therapy and it has given me insights into how the mind operates. Not always a pretty sight.

Oh, by the way, I want to point out that while the stories in here are true, the names have been changed to protect the privacy of others, and me from lawsuits.

GETTING READY

CHAPTER 1: WELCOME TO 50

(OH SHIT)

So now you're fifty. And single. Shit. Welcome, I suppose. What were formerly minor issues—like baldness and pot bellies—because neither of you cared while snuggly wrapped in the marital vows, suddenly take on catastrophic significance when faced with dating someone new. It's quite a daunting task to seek a mate again at this age. And it's not because anyone is rooting against us or conspiring to make us fail. We have just not been here in a very long time. Maybe decades. It will seem like a lifetime ago. But we are no different than we were, just older. What got us this far will serve to get us further. Gather, regroup, and get help.

If you are like me, you have, or will have, many sessions with your shrink. Do not take the reference to "shrink" negatively. I have the world's best shrink. I just don't know if he is a psychologist or a psychiatrist, and I don't care. He is amazing. His insights into what makes me tick and advice on how to make me tick differently because I was really screwed up, have changed my life. Twice. So I strongly recommend talking to a professional as you begin your journey, not into another chapter of your life, but a whole new fucking book.

But here you are, 50-something and suddenly single. Maybe you are happy, maybe not. Regardless, whatever you think it looks like out there, you are wrong. My second ex told me that she was jealous of her best friend who was online-dating and having a great time.

The grass is always greener, until you walk across the street. I am not happy to be single in my 50s. I was happy thinking I was going to walk into the sunset with my partner and not give a shit how old I was or how much hair I had left. But life throws us curve balls and we need to be patient to make contact.

I was 56 when my second wife said she wanted a divorce. I think I may be in the minority of guys dumped for reasons other than infidelity or general asshole-ness.

Okay, perhaps there was some asshole-ness.

That I had to regroup after such an unceremonious parting of the ways would be an understatement. Some of you might have left her, causing her to regroup. The perspective I share with you, while tainted by my hurt, is no less real regardless of who left whom.

Most of us don't have the same build we had at 30, or nearly the amount of hair. And the swagger that carried us to some level of confidence with women has been out of practice for a long time. We also are not sure how or where the whole sex thing will next occur. A whole lot depends on where your head, heart, and emotions are when you first get back into the dating scene. While you may think you know what is lurking around the corner for the next stage of your life, in reality, you have no idea. The woman you pursued in your 20s could now, in her 50s, be anything from a nun to a serial killer. Worse, you may be well into the 5th month of dating before you find out. She has no incentive to show her flaws—she is just like you.

Regardless of who left whom, the absence creates a void. Perhaps the void was already there before you left; maybe that is why you left. Or if she left, the void may feel like an abyss you can't climb out of.

The first lesson of dating is to recognize the void and come to terms with it. You can't try to fill it instantaneously or with the first person who comes along. That will not be a cure. You will need to heal the wound slowly and carefully. Even if you left her, there is a wound that needs to heal.

So despite not being emotionally ready to date, you decide to enter the battlefield. Wounded. You will be pursuing others who made the same decision and are just as fucked up as you. She will be feeling many of the same things and have many of the same issues and hang-ups. The first step is to understand that you are both scared shitless, unsteady and uncertain, but not unscathed. You both are very scathed. You need to know that because this isn't just about you, it is about her, as well. If you want to make any relationship work, it has to be about both partners.

SO WHERE IS SHE?

Theoretically, you know where you are (or think you do), but where is she? What is her emotional state? How different is she than the woman you may have known (and wanted) when you were in your 20s? How different do you want her to be? One important thing to remember is that women who are divorced (or widowed) and have been living on their own for a while, have *very* different desires and needs than when they were in their 20s. They are not looking for a clone of their ex. Neither are you. Throw all those pictures out the window, erase the slate, and start with a clean chalkboard.

Now, I am not a psychologist, but I like to think of myself as one. Years of therapy give me some reason to brag. I did do some actual research on the state of mind and emotional health of the typical 50-something woman, then added in my own experiences. Don't take what I say as fact, just my perspective on what you're up against. You need to be prepared.

Let's start with the one thing that is most universal among women who have been married for a long time, raised children, and are now free. They are free. *Now* is their time. The one thing they don't want is someone needy. It's like that commercial for satellite TV. If you are sick in bed, someone takes over your zoo job, and fucks it up, you are killed by the ape he let escape. Don't be killed by an escaped ape, get satellite TV. Or something like that. For our purposes, don't be fucking needy.

An AARP study (for $16 per year, you can be a member too— ouch) concluded that the majority of mid to late life marriages are ended by the wife. Why do I know this? Because *I* am free. After my second failed marriage and several uninspiring mini-relationships, I took up reading about issues women have in their 50s. Ugh. But I came up with some useful information. Maybe. Major reasons women leave their man appear to be infidelity, physical or emotional abuse, emotional estrangement, and alcohol abuse. Basically, you are an asshole.

No matter the cause, she will feel like a failure and the children will be indelibly screwed up. That feeling at the end of a marriage, regardless of who precipitated the break-up, can make women feel completely unattractive, incapable of accomplishing any goals, and diminish the confidence they had in their jobs and relationships.

Welcome to your first date.

Divorce is one of the three biggest life stressors next to moving and changing jobs. If she left, you have felt the devastation of being dumped. Even if you left her, you certainly noticed how she handled it.

This is who you are now looking to date.

Now that she is on her own, reality of day to day life creeps in. She may never have mowed the lawn, raked the leaves, changed a tire, dealt with a leaky faucet, or negotiated with the landscaper. I dated a woman briefly who had just been divorced and was living in a townhouse with her teenage daughter. When the first big snowfall of the year came, I offered to shovel her walk and driveway, but she declined because she wanted to learn how to do everything herself. After that, then maybe I could help. Of course, once they figure "everything" out, we become almost useless.

My second wife was quite worldly. She traveled a lot for her high profile job, dealt with the highest levels of corporate America, and made presentations in front of hundreds of stock brokers at a time. Stock brokers, who hate to listen to bullshit almost as much as they love to spew it. Nothing intimidated her. Except mouse parts. She had a cat whose only redeeming quality in life (at least according to me) was an ability to catch mice. We lived in a rural area of New Jersey and mice liked the warmth of the attic. A couple of times each winter, mouse parts were proudly brought to the bedroom and deposited at the foot of the bed. I had the pleasure of getting the elbow and hearing my wife say "Max has another one," with the expectation that I dispose of the remains, immediately. I am sure that my ex-wife has since figured out how to dispose of mouse parts on her own, but I think you get the picture.

Our worth as men and protectors of women is much less when they have things figured out.

Today's woman, despite the emotional scars, quickly becomes independent, learning how to focus on herself with a strong support group of friends and family. She will come to treasure her alone time and feel comfortable being alone. Some women like it so much they may never want to live with a man again. You need to understand what she is all about, and accept it if you want to have any chance.

So what do you do? First, take a long look at yourself and your role in the failure of your marriage. It helps to write down a list of your contributions to its demise, and accept your share of responsibility. She may have cheated on you for no reason, but she cheated on you and not someone else, so you were part of the process. Look for this trait of accepting responsibility in women you meet. It means they have a healthy perspective on their own divorce. Too many people bitch about their exes all the time. While it may be justified, if all they can do is bitch, let them bitch to someone else.

I know that I contributed mightily to my divorce and readily admit it. That level of honesty and introspection can go a long way to helping you heal your wounds. It can also demonstrate to a woman that you are ready to engage in a real, meaningful relationship. Finding this out about her does the same for you.

I have met many women who seem to find it easier to be happy alone the older they are. Certainly more so than men, who seem to have a constant need to be with someone. A woman's need for what a man brings to the table seems to decline the longer they are single, while their need for their own space surges. The older women get, the harder it becomes for them not only to find a mate (simply because there are fewer of them available), but also to make the compromises necessary to sustain a relationship. Some, however, do get to the point of acceptance.

I dated a 59-year-old woman who had been single for over ten years. She acknowledged that she had begun to give up hope of finding a permanent relationship. She began to accept the fact that she may grow old alone. But she was attractive, fun, financially secure, had her own life, and plenty of space for a relationship. Certainly a prime candidate for any man.

She was not letting the lack of a relationship get her down, though. She was constantly on the go visiting her kids, grandkids, nieces, nephews, friends, siblings, etc. As a matter of fact, she was always prepared to go anywhere. She drove a large car with a large trunk. Thankfully. It was always completely full of clothes so she was prepared at a moment's notice to make or change plans. If you have ever traveled with a woman, you know their packing habits. This had to be a pretty big trunk. Good thing she was petite. There were more clothes in her trunk than in my closet. You don't want to know what was in the back seat.

The point is that she had built a life with room for a man, but did not need one. She was mentally ready to live her life alone. She would never be void of something to do or somewhere to go. She altered her lifestyle to make room for me, which was something I needed and appreciated greatly at the time. She was willing to make the man her number one priority, but if there was no man, there were plenty of other priorities.

Not all women are as flexible as she was. I dated a public school teacher whose district was one of the poorer ones in New York City. She had made her mark in the business world and was teaching out of love, not necessity. Most of her students had an uphill battle to make something of themselves, but she relished the challenge and was completely moved when even 1 out of 20 did something special. But it was hard work, and stressful. So on Friday nights, she had martinis with her fellow teachers to toast the weekend. Every Friday.

On Sunday mornings, she buried herself in the *New York Times*. For hours. We never had a date on a Friday night and there was only one thing that could distract her from the *Times* on Sunday morning….

On top of that, she liked funky food. She was into every foreign-sounding, difficult-to-pronounce menu item she could find. The smellier the restaurant, the better she liked it. Sorry, the more *aromatic* the restaurant, the better she liked it. I hate funky food, but it was all she suggested when it was time to go out for dinner.

She wanted me to shave my back hair, watch only her TV shows, and was very opinionated. She had no kids and had been single for a dozen years. She was set in her ways. If I wanted to come into her world, I was welcome, but she wasn't coming into mine.

Whether the woman you meet is set in her ways or flexible, remember that you and she are really in the same place. You both have gone through divorce and are dealing with many of the same emotions. A healthy dose of psychiatric counseling will be very worthwhile. A female confident will help too. I have my sister, who went through a divorce before I did and knew what it felt like. Mom was also a big help. It will be important for you to get a pulse on what is going on inside you and become self-aware of those things. I hope I can help you with that along the way here.

SOME SOBERING THOUGHTS

If you pursue online dating, which has become incredibly popular, you will need to have patience. First, it has been my experience that you (as a man) will make the first contact 90% of the time. I hardly got any emails from women, and when I did, they were usually not ones I was inclined to respond to. Women do not seem to want to (and usually do not need to) make the first contact. If you are going to sit around waiting for them to say "hi," be prepared for a long time between really bad dates.

So you are stuck winking, poking, or trying to be clever in email. And your emails will get a very small percent of response even if they are Pulitzer worthy.

There are a lot of studies out there on dating, in general, and internet dating, specifically. One study noted that over half of all single men and women in the United States have not had a date in over two years. Yikes. I can't last two weeks without a date before I need to go see my shrink. But on the bright side it appears that 50% of today's relationships began online. Not unexpectedly, the internet is a relatively safe way for people to get to know each other, and except for those with narcissistic tendencies, is a lot more comfortable than the bar scene.

Guys who note in their profile that they make a lot of money get more email responses than those who don't. Duh. And let's face it: it will be a long time before she really knows how much you make. In between the time you told her you were rich and when she finds out you're not, perhaps, you can get away with telling her that Bernie Madoff made off with your entire fortune, or the fucking Democrats raised taxes again, or your ex found that offshore account of yours. I don't recommend lying on your profile, but even I have, in a moment of weakness, stretched the truth a bit. But only a bit.

More studies. (God, I wish I had a life.) Several studies showed there are more single women out there than single men. Finally, something to cheer about. A woman's most common fear when meeting a man from an online site is that he is a serial killer. Seriously. Roughly 3% of men are indeed psychopaths. Is serial killer far behind?

What is a man's biggest fear? Fat. She looks great in her profile and shows up looking like Shamu.

One study listed the ten things that turn women off the most. They included the obvious (farting, body odor, and missing teeth), but a couple of my favorites were hairy nostrils, man boobs, and raggedy nails. If I grow man boobs, you have my permission to pretend I am a wounded animal. Of course, the same survey with men led to the number one (and 2 and 3 and 4) answer: fat.

Another survey asked women: Where was the worst place your date took you on the first date? The answers made it believable as to why half the single women have not been on a date in over two years.

There were some obvious ones, like strip clubs and swinger parties, but who would say, "Hi, Dana, let's visit Mom on our first date" or "Let's meet at the hot dog stand" or "I know this nice restaurant, I hope you don't mind that my ex waits tables there." Oh yeah, these were some of the actual responses.

My favorite statistic is that over a third of men think sex on the third date is fine. Unfortunately, nearly half of women think that waiting one to three months is appropriate. That's a lot of porn watching between date three and three months. On the bright side, the average is 4-6 dates and what is blindingly wonderful is that nearly a third of women have sex on the first date.

Just where are *those women*?

NEW AGE COMMUNICATION

If you are online dating, you only get to know one another through the written word. You do not have the benefit of seeing the person and their body language as they try to bullshit your pants off. The written word allows you to take your time and make sure you communicate exactly what you want. But if words fail, all hell can break loose.

This has led to my cardinal rule of modern communication. Never communicate bad news or serious stuff through texting or email. No one seems to practice this despite one disaster after another. It is too prone to miscommunication or even misspellings. iPhones have a spell correct feature that works against us sometimes. I was having a text fight with a girlfriend and at some point she wanted to apologize and make up. She tried to say something like "I am an idiot" and it came across as "U am an idiot." So much for making up. So no downers in a text. Not illness, not conflicts, and especially not ambiguity. "Hi Joe. Listen, I need to talk to you about something. Call me tonight." That sucks. Pick up the phone or, here's an idea, wait until tonight.

And there is the "I don't want to see you again" excuse. Maybe. "Hey Mitch, I can't see you tonight. My Aunt Martha just flew into town and sis can't pick her up at the airport." Is she blowing Mitch off or is Aunt Martha really stuck at JFK?

And my favorite: "Sorry Nick I can't see you tonight. My son cut his finger." For the third time and always on a Friday night. You may get the picture, but it's a shitty way of getting it. If you don't want it done to you, don't do it to her. If you are going to text, at least be honest. Better yet, pick up the phone.

While we will get to all the steps from the first email to what to do after a great first date and thereafter, these texts can't help but make me think about breakup etiquette. Texts like the above suggest you prepare yourself for the inevitable; she is *not* into you. And if you are not into *her*, how do you break up with her? Everyone will feel a little different about this. With the proliferation of emails and texting replacing phone calls, a written "break-up" is the easy way out. But is it appropriate? Perhaps with younger generations, but we are 50-something. I know it's not easy breaking up face to face, or even over the phone—we have been on the other side of those communications and hate them—but by the same token, we have appreciated them, or at least I have.

So, how do you proceed? Well, if it's been one date and you don't want to see her again, a simple text is fine. Some suggest that you just don't call or text and she will get the hint. If you know she would like to see you again, it's kind of cruel to leave her hanging. C'mon, guys, it's not too painful to write a text. You don't have to look at her and there are no sharp objects around.

What do you say? I try to keep them all the same. You don't need to be verbose here. You will never see her again and she does not have a lot invested in you, so just be quick and nice. You don't have to drone on about how wonderful she is and how lucky some other guy will be to meet her—she doesn't give a shit.

Be nice on that first date even if when you meet her, almost instantly, you know that you will never see her again. I could never bring myself to say before even the first drink, "I'm sorry, Rachel, but this will never work," or excuse myself and just leave. I always, perhaps for the worse, provide no evidence that I think we are completely wasting our time. So if you give her hope during the date, keep the dump text short and simple.

I have been on the other side of this.

I met a woman who was into *Star Trek*. I am a true Trekkie and can hold my own in any *Star Trek* trivia contest, so this was easy prey. She bought my "I cry whenever Spock gets emotional" routine (I really do), and we met. We spent some time talking *Star Trek*, our favorite episodes and even which character would we like to have sex with the most. I was surprised when she liked Bones, the straight-shooting, conservative doctor. Of course, I wanted to bone Yeoman Rand, the hot blonde Captain Kirk concierge. She couldn't quite keep up with the trivia part, but we were having fun.

We ended up back at her place and I was beginning to think she was one of those delightful first date chicks. While we did not quite get there, I left feeling for certain that we would see each other again and carnal knowledge was sure to follow quickly. Until I got a text the next morning. "Hi, Paul. It was fun to meet you and I had a great time. Wow it was fun to talk about *Star Trek!* You are a great person but I am sorry, but I am just not attracted to you. I know you will find someone who will make you happy."

Great person? Not attracted to me? Fuck off. How long did it take for her to come up with that? I would have preferred "I had a nice time, but I don't feel a connection." I don't need to hear bullshit to make me feel better. And she won't want to hear it from you. Be short and sweet, but don't patronize her.

At the opposite end of the spectrum, if you are in a relationship, I think it's obvious the right way to break up is to have a conversation. But what if you are just sleeping together? She would probably appreciate an in-person conversation, but sometimes that won't be practical. You don't want to make a special trip on a Saturday night to sit her down and break up with her. It ruins both of your Saturday nights. For Christ's sake, don't go out with her Saturday night, bang her brains out, and then break up with her over coffee on Sunday morning.

Unless she is reading the *New York Times.*

If breaking up in person just doesn't seem right—maybe you won't have an opportunity to see her for a while—at least call her. And be prepared to let her vent. I have offered and been offered friendship, and while that sounds nice, it may not really be practical. If you were the one dumped, you don't want to hear about the other's new relationship.

Sometimes we have "the more than one date, but no sex yet" situation. This one is a toss-up, and it may come down to how much respect you have for her. I think that after two dates, a phone call is in order, but a text is not necessarily inappropriate. If you haven't slept together, she may not be that emotionally invested yet. But if you do the text thing, be prepared for a text tirade in response. It won't happen all the time, but there are women who can't imagine why you don't want to see them again. This will likely reinforce the reason you don't want to see her again. I had a woman send me a text hoping that a vampire finds blood on my testicles. If women can be that crazy, you know they think we are worse.

So here you are a 50-, 60-, maybe even 70-something, and life has sliced up a lemon and placed it right next to you on the counter. Can you turn it into lemonade? Sure. It will take some time and healing, but with the right attitude and a smile, you can get there.

ON YOUR WAY UP THE RABBIT HOLE

I know you can do it. And I know you know you can do it. It just may not feel that way at first. As you scramble your way back up the rabbit hole, remember the following:

- Take responsibility for where you are now and don't be afraid to admit it out loud.
- She is just as scared and scarred as you are.

- Patience is critical if you pursue online dating. Think before you press "send."
- Breaking up is hard to do.
- It is much more painful to fill out the application than to send the $16 check.

THE OTHER SIDE

You will feel guilty for the break-up of the marriage regardless of who wanted out, and especially if there are children. You have kept the family together through the latter part of the marriage and its end will feel like failure. It isn't. Get help. A good therapist is worth every penny she/he costs.

Just like you didn't care about his baldness and pot belly, he didn't care about your greying hair and a couple of pounds. But that security derived from growing older together is in the past and your next date will expect your best. If you are going to get back into dating, doll yourself up, but do not present a picture that is not reality.

Be very mindful that your children will always want Mom and Dad together, so any introductions to new potential beaus will be frowned upon deeply. Do not be upset with them and do not force the issue. Imagine being them.

Don't let texting get the better of you as you move from texting friends and family to texting total strangers. Remember always that texting can and will breed misinterpretations. Recently, my daughter, who at times at least, is in the friends and family bucket, texted me asking for some advice. After I responded with some ideas, she got very upset. Later when we spoke, she said she thought I was trying to control her life and the "tone" of the text was demeaning. She read my words differently than they were meant and not until we chatted live (imagine that) did we straighten it out.

I didn't know texts have tones. Mine just have words. Yours too. Don't try to interpret them, just read them. And if you are now texting with an almost total stranger, the "tone" will take on an even greater significance for them too. When our emotions are raw, which they will be, our interpretations of "tone" may well come from insecurity and defensiveness. You don't get to fix it until you chat or your fingers fall off.

By the way, break up with assholes any way you wish. I never really had a date with a woman I would describe as such. You may not be as lucky. You can actually have some "text" fun with him, if he is so worthy.

CHAPTER 2: ARE YOU READY TO DATE?

(DON'T WORRY TOO MUCH, NEITHER IS SHE)

First, make sure you are ready for a date before you go out on one.

You won't. It's okay. I didn't. You have a void. You have begun a very scary part of your life. You are hurt, sad, confused, and wondering what the hell happened. Again, it doesn't matter who left whom. These feelings will come to the surface unless you are a complete asshole.

After my second wife, I felt like I failed and was not sure of anything. My reaction was to go out and fill this huge void in my heart as soon as I could. It did take several weeks before I could even think about going out and trying to meet someone for real. Actually, it would have taken months, but I was angry and wanted to get back at her. "Huh! You think I need you? I will show you." I did ask her if she was sure she wanted a divorce before I went out on my first date. If she had said "not sure," I would not have gone and might not be writing this book. Oh well.

How did I meet this first date? You would think that the king of online dating (me) would have met her online. Not. It was another Saturday night and the ex was doing her thing (we were still living in the same house) while I sat at home pining. I decided to go to my favorite Jersey Shore bar. Every Friday and Saturday in the summer, they have live music with a big dance floor that is always full. And the crowd is perfect. There are all ages there, 20-somethings to 70-somethings. Single and looking. I suck in bars, but even I could have fun there.

I was hanging at the bar and chatting with another single guy about internet dating. He was telling me some war stories when two women walked in and staked their territory close by. One was a hot Spanish type. Great body, cleavage, and oh, what an ass. Perfect for my anger-induced fantasy fuck.

I am intimidated by hot so I hit on her librarianesque friend. She was a bit whacky, but said yes when I asked her to dance. She was my new soul mate. I had no idea if I liked her. I didn't care. She said "hi."

Meanwhile, my buddy was getting very cozy with the hot Costa Rican.

I asked my new friend for her phone number, but she wouldn't give it to me. She took mine. My first introduction to the new dating paradigm. She called and we made plans. My first date in 15 years. Yikes.

Instantaneously, my wheels began spinning out of control.

Are the jeans I wore to every dinner with my wife for the last five years okay to wear on this date, or should I update my wardrobe? I always unbuttoned the two top buttons on my shirt because I had lots of chest hair and thought it was cool to show it off. One or two buttons? What do I do when we meet? I had already met her so is a kiss okay? Bring a flower?

Fuck! Oprah, where is the "how to" book?

Forget the clothes and the greeting, how do I stop from shaking uncontrollably? How do I stop my head from spinning? How do I relax and just be me?

Shit! This sucks!

Unfortunately, I was still so angry and hurt that I could not enjoy the exhilaration of a first date. And that is what you should feel on a date—exhilaration. It is only the first date, but understanding that this is the beginning of the journey is very difficult. It feels like you'd better make this "the" one because who knows when the next one will come along.

Relax.

So we met—no kiss. We went to a local spot for Fourth of July fireworks, dinner, and then a walk around town. We had a nice time, and when it came time for goodnight, I hadn't a clue what to do. We sat in her car and I went to kiss her. She accepted. Now what? Should I give her some tongue? Do I go for a breast? What about the crotch? She had been divorced for a while, had a few relationships, so she had her shit together. I felt like a 16-year-old.

I opened my mouth and groped for a breast. Christ, I hadn't tried to put my hand under a woman's shirt or unbutton one in forever. Oh God, was I going to be able to undo her bra? This is the number one fear men have when making out in the front seat of cars. The fucking bra hook. And how many times do we grope only to find out it's a front loaded bra? Shit. Who came up with *that* idea? It should be a law that women have to disclose if they are wearing one of *those* kinds of bras.

Fortunately, my nipple radar had not lost all its mojo and I got there. Holy shit, that's what they feel like. Is she just letting me have some fun or is she one of those first date fuck fantasies?

I don't know. I gave up and backed off because I was now officially in love and didn't want to screw things up. In love. First date. Yes. Of course.

I think you are getting the picture. I wasn't in love, and she had already made up her mind to see me again no matter what part of her body I went for. She had a limit and knew I would honor it. My mind was totally fucking with me. You will feel the same way. Don't worry about it. Dating isn't natural, and it feels like the rules change every few years. And remember, while my date had gotten her act together, many women are going to feel the same way you do. It may be their first time too, and they feel like they are 16 years old while wondering, "Should I open my mouth if he tries to kiss me" and

"What the fuck do I do if he goes for a nipple?" We are in the same boat, paddling across the same lake.

I thought I was ready to date, but I was not ready to have an emotionally-mature relationship. I was ready to fill a void and did so with the first reasonable opportunity that came my way. It actually took several short-term relationships before I became emotionally ready to take on a woman who was emotionally stable in her own right. If neither of you are ready, you are just two ships passing in the night.

OR A CAR PARKED ON THE BEACH

In retrospect, it would have been nice to have the ability to look back at my past and the results of some of my dating experiences and actually learn from them. Not learn how to avoid saying something stupid or to be a nicer guy, but learn from the fact that it was a horrible date and I survived. Or it was so bad that I can now laugh at it now. Know that you *can* laugh again. Think about the worst or strangest date you were ever on. Revel in it. If this one doesn't work, there *will* be another one.

For me, proffering advice on the efficacy of searching for nipples in the front seat of a car in the 21st century reminded me of another car story that was scary for different reasons, and that turned out not only okay but memorable. I wish I had remembered it that night.

THIS WAS NOW AND THAT WAS THEN

I lived in Jacksonville, Florida after I graduated from Rutgers University. I kept the Jax cops busy during my brief stay there. Okay, for two nights, anyway.

One of the nights was with my college girlfriend. I was living at home in Jacksonville and working at my first real job. The girl I was dating was a Douglass girl. What's a Douglass girl? Douglass College was the all-female, sister college to Rutgers, the New Jersey State University. Douglass had a reputation as an excellent academic school, which came with the reputation that "smart equals ugly." There were thousands of women there and I am a math geek—they can't all be ugly, right?

My sophomore year, my roommate and I spent a lot of time on the Douglass campus. Rutgers and Douglass were cross town from each other and shared facilities as well as curriculum. We played tennis at Douglass and then went to the dining hall for dinner, with visions of meeting really smart beautiful women. As stupid college guys do, the first night, we created a contest to see who could find the best-looking woman in the dining hall. We would debate who was an 8 versus a 9, and challenge each other to go up to one of them and say "hi." Ultimately, we would crown one of them the Douglass "Queen for the Night."

At least that is how we thought it would go. We looked around as we ate gamey chicken parmesan and, for the life of us, we could not find a good-looking woman. They all looked smart, and maybe there were a few you wouldn't throw out of bed. We just weren't there to find a "You-Would-Do-Her-On-the-Floor Queen," and we were patient. We finished eating and sat there, watching hundreds of women. You would have thought, one or two 9.5s was not too much to ask; maybe with a few 8s. Every time we got excited at someone's ass, she turned around. And every time we saw what appeared to be a pretty face, she stood up. We tried and tried, and debated, but all we saw were a few "wouldn't-throw-out-of-beds," which could be anywhere from a 2 to a 6 depending on how much alcohol one had consumed. Our search for the Douglass Queen went unfulfilled.

Ultimately, we were forced to face reality and change our goals. We changed the contest from searching for the best-looking woman at dinner to searching for the Limp Queen. She was so ugly she would make you go limp.

This was college. It was hard to go limp. We were jerks. Hopefully, you had a better upbringing.

I eventually met my Douglass girlfriend my senior year. By then, the state of New Jersey was allowing smart *and* pretty girls to enroll at Douglass. Later in life, I married a different Douglass girl. (I had developed a pattern.)

Meanwhile, back to Jacksonville. The Douglass chick (not the wife) and I stayed together after I graduated, but hadn't been able to get together until winter break when she came to visit me in Florida. Dad was cool enough and said we could do whatever we wanted to do, just not in the house. My sister was about 12 so I got the message and looked for other means. I was working but not making enough to consider a hotel room, especially when I had a monstrous back seat in my car. At that time in Jacksonville, you could drive on the beach anytime, day or night. And the beaches were wide with lots of high sand dunes. We hadn't been with each other in several months, so it was "let's go to the beach."

I guess I should have known that at night, the beach, with the sand dunes and lots of brush and other flora, gets "buggy." Real buggy. There we were in the back seat, windows down, and at some point, my ass becomes exposed to the air. And the bugs. Those bastards nipped at my cheeks like Pilgrims with a fucking Thanksgiving turkey. If the bugs were not distracting enough, suddenly a flashlight appeared. I was almost relieved because I wasn't getting anything accomplished that night anyway.

The friendly neighborhood Jacksonville police officer shined the light directly on, well, everything. And it shined in one area on her just a bit too long for my liking. I had no choice but to wait it out. Finally, he put his tongue back in his mouth and asked us what we were doing on the beach late at night by ourselves. Was he really expecting an answer? He should have asked his flashlight. He gave us the usual lecture, saying it could be dangerous being out on the beach late at night. And buggy. Thanks, officer.

Not being one to learn my lesson, several months later, I was dating a local woman from Jacksonville. Of course, my back seat remained tempting. The new girlfriend and I found a deserted street right next to the St. Johns River, which runs through Jacksonville. Knowing we were somewhat close to a residential neighborhood, expediency was a priority. We both were thin so we decided to stay in the front seat. This time no bugs and things were working.

Right about the time we were "done," a car pulled up about 50 feet away from us with headlights glaring. I wasn't even thinking that the officer could see us; I just wanted to get composed so when he got to my car I could plead innocence. Of course, he could see every move we made. She jumped off, back to the passenger seat, and quickly composed herself. I was sitting in the driver's seat, so my avenue to composure was a bit more difficult. To the officer's credit, he gave us a couple of minutes before opening his door and getting out. Despite the struggles of pulling one's pants up in the driver's seat, I was almost there. I figured, if my pants were on, I could deny, deny, deny, even if he made me get out of the car. As he was about to reach my car door, I took a deep breath and finalized my preparedness. As I reached for the final step, I realized I was sitting on my fucking zipper.

I will say one thing for Jacksonville cops: they are cool.

Knock, knock on the window. To his credit, he didn't ask what we were doing. Nor did he ask me to get out of the car. He said that it was a bit deserted in this area and we should be careful what we do in public, then told us to leave with no summons or other harassment.

He didn't even ask if I had any "priors."

I offer these stories as a way to help you relax. Things always seem worse than they are. You survived your own sex on the beach story when you were young. I survived "searching for nipple;" you will too.

STARTING OVER

How do you know if you are ready to date? You don't. Just go out there thinking you are. It's okay. As you embark upon this new dating chapter of your life, remember the fun times you had in the past and make sure you recreate them now. It is too easy to take this dating thing too seriously at our age. Women are no different. They are trying to find someone too, and it can be stressful. If you open up the fun side of dating and sex, women will embrace it. What the hell, they are no longer 20 either. Maybe you have graduated from back seats to bedrooms, but don't forget the kitchen, the bathroom—or the beach.

Ultimately you have to go through the four stages of Re-dating. Like the four stages of mourning. These are mine. I made them up.

1. Cluelessness—21st century bras and panties work differently than years ago. So does her mind. You don't want to act like a dork. Nor are you trying to be a stud. You just want her to like you, but don't know how. Be yourself. Let the real you show up. No bullshit. No games. And know she is just as clueless.

2. Euphoria—It's going to happen. Guaranteed. You will hit it off with her and you will go to the moon. "Wow, that was fast. I didn't think I could feel like this again so easily." Love at first sight really is true. Then you really get to know her, or perhaps she really gets to know you. Or you just have a second date. Poof, the bubble bursts. There was no bubble to begin with.

3. Here We Go Againness—So it didn't work out. You will feel like you are back at square one, but you are not. You have had your void filled, albeit temporarily. It still helped heal the wound. It may hurt, but it is a good hurt. A necessary hurt. Part of the process. You are much further along than it feels. Take a deep breath, gain some self-awareness, and create some…

4. Balance—This will take awhile, but at some point, you will gain a life of your own and won't "need" her. She will take her rightly place in yours and you in hers. Along the way, you will date a couple of "clueless" and "here we go again" chicks. You will feel their pain.

You will date before you are ready for a real relationship. Temper your expectations no matter how good it feels. The only good an early post-divorce relationship will do is to prepare you for the next post-divorce relationship. At some point, you will become ready and thus better equipped to make a relationship last.

YOU SOMEDAY, INEVITABLY, HOPE TO BECOME…
THE MOST INTERESTING MAN IN THE WORLD

It would be nice to be The Most Interesting Man in the World. Attractive and worldly, no trouble getting dates. Well past Cluelessness. Most guys have seen the beer commercial with the commentator saying things like, "*His* 10-gallon hat holds…13 gallons" and the like. He is "the most interesting man in the world." He appears at the end of the commercial as the elder statesman type with two beautiful women on his arms and says, "I do not drink beer all the time, but when I do, I prefer…." Even I swoon. But as I think about some of the traits of the most interesting man in the world, I have come across a few that have not yet been used. Perhaps the cable TV version could add a couple of items to the list of things that make him most interesting.

"He can shit and get off the pot at the same time."

"He has two middle fingers on each hand."

"His shit really doesn't stink."

But alas, mine does.

DESPERADO

"Desperado" is an Eagles classic about a man who seems to be always chasing something he doesn't really want and doesn't know it, so he ends up lonely and doesn't know why. Talk about confused. I originally thought "desperado" meant "desperate" in Spanish and wanted to assimilate my tremendous music knowledge into a point to be made. Alas, the definition of "desperado" is "an outlaw." However, some may attest there is plenty of desperation to outlaws.

We continue with no further musical interludes.

Webster's online dictionary defines "desperate" as "very sad and upset because of having little or no hope: feeling or showing despair." Having been the dumpee in my second marriage, I was filled with feelings of hopelessness and despair. I resorted to self-help books on self-esteem and did all the little exercises they tell you to do, like make a list of all the things you like about yourself and tape it to everything in your home. Mirrors, refrigerator, doors. Carry it with you and repeat it while you are driving, eating, falling asleep. I had little pieces of paper stuck everywhere I could find. I put the original right next to where I kept my condoms so I could gain the maximum benefit from my new found self-worth when I got ready for a date.

Clueless.

If you are the one who was left, you may feel the same way. Don't feel bad. It takes time to overcome. If you decide to go out into the dating world while still feeling this way, you may find yourself appearing desperate. What does "desperate" look like? It looks like when you meet someone for the first time, you want to be with her all the time. And you nag her about it. You find yourself putting your life on hold to be available for her when she is free. You may not even really like her, but she gives you the time of day. Even after a few dates and things are going well, you remain nervous about where you stand. You begin to wonder why she doesn't respond to your texts right away, or where she is when you are not together, or who her exes are, are they still in the picture, or what she had for breakfast, or if your penis is too small. You are officially desperate.

While this is okay to feel, she cannot know. Do not ask her why she didn't text you right away. Do not challenge where she was. Don't bring up exes. All the other "don'ts" are basically anything that has you wondering or feeling insecure. They are your issues and should not be brought up. That's what shrinks are for.

We all know that communication is important in any relationship, so why not communicate this? We need to distinguish between real issues in a relationship versus acting desperate. If you are at the "significant other" stage, then, yes, some of these feelings may be worth a discussion (except, I'm pretty sure by now she likes your penis). Your feelings are caused by the insecurities, hurt, and emptiness that came from your prior relationship. You become needy. Women do not like needy.

At this stage in their lives, many women have already been a mother to not only their children but also their former husband. These women now have their own lives. They naturally took a break from dating to get their act together and established a lifestyle that does not include men. While that life will eventually have time for them, it will always have other priorities. She will make it work for the right man, but is not going to react kindly to desperation or neediness. And they are obvious to her. I want to help you understand how desperation might look so you can recognize it and hide it. If you feel desperation happening (it may not feel that way, so this could take some work and self-awareness), get help. You need to be able to distinguish a feeling of desperation from true feelings of affection. If you don't, bye-bye girlfriend.

I was dating someone shortly after my separation who I knew was not for me long-term, but boy did she do a good job of filling the void. I wanted to be with her all the time, wondered what she was doing when she wasn't with me, and grew anxious when she didn't return my texts right away. I knew I didn't love her, but I walked on egg shells all the time so as not to chance losing her. After a few months, I had thoughts of moving in with her.

The woman kept her house at 50 degrees in the winter to save on heat. She wasn't poor. She had a 25-foot boat that cost a fortune. She was tiny and there she was huddled under the covers all night. I am tall. My feet hung over the bed and were not always covered. Or my arms hung over the side. It was not a king bed. This was a small house. I was cold. The only good thing was that the walk to the bathroom for a hot shower in the morning was quick. George Costanza would be happy to hear that I redefined "shrinkage."

While we were dating, she listed her house for sale with a local realtor. She was not looking to sell her house, just curious as to what it would go for. This was the middle of the financial crisis and no one knew what real estate was worth. I couldn't cook bacon on the weekend. Why? She was concerned that someone might come by on Sunday, interested in making an offer on the house, and be deterred because we had breakfast. And the dishes had to be washed and put away immediately after a meal. She had a dishwasher, but the same prospective buyer who might smell the bacon was going to open the dishwasher to make sure the person she was buying the house from never ate at home.

I was considering moving in with her. Into her tiny home that had no room for a second person's stuff. At 50 degrees. Moving to a place that was even farther away from my work than I already was. Considering something semi-permanent, with the global opposite of what I wanted in life. And no bacon on Sunday's.

I was desperate.

We didn't make it much longer.

Many guys are insecure and needy when they become newly single. Insecure can be handled, needy should be avoided, but I don't have to tell you that.

So, what are some of the signs of desperation? They include:

- **Answering her texts within seconds of receiving them.** Every time. This makes you look like you have no life. You don't. I am not suggesting you play games like "she doesn't respond for an hour, so I am going to sit here and do crossword puzzles for an hour before responding." No, when you see it and it is convenient to respond, then you respond. If you *always* see texts right away and it is *always* convenient to respond, you need to get some hobbies.

- **Wanting to be with her all the time.** You may feel this way, but don't let on. While this is not easy, let her take the lead in terms of how often you see each other. If you sense she likes you, be patient. Women are typically not serial daters. If you are sleeping with them, they are probably not dating anyone else. Your insecurity is worrying that she doesn't like you enough. Chill. Time will tell. If need be, have the "is this an exclusive relationship?" conversation, but not after the second date.

- **Questioning what she is doing when she is not with you.** When you didn't speak to each other on a Friday night, it is a fine art to ask what she did the night before without sounding jealous. It can be done. Start off with what you did and hope she volunteers what she did. Don't make accusations.

- **Offering to introduce her to your mother after the third date.** Or your kids on the second date. Leave the fucking family out of it for now. I briefly dated a woman who introduced me to her kids on the first date (I picked her up at her house and she paraded me around) and invited me over for Mother's Day after the second one. I never saw her again.

- **Showering her with flowers, gifts, or offers of vacation.** This may seem like love to you, but she may interpret it as desperation. Do the flower thing in moderation. It doesn't have to be roses. Find a subtle, yet engaging way to show her you care without going overboard. Remember it is the thought that counts and thoughtfulness only needs to be thoughtful.

Now it's time to jump in.

ON YOUR WAY UP THE RABBIT HOLE

- She is struggling as much as you are. Empathize. Commiserate.
- Embrace that first date—feel and enjoy the excitement.
- Recognize feelings of desperation. They are okay to feel; try to camouflage them from her.
- Nipples still feel the same as 30 years ago.
- Bacon is no good for you anyway.

THE OTHER SIDE

A lot of what applies to men also applies to women when preparing to date again. Whether it's how you react on a first date or even a first contact, or how you feel after such firsts. If you are fresh off a divorce from an asshole, you may think all guys are like that ex. All guys don't necessarily think like he did, so you are more likely to get a fresh perspective if you allow yourself to be open to it. Viewing someone new from the same lens as you did your ex-husband isn't fair to either party. This may give you an advantage in protecting yourself from more pain, but that pain is only assumed. You will be preventing yourself from engaging in a real dating relationship that may well be much better than any relationship you've ever had before.

Having said that, you need time to heal and to figure out why you are feeling the way you do after a marriage ends. You won't know, you will just feel. It will affect your desires and ability to get close to anyone.

By the way, acting needy is not gender specific; anyone can behave that way, assuming a risky position while getting to know someone new. The woman who wanted to bring me to Mother's Day dinner on the third date was particularly needy. It was easy to read and could have been taken advantage of.

Avoid projecting the feelings of despair that your breakup created. Focus on the here and now; pay attention to what is good in life. There are a thousand things to be thankful for. New experiences not jaded by your past can replace those bad memories and allow you to enjoy the future more than you realize right now.

How do you avoid these feelings of neediness, desperation, and having fallen in love before the first date? Follow some simple practices:

- Stay busy—hobbies, dive into work, clean the house, whatever.
- Get some toys. Yeah, those toys.

- Accept feeling in love even if you fall too early. Or feel desperate. Give yourself a break. In time, it will get better.
- Don't be on a rushed, or even specific timetable to fill a void. Let nature take its course.
- Bring bug spray to the beach.

And don't worry, your penis radar has not lost its mojo.

ULTIMATELY, YOU HOPE TO BECOME THE MOST INTERESTING WOMAN IN THE WORLD.

- Your hair never turns grey.
- Botox is nothing more than a 15 point Scrabble word.
- You get to dump beer on the Most Interesting Man in the World.
- You have an automated toilet seat always in the "down" position.
- The only cellulite you have is on your phone.

CHAPTER 3:
DATING IN THE 21ST CENTURY

(AKA ONLINE DATING)

So now you are ready. Bars? Bowling? Church social? Nah, welcome to dating in the 21st century—online dating. When internet dating first came on the scene, I was happily married. But I was the first to understand that it was God's gift to dating as it instantly beat the hell out of bars, church, and bowling as a way to meet people. While I did not use too many online dating sites, I did use a few of them quite a lot. I will share some of my insights from those experiences.

Warning: online dating can be very addictive.

According to the dictionary definition, addiction is a strong and harmful need to regularly have something (such as a drug) or do something (such as gamble). In 21st century dating speak, a strong and harmful need to ruin one's life could manifest as emailing 500 women a day. Facilitated, of course, by dating sites.

There are different types of dating sites. Some are advertised on TV and some couldn't buy ad time if they tried. There are dating sites for those who want to cheat on their significant others, sites where 90% of the pictures posted show genitals, sites that claim to find the perfect match, and everything else including www.hooker.com. I "Binged" "hooker" and was surprised at the results. The results page tried to convince me that I wanted to Bing "hoover" not "hooker." Vacuum suction is not the topic at hand. There is another chapter for that. There was a hooker.com link, but it was to a rather benign dating site. Bummer. My favorite, of course, was a link to *T J Hooker*, a cop show from the 80s whose star was William Shatner—Captain Kirk from *Star Trek*. If I was interested in finding a hooker online, it does not look like Binging it is a good way to find one. And street corners are so passé.

As far as legitimate sites go, some are free and some come with a fee. I have always believed that you get what you pay for, and that holds true here too. Some of you may decide that you want to hit one of the sex dating sites first. Might as well get laid. Despite the ads for those sites, don't expect much to choose from. It is 90% guys (who by the way, post pictures mostly of their private parts) and the women are not "take home to Mom" types. I didn't even want to post a picture of myself, and pictures of my privates will not invoke much enthusiasm, I am afraid. I tooled around there for a while and met no one of interest. I actually met no one.

Back to the mainstream sites. While I am not going to review the sites in detail, a quick overview of the three that I have used may prove useful.

I started with eHarmony and found pretty good success. They send you several matches each day—I typically got three to six. The more flexible your profile is in terms of who you want to meet (age range, geographical proximity, race, religion, etc.) the more matches you will get. You are not able to scroll around and contact whoever you want; you can only contact those you were matched with. eHarmony also has a guided communication program that includes asking and answering some preset questions before you can email directly. You can attempt to circumvent that, but only if your match agrees. It is a positive that you have already been matched with someone. This naturally creates an initial level of interest not present with other sites, but you are limited to contacting matches their program defines.

I also tried Match.com on two separate occasions. The first time I was overwhelmed. You do a search for women with age ranges, location, etc., and you get hundreds of matches. This makes it extremely time consuming to go through all the profiles to find a couple you might be interested in. I became exasperated and eventually gave up, then went to eHarmony. The second time I did Match.com, they seemed to have changed their process. You could still do a search and come up with your own list, but at least they were sending me an email every day with 15-20 women who they thought met my profile desires. It was kind of the best of both worlds. I could search and contact anyone I wanted, plus they sent me a list of women. I found that just by using the list of matches they had created, there were plenty of opportunities without being overwhelming.

I tried the free site, Plenty of Fish (POF). Like Match.com, you could search for women based on whatever criteria you choose. While they provided a list of matches, the women that I was matched with at times seemed random. Suffice to say, the overwhelming majority of women I was matched with had nothing in common with my profile. I will admit, however, that I was matched with a former girlfriend on POF.

It was a little awkward because we had just broken up. Again. We did that frequently, but neither of us was ever quite sure if we really had broken up. Tearful goodbyes and good luck in life. If only the timing was better. Then it was inevitable that within a week, one of us would email the other wondering if we had left blue panties or black socks at the other's residence. We just couldn't live without our favorite underwear. Not at all. It was a way of maintaining innocent contact under the guise that we had broken up. And since we had parted friends, this was okay. Actually, we were gauging where each other's emotions were since neither one of us really wanted to break up. We were both so confused that this happened several times. The lesson to be learned is that if you break up with someone and get a text from her, she is probably still emotionally engaged. If you respond, so are you.

On another occasion, my girlfriend and I had quite the fight and it looked like it was over. No hope. She was rightfully furious with me for one of the many faux pas I have committed in my dating career. (I was trying to maintain an innocent, yet too friendly relationship with an ex-girlfriend. As I later found out from my shrink, "currents" don't like "exes.") After telling me she never wanted to see me again, she texted. Good sign. She wanted to meet to find out why I would do something like this to her. Good, I can convince her it was innocent. I never got a chance. She completely ripped me a new asshole and walked away in total disgust. Again, I thought it was done. Until she texted me. Again. We eventually got back together.

Back to POF. Since this was a free site, it showed in the level of women on the site. Not that it was bad, it just seemed that the women on eHarmony and Match.com were of a higher caliber.

Let me reiterate, the real point of this chapter is not which site is the best site or which one is right for you, but how you can be successful at online dating. First and foremost: take some time filling out the profile information and for God's sake be honest. The more information you include and the more flexible you are with who you are looking for, the more successful you will be. I know as a guy all you care about is how she looks, but trust me, they go a lot deeper. I have had over 100 internet dates (and read thousands of profiles) and many of them have shared stories in their profile that would make you want to laugh (or cry). Definitely avoid the tearjerker profiles—women hate "woe is me"—but take some time writing a thoughtful and honest profile. You will get a lot more responses this way.

Don't restrict yourself in choosing types of women, though. My sister has this thing about short guys (she's 5'9"). She won't date anyone shorter than she is and is anal about it. Who cares? It's online dating. I dated a 5'0" woman and I am 6'2". Did I ever think I would like slow dancing from a crouching position? No, but she had some very nice redeeming qualities and it almost worked. You don't have to marry her, but give yourself the best shot. Who knows, it could make a great story that you dated a 6'4" albino. If you have certain things that are required, fine, but keep them to a minimum.

You have to post a picture. If you don't, the ladies will think you are either married or an ogre. Neither is going to entice them to respond. They like both head shots and body shots so you don't show up to the first date at 400 pounds. Try to show them your personality. If you like to do something, have an action shot showing that. For example, if you like boating, post a picture of you on a boat. If you like to golf, show off that Phil Mickelson swing.

I have found that moustaches are passé. I had one in the beginning, until enough people suggested that I bag it. And I am the most un-photogenic person in the world, but I got a professional photo taken and at least it made me look human. So invest the $100 with a photographer and look your best. Just remember what you might think about a woman who doesn't post a picture. You will simply think she is ugly (or fat); she will think you are a degenerate.

So now you are ready to take the plunge. You have chosen a site and created a profile; time to sign in and start trolling. There will literally be thousands of women to choose from. I remember talking to my sister about internet dating. She lives in Arkansas and we got on one of the sites I had joined and did a search for men in their 40s. You can be as narrow or expansive in your search criteria (actually in Arkansas, you can include cows in your search, but she opted to keep it to humans). Virtually every man that came up had a 10-gallon hat on, wore cowboy boots, and had some kind of facial hair. Her choices were not particularly robust. Not that there is anything wrong with 10-gallon hats, cowboy boots, or facial hair, it's just that they all looked alike. Fast forward a few weeks and she decided to join Match.com. This is a woman who is in bed by 10 PM, but the first day she was on the site, I got a text from her at midnight telling me she just signed on and "OMG what a pisser this is!" She was an instant convert.

The contrast between what I was used to in the New York area and what my sister found in Arkansas was interesting. I am not sure how she would react to a picture of a guy in a suit and I am not sure how I would react to a woman in chaps. I would not exclude her, but I would be surprised. There will be other areas of the country that will have other differences. Perhaps in Vail, most people's pictures will show them in ski suits or hiking gear. In Utah, being married won't be an exclusionary trait. I had a client in San Francisco and for a while, I was visiting them on a regular basis. Not having a girlfriend at the time, I searched Match.com in San Francisco to find compatible women. My goal was not to find my soul mate, but to meet someone to have dinner with or show me around when I was out there. It was interesting to see differences in profiles and desires. I never met any of them, but did chat with a couple. The point is, if you move or even visit a different part of the country, you may very well find a different kind of woman than you are used to. Keep an open mind.

Chaps. Hmmm.

Now that you are officially trolling, here is where the addiction can take hold. You can spend untold hours just reading profiles and trying to figure out if you would prefer to marry each one or just screw them. And then you have to figure out how to meet them.

You need to temper the excitement of the *prospect* of meeting new women with the reality of the *odds* of meeting new women. Or maybe the time it takes to meet those new women. The time this takes can't be suppressed into one night, as I tried early on. Once I got my feet wet and saw pictures of the bevy of beauties lining up to be my next wife, I could not go to sleep. I was intoxicated by the seemingly infinite number of women available. Take a deep breath.

Some Dos and Don'ts on meeting women online. This is why you bought this book!

THE DON'TS

- **Don't ask for sex right off the bat.** Even if you want it, you will be ignored. Try to get a first date and then use your George Clooney personality to get her into bed. If fast sex is your main goal, I would try other means. I had a friend, a very incredibly good-looking male friend, who said 90% of getting laid is "showing up." This was before the internet, and he would go to bars and pick up anyone he wanted because he actually did look as good as George Clooney and had a great personality. However, to his point, if you show up at a bar and ask everyone there to go home with you, you might get lucky. At least you will know what she looks like and the investment will be very brief. If you ask every woman on line to have sex with you, your odds are much lower, and if you do get lucky, *she* might look like George Clooney. Stick to bars or sex sites if that is what you want.

- **Don't post misleading pictures.** One of the worst fears a woman has is to show up for a first date with a guy who has a "movie star" like picture on his profile, but looks more like Tom Thumb than Tom Cruise. I went out on a first date with a woman whose picture must have been airbrushed when she was 17. 20 years and 40 pounds later when I met her, I did not recognize her. Needless to say, there was no second date. It never ceases to amaze me that people think getting a date under false pretenses is worthwhile. They should know the person they are meeting will be disappointed and the date will begin on a very sour note.

- **Don't post misleading information on your profiles.** Lies will inevitably be uncovered. Put your best foot forward. You can wait until you're dating to disclose that your mother was a transvestite, but don't lie. At some point (usually very quickly) you will forget what you wrote on your profile. Sure as shit, she will nail you. So, for example, let's say you note that you know Mick Jagger. You better know the other band members, his mother's name, and where Bianca was from (Nicaragua). At some point, she will ask you and when you don't know, you are screwed.

- **Don't show up for the first date without looking your best.** Wear your best outfit, shower, shave, brush your freaking teeth, and try to cover up any warts, literally and figuratively.

Online dating is God's gift to shy people, but it's not God's gift to lazy or stupid people. I have been dating on and off online for several years and have seen a lot of bad habits. Some guys like to get online, find a cute chick, and send her a "wink." That's creative. And who do you think will respond to that? All right, what's a wink you ask? On some sites, instead of sending a message that takes some written words and just a touch of creativity, you can prod someone with a poke (see Facebook), or a wink or a smile, or something else that takes no time or effort.

Sometimes, guys will actually come up with a word to say, but do you really think a hip, fun lady is going to be impressed with "Hi?" If she is, she either posted a picture of herself that was stolen from Kathleen Turner's promo pics from *Body Heat* (of which I have one), or is a Lithuanian looking for a way to stay in the country. (*Body Heat* is one of my favorite all-time movies and Kathleen Turner was hot. Was.)

To prove my point, I tried an experiment. I went to one of the free dating sites and randomly contacted eligible women. I chose women who a guy like me might normally reach out to and who I felt might have some chance at responding. I kept it to ones that were geographically logical, reasonably attractive, and age appropriate. This particular web site did not have winks but you could buy various "gifts" and send them to someone you liked. In the interest of literary history, I allowed myself to be ripped off and bought several gifts. I chose a "key" as in a key to the future or a door to a new beginning or to someone's heart.

I sent emails to over 100 women with either a key and no message, a key with a "hi," or just a "hi." My profile was complete and I had a good picture of me loaded up. My calendar was ready and my supply of condoms was at an all-time high. In reality, I expected no responses except from women named Nadia. The results were a little surprising as I did get three responses. One was a thank you for the key, one was a "hi" back, and one was from a Nadia. I ended up having a date with the "hi" responder, but it led nowhere.

So was my point proven? Should you send some kind of thoughtful note instead of just a wink? I think so. If you want to go the wink route, feel free, just don't blame me when you get a lesser class of woman. I say, don't "wink." Write an email that is honest, includes stuff about her profile, and is of enough length to show effort and substance. If you write well, you will be off to a good start. If English is a second language, enlist someone to help or reduce your expectations.

THE DOS

- **Honesty.** Women love honesty. Number 1. No doubt. Other than fidelity, nothing comes close. I have found honesty, even if it discloses a flaw, is extraordinarily endearing to women. Tell her you are an alcoholic but have joined AA, and you get lots of points. Order your seventh drink and slur your speech, no points.

- **Find something in her profile to talk about.** This can be the topic of your first email communication or when you first talk on the phone. Women love that you actually read their profile. You don't have to really like cats, but if she says she does, go with the flow. I don't like cats, but my cat stories are very entertaining, and at least I acknowledge her love of cats.

- **Learn to listen.** This is true with everyone. People like to talk about themselves. It makes them feel good. Listen to your date and her stories. Even in the beginning, when it is just emails. Empathize with her, ask follow up questions. Be real and natural. You have to want to listen and put your own desire to impress her with your stories on the back burner. You will endear yourself more by listening to her than by telling her your stories, no matter how good they are. You will get your chance, just be patient. Trust me.

- **Be yourself.** You have very little emotionally invested when you initially contact someone. If they don't like you, it doesn't hurt too much. So why not find out if she will like the real you? Let's say you present someone other than yourself and you hit it off. When she finds out you're an asshole, it will hurt a lot more by then because you have invested emotionally. It is better to see if she is the kind to like assholes right up front.

The ups and downs of internet dating can be dizzying. Be careful not to get caught up in the roller coaster ride. One day you will be on a high with three potential dates, and the next, they may all disappear. This is frustrating, but don't take it personally. You can exchange emails with someone for a couple of weeks, even progress to talking on the phone, and start fantasizing that she is the woman of your dreams. And before you even meet, poof, you never hear from her again. It's almost impossible not to build up expectations about a woman you have been in contact with and begun to like, even if you haven't met. Then you feel really let down when she dumps you. Dumps you? You haven't even met. What is this fucking world coming to? The reality of the internet is that there is no reality. Don't get too excited, too early.

FINALLY WE MEET

When you do finally get the opportunity to meet, you will have already conjured up some idea of this woman. Even assuming that her picture is representative of how she looks, you will have created a total picture of who she is. You fantasize that she likes Breyer's coffee ice cream as much as you do, or that she will so enjoy that steak house you love. And you will be wrong. She is a vegan.

We all know we are on our best behavior on the first date. We tiptoe on the first phone call. Think of how high you are tiptoeing on the phone the night before you first meet. You are doing nothing to screw this up. You aren't telling her anything bad about yourself—as far as she knows, you are perfect. Guess what, she is playing the same game. So try to go into that first date muting your expectations.

Remember what we learned from Psych 101. It's not what we say, it's how we say it. It's what our body language says. That really sucks for a lot of us guys because women are typically pretty good at interpreting our body language. So that leads us to an opportunity for some tips when you first meet (of course, these pertain to all facets of life):

- **Never slouch when meeting someone for the first time.** Actually, never slouch period. It makes you look unsure of yourself. You are not really interested in attracting someone who is attracted to someone who is unsure of himself. Even if you are unsure of yourself, sit up straight.

Eventually, Mike will begin to desire more or different things from the relationship than Sue. The first challenge will be to recognize this. If you don't, you may break up over reasons you were not aware of. If you can recognize it, you can discuss the compromises necessary to enable the patience needed so you can catch up to one another. Patience and understanding—undeniable musts.

Defensive Peter meets Defensive Linda. Here are two people who can become co-dependent in a hurry. Spending all of their time together, ignoring friends and family because they have found someone who makes them feel good. They replace the incredible void felt when they were dumped. The sex will be off the charts. You hear the stories of couples who meet and are married in three months. Then one morning, balance begins to return for one but not the other. The end is near. If only you could communicate all of this, but you are so "defensive" and it feels so good that you are afraid to talk about it lest you screw it up. Until that morning.

So we know Offensive Mike can't date Defensive Linda because she wants to fall in love and he just wants to have sex. And Mike is going to have trouble at some point dating Offensive Sue. Poor Defensive Peter is going back to live with Mom. Just who the fuck is there left to date?

Rebounding sucks. Actually dating in your 50s sucks. But this is what you have to deal with. So, we learn that we need to figure out if we are an Offensive or Defensive Rebounder. Just as important, is your date an Offensive or Defensive Rebounder? You will encounter struggles and differences along the way regardless.

Don't give up. Acknowledge, understand, and communicate.

THREE DATE RULE

You know not to ask for sex when you first communicate with a woman, but what is the expectation regarding sex when you date in your 50s? Here's my secret: a nice goodnight kiss on the first date, major make out session on the second date, and sex on the third date. It's my formula and I'm sticking to it. It hasn't always worked out like this, but that seems to be the natural progression.

Is the Three Date Rule etched in stone in my dating playlist? No, but plus or minus a couple should be all that is needed. I have found women at this stage of their lives want sex and want a lot of it. They are just also careful about who they have sex with. It won't be easy if all you want is sex. If you are real and engage her honestly and have anything going on in life, you have a shot. If you can be patient and put it in her hands with no pressure, she will come around a lot quicker than if you pressure her. Understand that she does want it.

If she is an Offensive Rebounder, in her mind, past sex was poor, non-existent, or not enjoyable. Now that she is free, she has purchased multiple toys and can't wait for the real thing. You have to understand her mindset. She wants it, but needs to be careful. Give her the power to control the decision and the desire for it will overcome any hesitancies. If you pressure her, she will resist and you may have shot yourself in the foot. I know it is hard not to pitch the benefits of a lustful night in bed, but trust me, she will be fantasizing about it herself. She will come on to you in short order.

The Defensive Rebounder is a different story. She is heartbroken and will be clingy early on. She will be leery of sex, unless you show her signs that you are falling for her as quickly as she is falling for you. If you do, you will not need a Three Date Rule. But don't be an asshole and take advantage. If you get involved with her, she is going to be needy. For the relationship to work, you will also have to be a Defensive Rebounder. If so, you may find yourselves having wild sex very early on. But it will not be a healthy relationship in the beginning. You will need some hard work and good communication to make it work.

Remember, there needs to be a connection for sex to occur, and you have to be a nice guy. Assholes need not apply. My point is, we are dealing with 50-somethings who probably have had lousy sex for a long time. They still love sex, but women naturally don't give it up easily and their past could make them even more hesitant. Cede them control and they will not disappoint.

THERE ARE NO SLUTS AT 50

When we were young, we were told that if a guy sleeps around, he is a stud, but if a girl sleeps around, it means she is…not with me. Or labeled a slut. I find it a shame that society puts negative labels on the most pleasurable experience known to man and woman. I mean, society does have its place in making laws so we don't run red lights and kill people, but telling women they should not sleep with someone unless there is love was a bad move. And we guys do have to take responsibility for this. I mean, forever, men have been making all the rules. Each year, men who run the fashion world tell women what they should wear and how short their skirts should be. Mini one year, maxi the next. Cleavage is in, cleavage is out. Women couldn't vote until the early 1900s, and seemingly half of the men in this country have the nerve (and try to create laws) to tell women they can't terminate an unwanted pregnancy. Society (aka men) did create the "girls who sleep around are sluts" thing and, when this stuff was happening, girls had no say in it. If women were in charge, either men would be sluts too (perish the thought), or we would all be having a lot more fun. But guys have been in charge. Talk about cutting off your nose to spite your face.

Let's face it, do guys who committed adultery ever walk around with a big scarlet "A" on their shirts? No.

It's time for society to free those women from sluthood. If I were God, I would proclaim that there is no such thing as a slut, at any age. If a woman wants to engage in the pleasure of sex, she has my blessing.

And hopefully, my phone number.

ON YOUR WAY UP THE RABBIT HOLE

- Embrace online dating. Take it seriously but have fun. There is no "Daters Anonymous"…yet.
- Be honest, be honest, be honest.

- You will need to be introspective and communicative to get through rebounding.
- Make nice, make out, make love.
- My phone number is….

THE OTHER SIDE

Don't be afraid of online dating. Posting a picture and your life on the internet for the world to see is quite daunting at first. But you do get to control the message (and picture, but don't lie) and it is an incredibly efficient way to meet men. One of the safest and easiest ways as well.

If you are worried about how you look, be creative. Post a cool action pic of you doing something you like, enjoying life, if you are not comfortable with close-ups. Even if you are heavy, you will look better doing something cool than just standing there.

I have always been particularly impressed when a woman reaches out to me first. I know my sister does this unabashedly and usually receives a favorable response. You may not feel a need to do this, but at a minimum, if someone contacts you and you are interested, reply with more than a "hi." Endearing and funny emails are good to send; I have always found self-deprecating appealing. Think of what you like and don't like. Men are not that much different.

Don't read too much into a man's profile and don't feel the need to write a book for yours. Most guys do not care about all the little details, and I sense that women with enormous profiles wrote them to please themselves, not to inform a potential date.

Don't dote on your kids in your profile. Do remember, your profile is an advertisement about you, not your mothering skills.

While most of the "Dos" and "Don'ts" apply to women as well as men, ladies should feel free to ask for sex on the first date. You may be surprised at the answer from many men.

Don't harp on his ex(es) and don't conduct an interview.

But if you absolutely must interview him, don't ask: "Are you a family man?"

Ask: "What did you do for the holidays?"

Not only will you find out if he is a family man, but you may find out how big a family you may eventually have to deal with.

Don't ask: "How much do you make?"

Ask: "Where was your favorite/most recent vacation?" Get details in a conversational, get to know you way.

Don't ask: "Are you sloppy?"

Ask: "Do you have a cleaning lady?"

Don't ask: "What happened with your ex?"

Tell him what happened to you. But no details because you don't want to be the angry complaining date he dreads. Just enough to bait him to tell you his story. Now you have the opening to ask your questions.

Do ask if he is divorced or just separated.

Be wary if he is only separated. I had a potential date ask me that, and I was honest and said "separated." She said, "Call me when the divorce is final." I knew (ha ha) that I was ready for a relationship, but she did not believe I was. Actually, she was much more advanced emotionally and much more ready for a relationship than I, but I did not know that. I said "Harrumph!" and moved on. I know two women who dated separated but not divorced men. Both still lived with their wives. Very sticky. There is still a bond there that needs to be broken before he can fully engage. Tread carefully.

Dial in on your rebound status. Guys are less likely to do this, so you get an advantage if you do. Men are better at hiding their emotions (or worse at recognizing them) and may appear aloof, when in reality they are hurting and hiding it. They may be fooling themselves. Don't fall in the same trap. If you see Defensive Rebounder in the mirror, do not go out. You are far from ready. Ask someone who knows you well what they think. A confidant will come in handy with helping you read yourself. Embrace this.

The three date rule is mine—set your own. It may be difficult to transition from sleeping with your partner to sleeping with someone new. Rediscover your sexuality, but do it sensibly and with knowledge of whether you are ready for true intimacy or just a good time. Either is fine when there is honesty and a mutual understanding of the boundaries.

CHAPTER 4: DATING LADIES IN THEIR 40S, 50S, OR 60S?

(OR YIKES! THEIR 30S)

As you know, women come in all shapes, sizes, and ages. I have my shape and size preferences, but I wasn't sure about the age thing. Do you target any particular age or just go with the flow? When you're online dating, you do have to note some kind of preference for matches to appear.

It was easier when we were younger because the goals were the same. Find someone to build a life with, marry, buy a home, have rug rats, etc. Now we are dealing with women who are out there because they want to find someone, but they have baggage, and just like we don't want to acknowledge our baggage, they don't like to either. Most are divorced and have been hurt (either she left because he pissed her off or he left because she pissed him off), have kids, are mad at men, have some money in the bank, have become extremely independent, and are generally ready to take no prisoners. Tread carefully if they've never been married, too.

THE 40S

When I started online dating, I actually began by looking at the early 50s/late 40s crowd. I'll bucket them by decade to ensure that my obsessive sense of numerical correctness is maintained.

So who is this woman in her 40s you are about to have a date with?

If she's never been married, there is probably a reason. It doesn't mean you can't date her, but before you get serious, you might want to explore why. If you are single and have never been married, think about yourself. Enough said?

She likely has tons of girlfriends, is very active with hobbies/local activities, and has perhaps been engaged. She never married for a reason you should know about. She may be a confirmed bachelorette. And be wary of her picture. If she looks too hot, she may not be that way in person. And if she is that way in person, bang her quickly and then head for the hills. I wish it were that easy.

Once I met a woman after seeing her pretty picture on the internet and chatting with her several times. She was spunky, funny, and intelligent, and had never married. Uh-oh. She was hesitant to meet at first, almost scared. *Why are you online dating?* I thought. And she told me about her family woes and mother issues. It seemed odd that she would share intimate issues with someone she had never met. The stories were not pretty. I am the quintessential Mr. Fixit when it comes to helping women deal with their emotional issues, and had hit the mother lode. I began to wonder if we would be able to sustain an evening of conversation that would be stimulating and woe free, but then again, I never minded banging troubled chicks.

We finally agreed to meet in a public area and take a walk. As I got off the phone to leave to meet her, she gave me a warning. It went something like this: "I'm not Twiggy, but I don't need to be wheeled down the street either." Shame on me. Unmarried and face pic only. Double whammy. Unhappy to boot. I quickly realized there was nothing I could or wanted to do for this woman.

It is not always that easy. Go slow with the "never married" type. Find out why. And if she is hot, go even slower.

I was walking to the bar for a date with a gorgeous blonde who was never married when she drove into the parking lot, spotted me, and rolled down her window. For a change, I was pleasantly surprised that she was much prettier than her picture. Nice. But she had this funny look on her face. It was a combination of menacing tempered by incredulity. Was she disappointed in how I looked or did she just smoke some bad weed on the way? I thought she might just drive away. Then she didn't. We sat at the bar and her figure was just as attractive as her face. Why was this woman single? We talked about music and found some common ground, but the conversation soon became a little disjointed and she seemed distant. Like very far away. She went to the bathroom several times, but didn't take her phone with her. Who knows what was going on in the ladies' room? I was torn between wanting to find out and leaving.

We ended the night without even a kiss. But she was hot. And wanted to see me again. Enough said, in my book. Then she got wackier. She would tell me to call her, but then never be around. She would call me during the day, even though she knew I was working. She never once responded to my texts. It was almost like she was trying to screw things up. We arranged to meet a couple of times, but she cancelled at the last minute. Finally, I gave up.

I can't say for certain that being unmarried made these two women "male unfriendly," but perhaps the issues they had that created their behavior kept them unmarried.

The more likely scenario for the 40-something is married-and-now-divorced. Tons of them around. She probably has kids, maybe young ones. If you have kids, you know they come first—if you don't, now you know that's just how it is, or should be. She is now single, away from her children's father(s). Her kids will now grow up in a single parent household, running back and forth between Mom and Dad. Mom feels tremendous guilt about not being able to give her kids the best household possible. It doesn't matter who left whom. She may try to make up for this by overindulging them. There may be some anger at Dad and maybe even some verbal altercations. Try to understand what she is dealing with. This will not be an easy relationship.

Don't be upset if she doesn't introduce you to her kids after just a couple of dates. That's a good thing. The kids are also dealing with a broken home and will always want Mom and Dad back together. So seeing Mom dating your sorry ass will not be taken kindly.

This goes for you and your kids, as well.

I learned the hard way when I told my daughter I was dating a few women who ended up being short-timers. She was just finishing high school and we didn't have a whole lot else to talk about. She would ask me who I was dating, how long, did I have a picture, was I going to marry her. I would go into as much detail as I felt comfortable. She was very inquisitive so it made for good conversation, but she got involved with my emotions and felt hurt when the relationship didn't work. She was sad even when I wasn't, just wanting Dad to be happy. I soon learned to be careful not to disclose too much too early. I learned to wait until I thought it might be someone that could eventually be permanent. Same advice for you. It will be healthier for her kids not to meet you until you have a firmly established relationship with real long-term possibilities. Don't take it personally if she waits.

Trying to date someone who is still hurting from a divorce and struggling with being a single mom will be a challenge, and you should be sure you are up for that. She has little emotional capacity left for a relationship, but doesn't know that. She may want to jump right in, then find herself overwhelmed and run. Alternatively, she may never jump in because her emotions are frayed and she needs time to recover. Of course, the closer she is to the separation when you meet her, the higher the likelihood that all of this will be exaggerated. She could just be confused as hell and thinking she has her shit together. Very dangerous.

The most important factor at this age is timing. Are you really ready to date? Is she really ready to date? Are either of you ready for the kind of relationship the other one wants?

There are a million people out there any one person could be happy with, but both parties have to want that same "kind" of relationship, at the same time, in order for it to work.

So what kind of relationship might she be seeking? She might not even know. Or she may want to date casually, where you are both free to see others. At the opposite end is the exclusive relationship after two dates. There is the once a week date because she has no time for more, or because there is no inclination for more. There is the "spend every minute together" kind, "spend a lot of money on her" kind, "I can't sleep with you till we're in love" kind, the "I think I love you today, but oops, I don't think I do tomorrow" kind, and lots more. 40-somethings are all over the place.

And to be clear: guys are exactly the same in this area.

So now what? Does this mean you should write off all women in their 40s? Absolutely not. They are hipper, more energetic, want a lot more sex, and are a lot younger than you.

- It is better to meet someone who has been apart from her spouse for years, not months.
- You want someone with her shit back together, not someone still raw from a broken marriage.
- You have to be supremely aware and accepting unconditionally of her kids. You will *always* be second. Accept that or don't get involved.
- Try to find out if she left him or he left her (is she an offensive rebounder or defensive rebounder?).

This is true at all ages, but more pronounced with younger women. Her parents will probably be alive and a bigger influence on her life. That can be a positive or negative for you, but as with any divorce, there is a tendency to rely on close relatives to herd you through the hurt and sorrow. Parents play that role very well.

THE GOOD, THE BAD, AND THE UGLY

The Good
- She is younger and less set in her ways.
- She is more daring and willing to try new things.

- She is into sex as it has not been good with the ex.
- She still has life fantasies (including sexual) and is willing to be more adaptable.

The Bad

- She has younger kids requiring large time commitments. Partly because of the kids, she has a busier life; there may not be much time left over for you.
- She is confused about how to handle a relationship, but thinks she knows.
- Parents may have an undue influence in her life.

The Ugly

- Look out if she has never been married.
- If she left him, she was really pissed off at the time and may harbor continued anger.
- If he left her, she has a painful void, and there may be a tendency to fill that by jumping in too fast. Desperate.

THE 50S

Women in their fifties have older children and have been separated from their ex longer or recently separated but married longer. Either way, more baggage. Women in their 50s are also more set in their ways and more skeptical about men and relationships. They may have gone through menopause, which decreases sex drive. Their attractiveness as a partner also depends on how long ago they got divorced and whether they have given up on meeting someone. Look twice if she seems overly connected to her best (also single) female friend of thirty years.

My singlehood got so bad that for a while I took to reading about divorced women and their issues. *How to Recover After Dumping His Ass. 50 is the New 15*. Fake titles, but not fake concepts. There are a lot of self-help books for struggling females—you're reading a rare one for men. She is now armed with all this renewed vigor and self-confidence. She knows what she wants and is ready to go for it.

I also read that women in their 50s may also begin to develop "traditionally male" characteristics. Just what we need. They become more outspoken, egocentric, and aggressive, while taking less bullshit. Meanwhile, men may develop "female" characteristics. Fuck, double trouble. We tend to become more needy and too invested in relationships too early. Just what she is *not* looking for. We have our work cut out for us.

For women with kids, hopefully the father is still in the picture. This can lead to some interesting scenarios. Her kids could be teenagers or in college, and if the father is still involved, there will be plenty of former husband interaction. There are college trips, summer jobs, and maybe even wedding plans or baby showers that will involve both parents. If she dumped him, her hard feelings may linger. Get used to hearing "He can kiss my ass" on frequent occasions. If he left her, it will be worse. There will be a ton of anger and hurt that you will have to deal with first hand. This is not that different if she is younger, but there are more decisions and financial considerations with teenagers and young adults that force more interaction between the parents. When the kids are 10, Mom just wants the support check to show up each month. It gets increasingly complicated.

Just wait until the first event you go to where "he" shows up.

With a woman in her 40s, you have to accept younger children. With a 50-something, you will have to accept more interaction with the father and less interaction with the children.

If you can get past the children thing, you may be hitting the sweet spot for success. You both were born around the same time, have a lot of common experiences and/or memories, were brought up in a similar society, and may have similar morals. Time may have allowed her to cope better with her divorce than someone younger. Her relative youth may have allowed her to fantasize about what life can be like with a good man better than someone older can imagine. Again, the key is timing.

I dated a woman who was recently divorced after a two-decade marriage to a mentally abusive husband. I don't think she realized how abusive the relationship was until it was over. When she did, she was ready to have fun and thought she was ready to be in a relationship. But she was clearly not ready for emotional intimacy. She needed time to heal. Time to accept that she was not at fault for the abuse. Time to trust that the next person she let in would not abuse her.

Our timing could not have been worse because I was seeking that emotional intimacy. We got along so well, had so much fun, and had so much in common. I always thought that no matter what happened, we would eventually get married. But she needed space in order to heal. The word "love" never escaped her lips in over a year of dating. I wanted more; she couldn't give it to me. She wanted me on her terms; I couldn't accept them. I knew someday she would heal and be ready for the kind of emotional intimacy I was craving, but our timing was off and never could get on track. We both moved on.

In addition to timing issues, 50-somethings may be emotionally void. We know jumping in too fast is no good. You don't want to be a void filler. She may still be angry at men and not realize it. This can lead to strange behavior that even she might not be able to figure out. I briefly dated a woman who was obsessed with my prior relationships. "So tell me what happened with your first wife." I could see her taking mental notes. Without even a follow up question when I told her about the threesome shortly after the divorce, she asked, "So tell me about the second wife." Okay, there was no threesome, but in retrospect, I wish I had said it did occur. She just kept taking notes. When it was her turn, she bitched about her ex. There was a lot of fear and anger there. She needed a date with her shrink, not me.

The 50-something may have passed the rebound stage, but may now doubt herself. "Why am I still free?" She may have been hurt by a couple of disappointing post-divorce relationships. She may have slept with someone too early and now won't sleep with someone unless she knows he is madly in love with her (lucky you, with that one…). I dated a woman who swore she was going to put her "chastity belt" back on when we broke up because she, in retrospect, felt she slept with me too early. I wouldn't want to be her next boyfriend.

An interesting dynamic around this age is the "cougar" concept. There are tons of younger guys interested in older women. Your competition for women in their 50s, especially ones that look much younger, may be fiercer than you expected. Of course, women who become cougars are not looking for a long-term relationship. If your competition's date of birth ends in the 80s, you don't stand a chance. But the good thing is that cougars are easy to recognize and therefore avoid. How do you know she is a cougar? She won't return your call.

Women in their 50s will be dealing with older parents and an impending need to care for them. Understanding, respecting, and accepting this dynamic is essential. And how does she feel about your need to care for your parents? This conversation is important. You may have completely different views on this, since caring for parents can last awhile and take up a lot of time. This can be a deal breaker.

My father's mother came to live with my parents after I finished college. It did not impact me directly, but I saw the impact it had on my mother. She provided most of the care and was miserable. Her mother-in-law was manipulative and mean and, of course, Dad did not want to acknowledge this. Granny took advantage of my mother when Dad wasn't around and then played the innocent, forgetful old lady when Dad got home. Mom would complain to Dad, but when Granny professed ignorance or flatly denied what Mom said, Dad couldn't believe that this sweet woman could lie. This led to many fights. Perhaps this situation was worse than others, but that experience has made me extremely wary of adopting a parent. You may feel different and be more accepting, but it is still important to know where each of you stands.

The above is not all-inclusive, but it demonstrates the range of emotional states that a 50-something may experience. It's wide. It becomes important to understand which state she is in at any time. Depending on that state, she will deal with the relationship accordingly. You also have your own state. The key to a relationship working is to understand where the other is living. If you are cross-country, you will need to compromise.

So while the 50s may be your sweet spot from an age perspective, there are a host of challenges.

THE GOOD, THE BAD, AND THE UGLY

The Good
- Because you are closer in age, you will have more in common.
- Her children are older, so she may have more time for a relationship.
- The further removed from her divorce, the more time she has had to heal and become ready for a healthy relationship.

The Bad
- She will have more baggage and may be skeptical of men.
- There may be an emotional void if the divorce was severe or her post-divorce life lacked positive relationships. She may have doubts about finding someone.
- She may have care considerations for her parents that may not agree with yours.

The Ugly
- Cougartown.

THE 60S

The 60s is a decade to be reckoned with. The first thing to know about dating women in their sixties is that they will lie about their age. Assume the late 50-year-old is in her early sixties, and the early sixties is mid to late sixties. I am a firm believer that you are as old as you want to be, so age should not be a huge factor, but it is a factor. Women in their 60s are also at an age where it is more difficult to find someone. She may be willing to settle, and you never want to be the settlee.

There are two types of 60-somethings. Those who want to jump into bed with you early and often, and those who want to fall in love with you first. There appears to be very little of the "three date rule" as with earlier decades. Women in this decade have been divorced longer and have had more long-term relationships since their divorce. Since you are meeting them, they are still single. There is more skepticism and hesitancy, and many of them have become comfortable on their own.

Many have even come to terms with the fact that they may grow old without a partner, thus establishing more long-term ways of living and deeper habits. These may be difficult to break and will require compromise—by both of you. If you think women have habits, we can't kid ourselves about ours. We are just as stubborn in not wanting to give up new found "freedoms" or ways of doing things. We are as set in our ways and hate compromise as much as women. Two immovable objects make for a larger hurdle with the 60-somethings.

Sometimes the sex drive is still high even after menopause, now without the worries about procreating. Women in their 60s tend to be less inhibited because the kids aren't going to walk in on them, they are more secure in who they are, and now it's time for them. They will be more aggressive than you are accustomed to, but that is a good thing. They will be upfront about it. We are all adults, after all.

They still have baggage, but have stored much of it away by now. Storing the baggage in the right emotional closet may be elusive, creating surprising issues. Your attempt to help might look too much like her ex's attempts to control. She figured out her husband was a control freak, but has not yet quite figured out whether someone else is being helpful or controlling. Patience is important. She will come around to figuring it out.

She will also be stubborn. Compromise will not come without some resistance. A younger woman may be willing to compromise more easily, maybe even over-compromise, to make sure she can be with someone. A 60-something will not.

Since they are older and have grown children, those children may have their own children and voila! We are dating Grandma. I have no issues with dating a grandmother, but there are now some little ones running around that need Grandma's help. There are brothers and sisters and cousins who have kids that are having kids and getting married, and surprise 50th birthday parties and surprise 50th anniversary parties. You not only have to deal with a woman more set in her ways, you have to deal with a shitload of family gatherings. Wedding here, surprise party there, annual barbeque at this cousin and then that cousin. If your family is big and hers is not, then you will have to deal with the opposite effect. You will be asking her to attend a *lot* of events.

This can lead to issues. If both families are the same size, there will be conflicts. If hers is much larger than yours, she will be used to going to every fucking event. And now she is dating you with the small family and inviting you to the second cousin once removed block party where you will know no one. Of course, you don't want to go, but then pouting ensues. Since I am the small family guy who has experienced this several times, I like to use the following logic: "Honey, you have a big family and lots of family events and I don't. But I have just adopted the New York Jets and we have a family event every Sunday in the fall. I don't expect you to go to all my events, so can I occasionally skip a grandniece's christening?"

Keep in mind that there is a 50/50 chance you will be on the big family side. Give her a break.

THE GOOD, THE BAD, AND THE UGLY

The Good
- She is more mature and honest, making open communication and a roadmap to a good relationship easier.
- Her children and parents are less of a factor.
- The sex is still good and she will be less inhibited.

The Bad

- She is set in her ways and stubborn; habits may be unbreakable.
- Too many family gatherings, yours or hers, will create issues.
- She is older than you, and you are not sure by how much.

The Ugly
- She can be an immovable object.

THE 30S

My daughter has one dating rule: I may not date anyone who is less than 10 years older than she is. At the time of writing, this comes to a 29-year-old lower limit. But do I even want to date someone in their 30s? I dated a 39-year-old once and felt a bit uncomfortable. She looked like Madonna looked in the 80s. Big hair with things attached to it. Metal dangling from her ears, neck, and arms. I managed to overcome my initial intimidation, but found it difficult to find common ground for conversation. She couldn't relate to the seven Jay and the Americans concerts I had been to. We had a fun night, which ended with a surprise make-out session in the parking lot. She said she wanted to see me again but was real busy. I said I wanted to see her again and would call. I did, halfheartedly, and when we didn't hook up, I lost no sleep.

I could not stop wondering why a good-looking 39-year-old would want to date someone almost 20 years older than she was. It made me feel pressure to be funnier or more entertaining, or smarter than I would have to be if I were 40. I finally relaxed when she told me her former husband was much older than she was. If she had not, I would have eventually calmed down and not given a shit. I think.

I have a friend who said if he ever got divorced, he would seek out a 30-year-old to date and have sex with. He thinks he is missing something. He has a wonderful wife who adores him and deep down, he knows it's just a fantasy. I am not the type to date a 30-something, but my friend and many like him think they are.

Three things to be 100% comfortable with before even engaging in the thought: tattoos, piercings, and texting.

We all know why *we* would date someone in their 30s, but why the fuck would they date us? If you consider dating 30-somethings for more than shits and giggles, you need to understand why they have chosen to sleep with fat, balding, emotionally scarred men when they have plenty of younger choices. There are usually two main reasons: daddy issues or sugar daddy desires. Neither of these is good. But think about it: why would an emotionally well-adjusted, normal 35-year-old date someone 20 years older than she is? I don't care if you are buffed, have all your hair, and look like a rock star. Don't you think those characteristics come in a 35-year-old brand?

Now, if you are doing it just for the experience, go for it. For all of us. The sex will be off the charts with twisting in ways you thought not humanly possible, and going out at 11 instead of coming home at 11. And lots of dealing with her friends who are just as young as she is. And eventually meeting her parents who are just as old…as you.

If you are considering a serious relationship, there is some real baggage with someone who wants to be in a serious relationship with someone 20 years his junior. Or her senior. You want to be a daddy and she wants a daddy. Or you are rich and want the trophy wife because that means more than having a substantial relationship, and she wants a sugar daddy. You both have your own set of issues. If they draw you together and you see a relationship in it, understand what it is. You will not find true love with someone who wants a daddy or a rich guy. If you are fulfilled being a daddy or showing off the hot young wife, go have fun. Then get some help.

THE GOOD, THE BAD, AND THE UGLY

The Good
- Sex.
- Sex.
- Sex.

The Bad
- You are emotionally fucked up because you want to date her.

- She is emotionally fucked up because she wants to date you.
- Short-term fun will not lead to long-term happiness.

The Ugly
- She dumps your ass once she figures out she needs neither a daddy nor your money.

WIDOWED VS. DIVORCED

Many of the age differences are subtle and overlap. The differences between a widow and a divorcee are not so subtle.

It is safe to start by saying a woman who has lost her husband doesn't have the same emotional scars as a divorced woman, though she is scarred. Let's assume that the widow had a good marriage and the death of her spouse was unexpected. She loved him, they never had issues that caused a divorce, and she's never gone through a divorce. The suddenness of the death of such a loved one leaves a hole so deep it takes a long time for her to recover.

The divorcee has gone through a divorce, which we all know can be hell. Whether you fled or she kicked you out, it was hell. If there are kids involved, more so. This creates a set of emotional issues very different from a widow's.

The widow has to go through the four stages of grief: denial, anger, depression, acceptance. The divorcee only has one—pissedoffness.

If you date a widow, you will be up against the man of her dreams and he will forever be her soulmate in her memory. How long ago she lost her husband may determine how big an issue this is. Time heals all wounds. Memories fade, focus changes; once the grief stages are complete, she may conclude it's time to move on. The variable is how long and everyone is different. It will be important for you to figure out if she is past the stages of grief and capable of loving again. That doesn't mean she will forget her late husband, she will just be able to open her heart to new possibilities.

Some women find out things about their dead husband after he dies that they didn't know (or ignored) when he was alive. One woman I dated found charges on his credit card from a sexy lingerie store and did not recall getting any fancy presents shortly before he died. That added another layer of denial to her grieving process.

Remember, you are competing with a memory. You may find that you can't live up to that memory, or you may find that she is looking for feelings she had with her husband. It may be difficult for her to recapture it with you (or anyone). You may find that she doesn't want that feeling again or that she feels like she is cheating on her husband. You may never be loved the way you want to be.

The woman who lost her man to death will not be angry at men. She may be angry at God, but not men. She will learn independence quickly, like divorced women. Actually, she may be more independent. It may take years before she is ready to engage someone new and during that period, she is living alone and building a life without a man. She may come to the realization that she will never be able to replace him, and learning to be okay with being alone.

Once she moves past the pain, hurt, and sorrow of losing her husband, hopefully she can become ready for someone else. She will still have baggage, but without the emotional scars a divorce can leave. So flip a coin. Heads, there is no divorce baggage. Tails, she lost her soulmate and you will never replace that person. Neither side is pretty, but neither is hopeless.

I can't tell you which I would rather be with, and I have been with both. The widow was single 10 years before we started dating. Her husband died suddenly of a heart attack, well before his time. She clearly loved him, but was over it. By the time I met her, she had had two long-term relationships. At first, I didn't know whether I was competing with his ghost or not, but over time, I knew I was not. Not all widows will feel this way. Not all men who date widows will be able to come to feel the way I did. And it may not be their fault or anything they can do about it.

Then there was the time I dated a woman who had been widowed...twice. She brought that up on the second date. I am not sure why, but it did make me pause. Bad luck, bad choices, or serial killer? I did not much care. There never was a third date.

When you date a divorced woman, your competition in her memory bank is most likely an asshole. Most guys will have a much better chance competing against an asshole.

The divorcee will be ready to date sooner than the widow, but may not be emotionally prepared for it. She is angry but ready for someone to "really" love her, not like the bastard ex-husband. The divorcee would love to have someone in her life immediately, to fill the void left by the emotional loss of her husband. She may not be ready emotionally, but she is going to think she is. She will think she can handle dating, loving, and sex before she really can.

Ultimately, if recently divorced, she will probably be unsure of her own feelings and ability to handle a relationship, but willing. Time and experimentation will help her figure it out. If you desire a real relationship, let her experiment with others. The widow will need to get through her grief and become ready to put herself back out there on her own time and schedule. There will be no pushing her when she isn't ready. The divorcee can be pushed to date too soon, and if she thinks she is ready but isn't, lookout. You are now the pusher and the experimentee.

THE CHANGE

The Change is a fact of life. You are dating women that may be going through The Change, have gone through The Change, or will shortly go through The Change (unless you hopped on that 30-something bandwagon). It sucks. For women. For men. You need to be at least marginally educated on the topic, so you know what she is going through and don't act like an uncaring pig. Acknowledging the issues that go along with it may actually engender a productive conversation about it and how it is affecting your date/girlfriend/partner. Educate yourself.

Men and women are different in many ways. How many times have you asked yourself, "why doesn't she get me?" She has asked herself the same thing about you. When The Change comes, she knows you don't get it and needs you to. So try. And if you can, it will be acknowledged. Understand the symptoms and you can be empathetic to what is happening. You will still have to deal with the moods, but at least you can try to understand. Dealing with it is not easy: it is a hormonal issue. But we guys tend to take things personally. So when we pick her up for a date and she gets pissed off over nothing, we get pissed off back. Why? Because we are insecure and think she is really mad at us. It looks like she's mad at us, she acts like she's mad at us, it feels like she is mad at us. Ergo, it must be something we did.

Like the time I was commiserating with my hormonal girlfriend who was complaining about her adult daughter's seeming lack of appreciation for all the things she did for her. It appeared to be a product of hormones because there was no other rational explanation. Her daughter had not done anything worse than not return a text Mom sent, within the required time frame. "Why can't she act like an adult instead of a 17-year-old? I just want to know that she got home safe." But there I was, the good boyfriend. I said that her daughter loved her, surely she got home okay. And all was right with the world. Then, I goofed. I tried to make her feel better by bringing my daughter into the conversation. "Meghan does the same thing to me. I ask her how school is going and she responds three days later." Oops. That gave her the perfect opportunity to tell me that I had no right to talk about her relationship with her daughter. "How can you tell me what to do about my daughter when you are the world's worst dad?" Okay, that is not an exact quote, but that is what it felt like. Here I am trying to make her feel better and she lashes out at me. Why? Hormones. Had I not known they were at work, I certainly would have gotten upset.

Moral of the story—if you didn't do anything wrong, don't get upset. She may have just gone through a hot flash or gotten no sleep last night. Try to understand and talk to her. Better yet, listen. If she remains mad, know that it's temporary. She will appreciate how you are dealing with it more than you can imagine. The most important thing to remember is that she is not mad at you. She is mad at God for putting her through this. And if she doesn't believe in God, she is just pissed off and we have to deal with it.

Be kind, be gentle, and know it's not about you.

TEENAGER IN LOVE

No matter who you end up dating, you will sometimes feel like a teenager in love. Being "out there" after a long-term marriage means there is a void of some description. Regardless of age, if that void is filled, you will find happiness. How that void is filled and by whom will determine whether that happiness is sustainable. Know what you are getting yourself into and go slow emotionally.

ON YOUR WAY UP THE RABBIT HOLE

- Embrace the positives of each decade and be aware of where difficulties may lie.
- Be sensitive to what both divorcees and widows have gone through. They have different emotions, feelings towards their ex, and men in general. With widows the memory is positive, not so with divorcees.
- Educate yourself about The Change, talk about it with her, and most importantly, don't take it personally—unless you should.
- If you want to date a 30-something, God Bless You.
- If you want to marry a 30-something, God Help You.

THE OTHER SIDE

And what about us guys? Are we different at 40, 50, or 60? I certainly was. I was divorced the first time in my 40s, the second time in my 50s, and quickly settled into a new relationship after the first divorce, but ran around like a Kentucky Derby winner put out to stud the second time. My rebound status was mostly confused.

Are guys any different than women in the same respective decade? In a word, yes. First and foremost, men often look for younger women and women are more open to dating older men. That brings the 70-somethings into the conversation for women. Talk about set in your ways. Is he open about his health status? How many times a week does he have to golf?

Do you care about finances? Are you financially secure in your own right? Do not expect a man to be your financial lifeline. If prior beaus have wanted to be a provider, it does not mean that future ones will. Even rich 75-year-olds can be cheap. Or perhaps just thrifty.

Being with an older guy can be great:

- They view you as beautiful simply because you are younger.
- They are more relaxed with sex and embrace toys and experimenting.
- They are more comfortable with themselves than someone younger.
- They are more financially stable.
- They are more cultural and classy.

With younger guys:

- Career is a priority.
- Rebuilding wealth after splitting everything 50/50 with the ex is a priority, and a source of great stress. I found this very true with my second ex. Our combined nest egg had been growing nicely and with our home paid for and respective savings, retirement was looking pretty nice. Then half of it was gone along with the paid up house.
- Just like you, younger guys will have less time because of their career and kids.
- They are more active with manly things still important and that mid-life crisis is still in front of them. Mountain climbing, helicopter skiing, scuba diving. Be ready.

- Be wary as guys play the victim really well. Do I hear passive/aggressive?

Okay, we need to talk about children. Do not be there Wednesday night and "that" every other weekend, at least early in the relationship. Wait until a long-term commitment is real. Respect his parenting relationship just as you need him to respect yours. Don't expect his kids to like you. Do not under any circumstance try to replace Mom. You can't, and will only be disappointed while screwing up the kids and maybe even your relationship. Listen to how he talks about his kids and his responsibilities to learn if he is a good dad. He could be your kids' stepdad someday.

Remember, you live with your kids, he sees them on Wednesday and every other weekend. There is a completely different mindset to caring for them, the need to be there, and the need to compensate for the lack of the other parent. You may look at the time your ex has with your kids as a relief; he may treasure the time he can spend with his kids. Respect that.

Daughters and fathers have very special relationships, more so than sons and fathers. Not that sons and fathers aren't special, but it will be more difficult for you to understand the father/daughter connection and daughters will need time and understanding to work through their feelings about another woman in the picture. Don't perceive that as threatening, but as an opportunity to show that you too believe the kids come first.

You will also see them deal with their kids on an occasional basis, not every day like your experience. Very different. There are a lot of Disneyland Dads out there because of guilt or just to make their time with the children as special as possible. For the most part, the everyday humdrum of cooking, cleaning, laundry, and homework do not permeate his life. You may think he is a lousy dad for indulging his kids because you discipline yours. It could be the opposite. Don't judge and don't offer your opinions unless asked—you are not walking in his shoes.

We have to end this with some fun. Wanna be a Cougar? It would be quite the ego trip having someone 20-30-40 years younger coming after me. My sister tried it briefly and enjoyed it, but took it for what it was worth. Temporary and fun—nothing serious. I say go for it if you are so inclined. Grrr.

CHAPTER 5: SPRECHEN SIE DEUTSCH?

(MEETING FOREIGN WOMEN)

You will find all types of women online. A subset that I found particularly interesting early on was foreign women. They come in all the same flavors as American women, but also have their own special characteristics. Ah, dating foreign women: something we all should experience.

I encourage new experiences and if you are going to get serious about dating foreign women, there are some things you should know. Let me start with some basics. If you are in the hunt for a mail-order bride, there are plenty of web sites that provide that kind of service, and you are free to troll around them. I respect the man who wants a 20-year-old Russian to fuck his brains out in return for supporting her and her family. No, I don't.

I am talking about meeting someone and she just happens to be foreign. And she is foreign and looking to meet someone, and it just happens to be you. It's random, you didn't choose to go in this direction, but it laid across your doorstep and now what do you do? I am describing a woman who is foreign born and has come to the US as an adult. The primary differences between her and an American-born woman are culture and language. I realize these are generalizations, but they are based on my experiences and shared in the hope of helping others.

You cannot obviously put all foreign women in the same bucket. There are many subtle differences between foreign-born women and American women. And those that are not so subtle. We will get into both. Some of those differences occur more frequently and some are more pronounced. Nothing bad, just different.

Some shit you learn in life by living, providing you are paying attention. Other stuff you just stumble upon. All the while I was suffering through my divorce and self-esteem issues, I was reading self-help books and seeing my shrink like he was the morning newspaper. Living. While I was getting some ideas on how to get better, I soon realized I was missing one of the most important avenues of awareness and information. I stumbled upon blogs. There are blogs about everything. At 50-something, one does not seek blogs for help, but when you sink as low as I did, you can amaze yourself by where you end up. I found a lot of guys out there blogging about foreign women. It helped put my experiences in perspective and really hone in on what makes foreign women tick.

One of them is that foreign women often have more of a traditional view of gender roles in society. I don't disagree with the feminist revolution, but it has not gained as strong a foothold in other countries. She likes to be treated like a lady, whether it's opening doors, ordering her meal, helping her on with her coat, or buying her flowers.

Another trait that is much stronger is communication skills. American women seem to play more mind games and are afraid to open up emotionally early on in a relationship. This is a honed skill from dealing with American assholes all their lives. Foreign women seem more comfortable telling you how they feel and demanding honesty from you. You will encounter less bullshit with foreign women.

Foreign women value family highly. Though American women do as well, their families tend to be more local, as in somewhere in the United States. Foreign women have family back "home," which will mean trips of a much longer variety, potentially multiple times per year. So either prepare to be alone for a couple of weeks a year or dust off your passport and figure out just how the fuck you are going to get from Rutherford, New Jersey to Dublin or Warsaw or Brasilia. She has probably been taking these trips by herself for years, so she may be fine if you don't go, but make sure you are up on the status of her childhood sweethearts before letting her traipse back to the homeland by herself.

Foreign women have lower opinions of men from their home country than American women have of American men. Christ, if American women think we are schmucks, guess how bad those foreign dudes are. This is a plus for us. Their expectations are lower. However, it will make them more aloof and untrusting as their frames of reference are the foreign schmucks. When we do attain their trust, they are more passionate and romantic, and exquisitely expressive in bed. And they like to walk around naked!

You will think they are exotic because of where they came from. But to them, you are what they have become used to—dating American men. They are different to you, but you are not to them. Do not make them feel different. Treat them special, but not because they are foreign. They know it. I dated a foreign woman with an accent and she would get annoyed when someone asked her where she was from. In her mind, the accent should no longer matter. I guess if I were in Europe, I would get tired of people asking me where in the United States I was from.

So this is new territory for you. You have to be prepared for some heretofore never experienced issues. Communication is a brand-new ballgame. If English is her second language, sometimes you will have no idea where she is coming from. How long she has been here and the degree of her English skills will determine the immediate flow of communication. She may have an accent and it may be thick. I met a woman from Poland and discovered that in the Polish language there is no "th" sound. So every word that has a "th" in it sounds like something different. "Thought" sounded like "fought" and "they" sounded like "dey." And so on. It took a little bit of time, but eventually I caught on.

There will also be nuances she may be unaware of. Many words and phrases have multiple meanings and she may not know all of them. It will be good to keep things clear, especially early on. I use the word "yikes" as a politically correct way of saying "Holy shit." And "Holy shit" can be used in a positive or a negative way. "Holy shit she's hot" is positive; "Holy shit, the New York Jets lost again" is negative. Well, I used the word "yikes" in a positive manner, but she assumed I was describing something negative. Daresay, we had a little communication mix-up that had to be straightened out. We did, but it was a lesson learned.

Accents can also be fun. I love Australian accents and could listen to them all night. I have never met an Australian I did not instantly like, so maybe I am positively prejudiced. An Irish brogue can be musical. I dated an Irish woman for several months and loved not only how she spoke, but also how her lips pursed in a very cute manner when she said certain words. I found myself thinking in Irish. When I thought of her, my mind was talking with an Irish accent. It was kind of like the song you can't get out of your head.

The novelty of a foreign woman may make the initial stages more exciting and interesting, as well as challenging, but all novelties wear off. You will need to see beneath that novelty and be willing to accept unconditionally her accent and cultural differences. These differences may create unexpected reactions between the two of you. Communication mishaps may create insecurities. You won't know how to read her or react to certain things 100% of the time, and you may think she is reacting negatively when what she is saying is positive in her mind. Confused? Exactly.

If English is her second language, then your emails and texts may create some interesting situations. It is easier to speak a foreign language than it is to write in one, so if you are exchanging a lot of written material, take care. She may easily use a word the wrong way or you may take it the wrong way. Do you correct her? I dated a Belarusian woman who told me that it was okay to correct her English, just not during a fight. So take what you read with a grain of salt and understanding. Clarify and ask questions before getting upset.

Embrace the differences and use them as a tool to communicate better. Agree to work together and you will have a fighting chance. On my first date with the Belarusian woman, we made an agreement: she would talk slow and I would listen hard. Imagine the frustration of trying to understand someone with an accent and not always understanding what she is saying. The tendency is to shake your head in agreement so as not to admit you didn't understand her, again. And she is thinking you are a total bore. Acknowledge what you both know up front. I am going to have to listen hard and she is going to have to talk slow. Bingo. Ten minutes into the date—no issue.

By using your differences in a positive manner, you are allowing yourself to be more vulnerable because of those differences. Open up. Talk about them. There will be plenty more than just language. By overcoming the vulnerabilities together, you build a closeness that was never felt with anyone else.

I have painted a pretty rosy picture of foreign women, but I do not wish to minimize that the cultural and language differences are difficult. Also, there can be a perception by friends and family of "What! You can't find an American woman? There must be something wrong with you."

A few final thoughts and then some real life experiences. Foreign women are more prone to like older men. The age difference does not seem to matter. It may lead to a different dynamic and kind of relationship than dating a 30-something American woman.

The next component is financial. Many foreign women who have come to the US settle into their ethnic community and work there initially. While they are fiercely independent, they may not have had the opportunity to save much or may not make a lot of money. If you are looking for an equal financial partner and are upper-middle to upper class, you may have to look elsewhere. They expect that you will pay for most everything, including vacations. They do not do this because they think they are deserving or entitled, but because it is where they are financially. Despite that, they will make a sincere effort to once in a while pay for something. They are perfectly happy if vacations do not include a five-star hotel. Going to fancy restaurants is not important. Cooking at home and watching a movie on the internet is a perfectly enjoyable evening for them. They are not applying for a sugar daddy.

Be prepared for the first time she chats with Mom on the phone. There will be silence, then all of a sudden...gibberish. She may even get a little animated. And if you have had a disagreement recently, you will sit there knowing with 100% certainty that your new girlfriend is telling her mother what a piece of shit you are. Chill out. She is probably talking about her stupid 50-year-old brother who is dating a 30-something.

Finally, she will melt if you send her a poem, email, letter, card, or some other written communication in her language. The translation does not have to be perfect; she will love the effort. Don't try this as a tactic to get her back when you fuck up, however, as her annoyance will dwell on your shitty linguistic skills. Instead, utilize this tool to push her over the edge.

The seeds of my adoration with foreign women began at a surprisingly early age. Well, before two divorces, funding my shrink's entire IRA account, and the invention of the Three Date Rule. My exposure at an early age gave me the opportunity to meet, become infatuated with, and ultimately respect foreign women before becoming jaded with age and insecurity. If you can find a similar experience in your youth, embrace it.

DOWN UNDER (AUSTRALIA)

I had barely left New Jersey in my first 21 years of life and for the first time, I was beginning to feel my wings spread. My father always had an unusually strong hold on what I did. I went to Rutgers University, near home in New Jersey, because he commanded it. My parents moved to Florida my senior year in college. When I graduated college, my father commanded that I move to Florida and work in his business. I succumbed to the pressure and moved to Florida. Fortunately, I was able to resist getting involved in his business. Barely. I found a job in Florida and it provided a springboard to a career without it being my father's career path.

I began to date a local woman and that blossomed into a nice relationship. After spending a year working where my first raise was $100 per month, I decided to pursue a graduate degree at Rutgers and moved back to New Jersey. While we never officially broke up, we both knew that a long-term, long-distance relationship would not work. We remained friends.

So much so that I wasn't afraid to ask her a favor. A really big favor. Things were going very well back in the Garden State. I had a job lined up with an accounting firm and was about to earn my MBA. I even had five weeks between the end of graduate school and the beginning of the job. I thought about driving cross-country, but knew my car would not make it. And I didn't want to go alone, but who would have five weeks off from work or school at the same time I did? And a car? Florida?

On a million to one shot, I called and asked her if she wanted to drive cross-country with me. She accepted. Bam. Okay, now the tough one: "Can we use your car?" "Yes." Bam. Bam. Holy shit, I was going cross-country and even had a partner.

Back then, people communicated by phone, and our trip was still three months away. I diligently called her every week to make sure the car was okay. Oops, I mean to make sure she was okay. It was. So was she. But then, three weeks before we were to leave, I got a phone call. "I'm sorry, Paul, but I can't go because I am pregnant." "Can I borrow your car anyway?" is what I wanted to ask her, but didn't.

Fuck. Now what? No car, no traveling partner. This was 1978 and I had a thumb. Hitchhike? Across country? Me, the shy nerd, meeting strangers. No way. But I didn't have a choice. It was either hitchhike or sulk. I was good at sulking. Always have been, always will be. Someone has to do it.

I sucked it up and changed my plans. I mapped out a route that took me to Chicago, up to Seattle, down the coast to Portland, San Francisco and Los Angeles, and back east through Kansas City where I had friends. I bought a backpack, sleeping bag, and a shitload of balls. The balls were free but painful. I had a friend drop me off near Route 80, heading west, and I was off on the adventure of a lifetime.

I was a nice kid, held the door open for old ladies, helped Mom with the dishes, did my homework. You would think the Hitchhiking Gods would smile upon me. No. Could my first ride be with Ozzie and Harriet or the *Leave it to Beaver* family? Hell, I would have taken the Clampetts. Nope.

I get into a car with a hippie, long-haired dad and his 10-year-old son. After Dad welcomes me, he tells Junior to show me his pet. Oh, how cute, father and son taking a ride with Fido.

Junior turns to me with both hands as if to say "Would you like to hold Fido?" but it was not Fido. It was a fucking snake. A big one. My first fucking ride.

After buying some more balls, things did turn for the better as I made my way from point to point. While I could write a whole book about this adventure, this prelude is to introduce "Down Under." In San Francisco, I toured the town on a bicycle. The hills are so steep you would think you would not be able to ride up them. My issue was riding down them. I was afraid to go too fast so I walked the bike down the hills. I also took a bus, looking around to soak in as much of the city as I could, and that's when I spotted her. Short, blonde, beautiful—breathtaking—and totally out of my league. I figured I would do what I usually do in these situations. A quick look, deep sigh, then stare at her ass as she walks away, and onto the next out-of-my-league fantasy.

But she said "Hi." And when she spoke her next sentence, I had my first full-fledged love affair with an accent. She was Australian. I had met an Australian earlier on my trip while in Seattle but of the male variety. He was as friendly a person as you could meet. So was she.

I thought I was on an adventure traveling across my country, but she was traveling across the world—in first class. Her father was a pilot for a leading Australian airline, and as a child of a pilot, she could fly anywhere in the world for free until she turned 21. She was 20 and taking full advantage. It was a three-month trip. Our time together in San Francisco was brief because she had to move on to the next leg of her trip. One of those legs was New York. Being the consummate gentleman (and horny 24-year-old), I told her to call me when she got to New York and I would show her around. I never thought she would call. I never thought I would ever see her again, and that would be okay because this trip was about meeting lots of people for a short period of time and knowing you were never going to see them again. Oh well. She was gorgeous, but out of my league. For the best.

Three weeks later, my phone rings at 8:00 in the morning. The voice is sobbing and stuttering about how no one will help her. She is lost and no one will help her find out where she needs to be. The voice also has an accent. She was smack dab in the middle of the commuting mob at Grand Central Station in Manhattan asking people for directions during the heart of rush hour. She had no chance. I calmed her down, helped her figure out where she had to go—and made a date.

I walked through Grand Central Station almost daily at the time. Being jostled and ignored was an art form, but this young lady had no clue. I know, if she were from Idaho, she may have been just as clueless. I would like to think empathy was the dominant characteristic, but it was probably hormones. Regardless, it gave me emotional exposure to a foreign woman for the first time and the "difference" stayed with me, and gave me insight later on in life.

The story continues.

She was in town for five days and we saw each other for four of them. We went to dinner, went out for drinks, went dancing. I had just quit smoking. She smoked. I started again. I had to work every day. She didn't. I didn't get much sleep. We had a lot of fun, but never got romantic. I felt she truly was out of reach and was happy she wanted to spend time with me. We kissed, but not passionately. I wanted more, of course, but sensed she didn't. On our last night, I could not resist at least a stab at it.

I can't say I imitated Burt Reynolds in any way other than having a moustache. Certainly not how to make a woman swoon. But I got to the point of asking her if she would like to sleep with me. It was somewhat unromantic, but since we never got romantic, it didn't feel that awkward. This was our last night and we may never see each other again. We got along so well. Wouldn't it be nice to make love?

I did not expect a positive response, but I also did not expect this: "I would have loved to sleep with you, but I slept with a guy I had just met in San Francisco. I didn't feel good about it afterwards since we would probably never see each other again. So I can't sleep with you." Why am I never the guy to screw up the next guy?

She was right. She left the next day. No tears, and we were definitely going to see each other again. It was fun and we'll write. We did for a while, but it petered out as I expected. To this day, I have never met an Australian I didn't instantly like. I will visit there and when I do, I may never leave.

My first real exposure to foreign women occurred at 24, and it was innocent. Many of the traits I subsequently learned, I did not recognize at the time, but it opened my mind up to the possibility. Open your mind up, whether you had similar experiences when you were young or even if you have not.

My youthful exuberance was subsequently tempered when I found out what dating a foreign woman was really like.

SPUTNIK REDEUX (RUSSIA)

Back to current day.

One of my experimental "hi" emails that went awry: She had a cute pic online and responded, starting an email exchange. There was a small hitch—her spelling and grammar sucked. I had never had a problem banging lousy spellers, so I persevered. She told me she didn't want to talk live because of her thick accent. Her foreignness intrigued me. She was Russian. I always like meeting people who are from somewhere I have not been, and Russia was in that category. She was interested in meeting me and her emails went from "you are very attractive" to "you seem like such a nice person" to "I can't wait to meet you and see how special a person you are."

As she got increasingly friendly, I began to get apprehensive. You hear the stories where the hot Russian babe destroys the life of some schmuck who can't keep his pants on. She was gushing with compliments when we finally agreed to meet. I began to think she was looking for a husband so she could stay in the US, or worse, wanted to get pregnant so she could literally have a sugar daddy. I wore a chastity belt to that date.

I picked a classy bar in Manhattan and got there early. By the way, guys, always get there first, especially on the first date. Woman are not typically comfortable sitting in a bar by themselves, especially when they think that they look like they have "first internet date here" stamped on their forehead.

She was late and I began to wonder if she would show up. I looked up and then did a double take. I thought all Russian women were supposed to be hot. Not. I sort of recognized her face, but only barely. While her face was not unattractive, she was built like a Russian wrestler. A male one. Almost scary. It was the only time in my dating career that I almost said, "I am sorry, but I don't think this is a good idea" and left. But the gentleman in me told me to be quiet. Of course, there was one other matter that helped. She brought along her incredibly attractive 23-year-old daughter. Yikes.

I had never had someone bring along someone else to a first date. Now, if I had my pickings of who should be that second person, she was sitting next to me. Her mother struggled with the language quite a bit and used her daughter to interpret both what I said and what she wanted to say. It was a bit awkward, but I learned a lot about her and the Russian culture. We ordered a second glass of wine. Nadia Jr. was truly overwhelming, but was 23—not even a 30-something, and younger than my daughter-imposed limit. Sigh.

Mom was here legitimately and honestly looking for a real relationship. Unfortunately, her accent was almost prohibitive. It would be hard for her to find someone on a traditional dating site, but I give her tons of credit for trying. I am not sure I could confidently go on a Russian dating site with my thick New York accent. After the second glass of wine, we parted and I never saw her again.

I would be remiss if I didn't end this story with some reactions from my friends. They, being bigger degenerates than I, admonished me for not being able to transition from the mother to the daughter. I do admit the thought crossed my mind. I guess you had to be there, but despite my proclivity for sarcasm towards the fairer sex, the only thing that felt right was to wish them both good luck in life. It was fun and interesting to meet them, but I let it go at that.

Then there was crazy.

RAF DIVE BOMBER (ENGLAND)

I never met this one, and I was skeptical of her story, but both she and the story were entertaining. She was 35, grew up in England, and was pretty. She noted in her online profile that she desired men up to the age of 60. I didn't need much else. I don't spend a lot of energy if I really don't think I can attract someone, so 35-year-olds like this one fall into this category. I said: "Nice profile, check out mine and if you like it, let's chat." I got a 500-word response. The giveaway was the way it was written. Some women don't use punctuation properly, or capitalize, or use spell check, but usually Americans conjugate verbs properly. Many of her 500 words were non-conjunctive. She noted that she grew up in the United Kingdom, but it did not seem like English was her first language.

She described herself in detail, and if it weren't for all the grammatical issues, I would have thought she had cut and pasted this to hundreds of emails. Then she finished it with the fact that she lived in Houston and asked, "Is this distance a barrier?" I live in New Jersey. Duh.

We exchanged a couple of emails and she suggested we instant message. We began to chat and I got a sad tale of how both her parents had passed away, and the story of her lousy ex who abused her, was found in bed with her best friend two weeks after he proposed to her, drank too much, smoked too much, and didn't come home. She had a dog named Bella. Mmm, Russian? Maybe she has a hot daughter.

Then she lays the following on me:

> "I see life as the pivot and the engine in the mechanism of human existence so I believe we should live life to the fullest with that special one that brings joy and happiness with that special tender loving emphatic emotions that make you wanna bring down the moon and stars just to give that spark and sparkle in our lives."

Now that's good stuff, but clearly unoriginal. Believe it or not, it was the most lucid sentence she wrote, and I wanted to know where she got it from. That was not forthcoming. She was willing to relocate after she got to know me better. By the time we were done, though, I had lost the passion to pursue this any further. I suggested that she figure out how to get to New York to visit me and once she was here, I would take care of the rest. Oops, I guess she wanted air fare included. So this one was a hot foreign babe clearly looking for a sugar daddy.

But then along came…

VIVA THE EMERALD ISLE (IRELAND)

When we first talked, I asked her where she was from. She replied "Ireland" with just a touch of indignation because I couldn't tell. I loved her Irish accent and she was very pretty. She had pictures online as both a brunette and a blonde. I didn't know which flavor I was talking to, and for the moment, I didn't care. She had been in the US for 17 years, became a citizen, and had settled into an Irish community. Her sister arrived before her and spurred her to come too. She was college educated, very well read, articulate, and intelligent.

Through some luck and connections (as well as her amazing people skills) she managed to work in corporate America for a while. Then she became a restaurant hostess for over 10 years at a neighborhood restaurant. Her world was mostly the Irish community, and cops and firemen who frequented her restaurant. She lived in a small one-bedroom apartment in Brooklyn with her two cats. She was in and out of relationships, and in and out of emotional dark periods.

She made enough to live on and occasionally pay for dinner, but had little in reserve and would probably have to work forever or survive on Social Security. She got stuck in her lifestyle. She was making decent money for what she did and would have a hard time replicating it doing something else. Restaurant work meant working weekends, which made sustaining relationships difficult. She had little in the way of marketable skills outside of her intelligence and natural charm. No one was going to give her a chance to start from anywhere but the bottom. She worked her tail off and was never afraid of giving it her all. She came here with nothing after her marriage in Ireland and made herself successful in her own right. She deserved tons of kudos, but she would struggle financially the rest of her life.

What does this mean if you meet her and start a relationship? You are entering a world you are not used to. Assimilation into society only changes someone so much, and she will retain many cultural differences from you. How you accept and deal with them will be a large part of your success. She will more easily deal with the differences between her and you. She knows American men because she has been dating mostly American men. You have dated very few women similar to her. The advantage is hers.

So, how did my relationship with the Irish woman end? For five months, I tailored my life to hers. I did it willingly because she was the kind of woman I wanted. She had Tuesday and Wednesday nights off, so I made myself available those nights and we went out during the week. She got off work at 11 PM on Friday and didn't have to go to work until 3 PM on Saturday. I would pick her up at work Friday night and we would party late into the evening like we were 30-somethings. I spent Saturday nights doing my own innocent things. As time wore on, I tried to get her to become more weekend friendly and she acquiesced briefly by changing her work schedule so she was off Thursday and Friday night. One night she called and told me that she felt I was trying to control her life and she could not accept it. She had lost herself trying to please me.

Her fierce independence and need to feel in control of her life led her to break up with me despite an attraction we both knew was real. I know plenty of American women who do not have that much respect for themselves or who do not know themselves as well. She was a gem and I hope she finds someone.

As you can see, cultural differences create positives and negatives. You will need to acknowledge that and be ready to embrace those differences.

But sometimes you just hit the lottery.

IT'S A TOUGH JOB BUT SOMEONE'S GOTTA DO IT (BRAZIL)

One night, I was at one of those networking events for meeting people that you don't know in an effort to market your business. It could be a seminar sponsored by a local business that is followed by cocktails, or just cocktails. You walk into a crowded bar, banquet hall, conference facility, or whatever, and everyone is talking to someone, except you. I hate it. I am not a natural salesperson; quite the opposite, I am shy by nature. I walk into a room like that and feel that everyone is looking at me, the loser, who is by himself. I have gotten better at it over the years because I had too. Most of the jobs I have had included this kind of marketing.

This particular night, I decided to hang out at the bar after the event was over. I usually have a ginger ale or water at the networking event to keep my wits about me, but once it's over, a drink is in order. Now I can finally stop being charming and smiling, pretending I am enjoying this bullshit. And maybe watch a baseball game for a while and say "fuck" once or twice without worrying if the potential client I was talking to will take offense. I squeezed into my seat at the bar, hair down, no more pretense, and ordered a vodka and grapefruit juice. A double. Heaven.

Little did I know how prophetic that last word was.

She was sitting next to me, but I was looking at the TV. Yankees were playing and I was ready to debate the nearest Mets fan. We caught each other's eye and I said hi. She said hi back and I instantly did not care if she was a Mets fan or not. She was lovely and exotic. Dark hair down to her shoulders, dark complexion, and I think, voluptuous. I could not be obvious and check out her cleavage on the first "hi," but it appeared ample based on peripheral vision. Love that peripheral vision. We began to chat and I found out she was Brazilian. You hear those stories about Brazilian women. Well, she was sitting next to me. Talking to me. We were hitting it off and she was not only hot, but fun and nice. I expected hot. I did not expect fun and nice. And I certainly did not expect hot, fun, and nice to be talking to my drunken ass.

We moved to a couch on the outskirts of the bar. We sat close to each other and were beginning to get friendly. I began to worry that some potential client I met at the networking event would see me and think I was some kind of womanizer. You only get one chance at a networking event to make a good impression, and you have to go to dozens of networking events to get business. Go to 20 events, collect five business cards at each. Follow up and get 10 appointments. Pester them and get one proposal opportunity, two years later. Shit. Sounds like online dating. I no longer cared.

Next thing I know, we are making out on our couch. Fuck business. I have confirmed the cleavage, and oh, what a kisser. She was way too hot for me. There had to be a dozen guys who could have sat in that empty seat next to her at the bar. Would she have said "hi" to any of them or was I special? Am I just a lesser asshole, or very lucky? I ordered another drink and didn't really care.

As we were tongue dancing, she told me that she was going back to Brazil the next morning.

"Wait, no, can't be. But when will you return?"

"Maybe in a year, but probably never."

"Why not?"

"I am not supposed to be here and probably could not get back into the country."

"Why are you going home tonight?" *Because I really think you are the hottest fucking thing I have talked to in a decade.*

"It's time for me to go home and restart my life there."

Fuck. I have always fallen hard and fast, often on the first date. Maybe not the first drink, but we were on our fifth. Shit.

But then, the following escaped from her lips: "Since this is my last night in the US, I want to make love to an American man before I leave."

Holy shit. I wanted to ask her to repeat herself, but realized this was not a Senate hearing. After scraping myself off the floor, I looked around and saw that I was the only candidate she was interested in. OMG, she wanted me to be her last memory of American men. I was now charged with carrying the torch for 100+ million American men. Sorry. That was way too intimidating for me. I struggled getting it up when the only torch I was waving was for me. If I have to take one for Mother America, I will do my best. I pumped my chest and asked for the check. We found a cab and headed back to her place. I was officially shit-faced. She opened another bottle of wine—just what I needed. But God bless Brazilian women. Before I finished the first glass, I had the torch of American men firmly in hand and she had that torch, well—you figure it out. I knew she wanted the total package, but the math wasn't going to work. When you add my age to the number of drinks I had and it comes to more than 60, ladies, don't get your hopes up.

I was flirting with 70.

But she was from Brazil. My new retirement destination. If you think American women are undaunted in their attempts to achieve their goals, imagine Brazil trying to achieve her goal. She was never going to be in America again. The memory of her last night was going to be making love to a hot American man—it was going to be great. But there she was, with me.

Despite way too much alcohol, or because she had to compensate for it, she became the most focused woman I have ever met in my life. She had goals to accomplish. And ultimately, aided by my overwhelming patriotism, she did. We never spoke again after that night. My loss.

If someone else had sat down next to her that night, he might be telling this story in his book. Sometimes one is just a lucky man. Hope she is foreign.

And, finally, talk about a double take.

IT'S ALL RUSSIAN TO ME (BELARUSIAN)

Match.com had started hosting "Stir" events where local members of Match.com were invited to a party, typically at a local bar where only members are allowed in. This may be the only time you go into a bar knowing all the women there want to meet somebody. It is like speed dating without the formality. You go up to someone and if you hit it off, great; if not, you move on quickly. At least in theory. I was never able to figure out how to extricate myself from a conversation. It's one thing if I am leaving the bar, but not if I am trying to find someone more interesting. It's not easy. I have issues.

This was the setting one night in Manhattan. I have never been comfortable in bars if my goal was to meet a woman. I am shy by nature, and rejection and I do not get along well. Despite this, I walked into the bar and said to myself, "If she's cute and age appropriate, I am going to go up to her and start a conversation." It did not take long for me to find her. She was blonde, thin, and standing under a spotlight, I could tell she was quite pretty. She was dressed in a short but classy skirt, hair down to her shoulders. She wore glasses and held a glass of red wine. I already had my fill of foreign women, so I hit the pause button when she laid another thick Russian accent on me. Didn't I just get over one of these? But no, she wasn't Russian. She was from Belarus. Now my only conscious reference to Belarus was the Olympics. I'm very culturally rewarding to be around. But nary a likeness to a wrestler here. And she didn't like being called Russian.

It started out a bit awkward, as all first conversations do, but she was readily understandable and ended up being quite endearing and witty. What made her different? She was from a former Iron Curtain country, came to the US in her 20s, and settled in an ethnic community in Brooklyn. She worked for a construction company, and now lived in an apartment in the lower east side—with a roommate.

I was quite smitten with her on our first date, and when she invited me up to her place for an after dinner drink, I was excited. But first, she had a confession. I liked her, so I was ready for anything. I thought. It was about her roommate. My mind couldn't race fast enough to think of anything too negative about a female roommate. Actually, a fantasy or two would have eventually made itself to my consciousness. But her confession came quickly.

"It's a guy."

"What's a guy?" I queried.

"My roommate."

"Oh." *Ooooooh!* That was different, though they weren't sleeping together. Maybe that was why she was still single. It's tough to bring a guy around when there is already one living there. It can be just a tad intimidating. Imagine my horror if while trying to make out with her, some guy came out of the bedroom sleepwalking in his skivvies. He didn't.

It wasn't until I woke up the next morning that I wondered what the real story was. I presumed the reason she had a roommate was financial. And here is the rub once again: you are not going to meet "rich" in the land of foreign dating. They seem to have a fierce desire to make financial ends meet by themselves. She offered to pay for things, so she wasn't poor; she just did not have a lot saved for those fabulous vacations you were hoping to split with your partner.

But I didn't care. Smitten grew into a lot more. I have found that love is nationality agnostic. To my utter amazement, as I got to know her more, I found we had so much in common. Not just in the usual way, like that we liked the same food and both liked to read. No, like in the things you would never think of. We both sniffled and farted and coughed and made other bodily noises on a regular basis. For the first time in my life, I could sniffle unabashedly knowing she didn't care. We literally got up at the same time every day to go to work. We loved to go just a little too far in whatever adventure we were on. We both liked to sleep on the same side of the bed. That one was an issue. She thought the only way lobster could be eaten was with butter. The list goes on, but I dubbed her "me with a vagina." And her roommate was a great guy. Look at me—not so insecure anymore.

LET ORIGIN BEGAT ORIGINALITY

Foreign women, excepting the whack jobs, are strong and seem to be void of giving and taking bullshit. They are sure of themselves and prideful. They won't be taken advantage of and may be overcautious early in the relationship, but are open communicators. Foreign women don't seem to have the issues that pervade American women who have been dumped or cheated on or feel sorry for themselves or hate men, yadda, yadda, yadda. Or at least foreign women have managed to deal with these issues better. I am becoming increasingly convinced that they may make for better emotional partners than American women. You have to decide for yourself and I hope you embrace the opportunity should it arise.

To honor foreign women, I leave this chapter with a positive thought: I love foreign women because they have added to my life's knowledge of the world and I want to experience everything the world has to offer. So, thank you, dziękuję, спасибо, grazie, buíochas a ghabháil leat, děkuji, and danke.

ON YOUR WAY UP THE RABBIT HOLE

- Foreign women are used to dating Americans, but you are not used to dating them. Don't let it show. Treat them special because they are women, not because they are foreign.
- Honest, fiercely independent, maybe even intimidating—those are the good ones. Enter the "no bullshit" zone with fervor. How refreshing.
- Embrace the cultural and language differences. Learn from them. Turn communication faux pas into fun and a chance to let go of insecurities.
- It's not all rosy. Money and family back home may be issues.
- They like to be naked. Their neighbors never move.

THE OTHER SIDE

I didn't think of famous attractive foreign women in the context of thinking about or dating foreign women. But who can help it. Geneviève Bujold, who is Canadian but seems to me much more exotic. She has that librarian look I love. I loved her in *Obsession*. Or Ingrid Bergman, she is Swedish and *Casablanca* is one of my favorite all-time movies. My point is that you may think of Antonio Banderas or Sean Connery when you envision foreign men. It is exotic and exciting to think of it that way, but ultimately you will just be meeting Jorge from down the street. Nothing exotic, but different. Foreign men have more gender separation than American men. Women are to be treated like women, and they should act like women too. This has plusses and minuses.

Pick up on cultural differences and see if they matter. They may be akin to religious differences—ways of life that will not change. What does he expect of women? Can you deal with his expectations? You should be able to discern this fairly early on.

What about language differences? If English is his second language, there may be obstacles, but there will also be opportunities to have fun. Most guys are like me, wanting to learn cuss words first. Perhaps this isn't so gender specific but a natural curiosity. The Belarusian woman I dated loved to curse in English. "Fuck" was a frequent utterance. Why? She liked the way it sounded. I asked her how to say "fuck" and she would not tell me because in Russian or Belarussian it was offensive. But in English, it sounded cool. At the first dinner with her, and my best friend and his wife, the "fucks" were flying so fast, he started laughing at one point, saying, "I have never heard someone use the word 'fuck' as much as you." She just smiled.

CHAPTER 6
THE "WHO" AND THE "WHAT"

(THINGS ARE NOT ALWAYS AS THEY APPEAR)

When we think of who we want as a partner, we often make a mental checklist. Pretty, check. Nice, check. Emotionally secure, check. Horny, check, check, check. I actually make a real checklist. Think column headings, bolded, and, of course, underlined. It isn't necessary, but I am the quintessential numbers/spreadsheet nerd. There is nothing wrong with the checklist concept and most people do it in their head, often subconsciously. A mental profile of plusses and minuses is a useful tool in evaluating whether or not to go forward with someone.

When you are young, you don't make checklists because you don't care. First we ask if she is free Friday night, and then we ask if we had fun. At our age, it becomes much more complicated. The subconscious checklist is rather large because we have been around a long time and, more importantly, have been by ourselves for a period of time. Solitude causes one to develop habits and ways of doing things that become important. Sometimes they become too important, therefore deal breakers. He doesn't put the cap on the toothpaste tube. She has 200 pairs of shoes I have to tiptoe through on my way to the bathroom every night. He drinks too much. She never puts the fucking phone down. At 20, we would all be answering texts as soon as they arrive, wearing sandals year round, and drinking on Tuesdays.

After age 50, having been alone and becoming good at not worrying about a partner, our life is ours, only to be shared if convenient. This doesn't just pertain to around the house. Outside activities are just as important. She exercises at a gym. Any guy she dates has to be a gym rat. She got involved with a local charity and goes to all of its events. He is welcome to join her or stay home by himself, but she is going to everything. And the worst, she has a freaking big family and someone—without fail, every fucking weekend—has a block party somewhere, and you have to drive.

Guys are no better. "Do I really have to start putting that fucking seat down again?"

We all go through our checklists of not only what we want, but what we like and don't like after we meet someone new. It is important to pause here and take a deep breath. There seems to be a lot of men and woman who look at their checklist and fail to do one very important thing. Rank the priority of each item. He doesn't like sushi—deal breaker! Her condo is not big enough to store my golf clubs—deal breaker! She won't go to my cousin Charlie's half-sister's boyfriend's son's Christening after spending the previous weekend with my parents—deal breaker!

As a famous person once said, don't sweat the small stuff. If she is sweating, tell her you won't sweat hers if she doesn't sweat yours. You are fucking 50, who cares what side of the king bed you sleep on?

This leads to a major breakdown of these checklists. I like to call them the "Who" and the "What." I have met several women who were the Who-but-not-the-What, and several women who were the What-but-not-the-Who. The difference may be obvious while you read this, but it will not be obvious when you are feeling it. You will think she is a great person, but there is something missing from the time you spend together. She is the Who, but maybe not the What and you can't figure it out. Your relationship is great, you like doing the same things, and the sex is off the charts, but you hesitate introducing her to your family and friends. She is the What, but not the Who.

I have found many Whos and a few Whats. The one you are going to be with forever needs to be both. For me, that has been elusive. Notice I said many Whos and only a few Whats. Why? At this age, the person she is (Who) has not changed and there are plenty of women I can be happy with. The What, because you are older and more set in your ways, is a much more difficult place to find common ground.

If the "one" is very strong, you may be tempted to ignore the lack of the other. If you do, you will be settling. You may not recognize the feeling, but will know something is missing. If you do settle, recognize and accept it. Settling and compromising are like night and day. Settling is willing to accept that pit in your stomach on an ongoing basis. You don't know what is causing it, but you are afraid to face it. Compromising is talking about it, knowing that you both have pits that need to go away, and figuring out how to get rid of them together.

THE "WHAT"

The What is the more difficult concept to understand. The What is the *type* of relationship you have. It includes what you do, how often you see each other, or if you like to do the same things. Do you stay at home or go out? Do you go to the movies or go dancing? Do you hang out with each other when you are doing nothing? Does she play scrabble? Do you watch HGTV? You get the point.

A critical aspect of the What is how often you want to see each other. Not how often you see each other, how often you *want* to. The difference is huge.

Do you want to see her just Friday night, but she wants to see you both nights of the weekend? Do you begrudgingly go out with her Saturday night, knowing you would rather be playing poker with your buds? If you do want to spend both weekend nights together, what about the days? Do you want to golf while she goes to the mall, or does she want you to go shoe shopping with her? Is it okay if you watch a football game at her place while she goes shoe shopping by herself? When you do go out, does she give you shit when you order a third drink? Or get pissed because you are talking to someone else (either sex) at the bar rather than paying 100% attention to her?

These are the What questions and dare I say, most of the time, the What that you want does not match the What that she wants. She could be the most incredible woman in the world, but if she wants you to garden with her the entire weekend and you absolutely hate worms, you are in trouble.

I spoke earlier of the "kinds" of relationships we want in the context of where you are emotionally. Here I am also talking about the type of person you are naturally. Your gene makeup. You may be in different What places because you and she are at different points emotionally, or you may just be different. If you are at different points emotionally, you have a chance to morph to the same point. If it's in the genes, you have a problem.

Some people marry and live together, but don't see each other very often for various reasons. Work, family, outside interests. Perhaps because they don't want the kind of relationship where they see each other too often. It's in their DNA. I knew a married couple where he worked in New York and his wife worked in Oregon. They had a place in both cities. Maybe they saw each other half the time. For them, this was completely natural and they were happily married. They have the type of relationship they want and it works. And if they later break up, it's more likely because of the Who and not the What, and their next relationship will be with someone who again is looking for the same What. They will need to figure out the Who.

If you are in different What zones either due to emotional timing or DNA, can you survive? If it is timing, one of you may come around, so you will need to be patient and willing to compromise. I was with the perfect Who for me, but the What was different. She wanted the Friday night only thing and I wanted to spend the weekend with her. I thought her What was due to emotional timing and I figured she would come around; I just had to be patient. A recipe for success. While I was partially correct and her What did move towards me, she had an innate What that prevented her from getting to where

I needed her What to be. It sounds confusing and felt even more confusing. Ultimately, her DNA prevailed and we never got on the same What page. If our What difference was solely due to her emotional state, the Who may have been strong enough to permit the patience necessary. We eventually broke up.

If the What difference is due to different emotional states, you stand a chance. If your difference is due to DNA, you are doomed. You have to figure this out, otherwise you will spend a lot of time trying to figure out why that pit in your stomach is so big. The innate What trumps the emotional What every time. Those kind of core differences will likely spell doom. And if you choose to persevere, make sure she is one helluva Who.

THE "WHO"

This is a much easier concept. Is she the right person for me? What are her core qualities? What are her non-core but desirable qualities? While the concept is not difficult, the evaluation often is. Again, we are now in our 50s, which has given rise to certain personality prejudices that should not be deal breakers, but we give them deal breaker status. This is where the "Grass is Not Always Greener" concept comes into play. We all want the perfect person. When we are young it is much easier not to find perfection, but to think we have found it. When we are older, we know perfection is a fleeting concept. How much below perfection we are willing to settle for is difficult because we have to compromise from our picture of perfection. Easy at 20, not so at 50.

We all know the basic personality characteristics we want from a person. I want someone who is nice, smart, funny, pretty, honest, etc. Your list is probably not too dissimilar from mine. But the Who goes deeper than that. At this stage in life, you have many beliefs that are core, you live your life a certain way, and you have added a lot of things to your Who list. You have political beliefs, how you deal with children and parents, financial concerns, what you do on Sunday, all things you never thought twice about when you were 25.

Does she share those same beliefs? Some will seem silly to you, but not to her. And some of yours will seem silly to her. But these desires and beliefs form the basis for the type of person you want to spend the rest of your life with. The Who.

Here is an example of a Who difference that could apply at 25 or 55. At 25, you have a fighting chance to figure it out. At 55, good luck. And it will seem silly to one of you, but not both.

She likes to flirt. It is always harmless and she is not a cheater. She just happens to be very friendly. Her Who craves attention. This drives you crazy. Maybe your Who is insecure. Maybe she does go too far and doesn't know it. You think it's completely inappropriate and yet, this is how she likes to have fun. Neither is wrong, neither is a bad person. How important is this to her if she knows it hurts you? How important is this to you if you know it is innocent and fills some void in her? You will have to answer these questions. If this becomes an irreconcilable difference, then she is not the Who for you. At 25 you will then agree to be friends and she will "hook" you up with one of her friends. At 55, you will "hook" up with your therapist and for several thousand dollars more you may figure out why you can't find the right Who.

I had a relationship with a wonderful woman who was the complete What that I was looking for. We made a connection, were attracted to each other, and had fun together. We wanted to spend both nights of the weekend together, as well as the days. It was okay if she read a magazine and I checked out the baseball box scores. Or if she wanted to sit on the beach and I needed a break from the sun. But as the relationship developed and we got to know each other better, major differences in our outlook on life arose. Neither of us was wrong, and we both acknowledged such. The differences were significant enough that one of us would have to change certain core beliefs in order to make it work. She believed that her man should be by her side in all things she did in life and was willing to do the same for him. I didn't want to be *that* close at this point of our relationship. Perhaps never. I had things I wanted to do and knew if I wanted to do "my thing," she was going to have an issue with it. She wasn't going to change and "my things" were not going to go away.

I struggled with the "grass is always greener" concept, as I knew I could do much worse than this woman. This may be as green as the grass gets, but I could not get to the point of doing things her way and she couldn't get to the point of doing things my way. We both acknowledged that it was a shame, but these truly were "irreconcilable differences." This is a classic example of the What being good, but not good enough to overcome the Who differences.

Think about the Who you have before deciding that the grass is greener elsewhere. I took my own advice and thought long and hard about this woman. We met and talked honestly and openly about the relationship. We gave it all we had, but finally succumbed to the Who differences. We remain friends to this day.

While the Who concept is easy to understand, it doesn't make it easier to figure out who the right Who is. I strongly urge open and honest communication as you explore who each of you is and what is on your checklists. Try to figure out Who and What you both want. Tell her and seek her feelings. This seems basic, but I have failed myself too many times to recount here. I also urge you to recognize and respect that you both are different and that there *will* be a need to compromise more than you initially thought, and clearly more than you had to when you were younger.

The younger you are, the more the Who matters and the less the What matters. You will figure out the What. The older you are the more the What matters. It will never completely overtake the Who, but will come close. Make sure you know where you are.

You'll never have to "settle" if you can keep an open mind about Who and What you want, understand and accept that there is no perfection, and fully embrace that you will have to give to get. If you want to wait for perfection, you may end up having to find it in yourself, because the perfect "she" doesn't exist.

ON YOUR WAY UP THE RABBIT HOLE

- The "Who" hasn't really changed from your 20s.
- The "What" is influenced by how long they have been single and any remaining emotional scars that need healing.
- The "What" can be hard to detect. You will feel it, but won't know what it is.
- The "Who" is somewhat immovable. The "What" can be discussed and worked on. You may not resolve it, but at least you gave it your best shot.
- "Who" gives a fuck? Find a foreign chick.

THE OTHER SIDE

The younger you are, the more the Who matters. The older you are and the longer you have been single, the more the What matters. Not because you have compromised on the Who (although you may as you get older), but because you haven't had a Who in a while, so all you had was the What. It took on significant importance. More so for women than men. Your independence gene kicked in after dependence caused you pain.

You have to make a decision about your goal. Find someone (Who) or do something (What). Why not both? If you are like me, finding both will be a fleeting concept. Don't try to change him to make him like what you do. You have things you have become accustomed to doing. Don't force him to participate. He has similar things. It's no longer the romantic ideal of doing everything together. When young, you build things you like to do together. You are both past that. Accept his, ask him to accept yours. Where they cross over, you have an added benefit.

At this age, you begin to lose the luxury of waiting for Mr. Perfect. Not so at 20 when you have all the time in the world. When you are 50, you may wonder whether you should "settle." You are torn. Grass has a little brown in it, but damn, isn't there perfect sod somewhere?

I have had several relationships where I thought I could be happy with my partner, but had some doubts. I wondered if the sod could get better, but was it worth the search? Tough question. Especially when the What is not ideal. But remember, the What grass can't seem that green when you have no other to compare it to. Your What has been nurtured by solitude. How much of it is really that important? Watch his reaction to changing the Whats in his life. If he is willing to compromise, you have a start. If not, go slow.

At this age, you may be unwilling to compromise on the What (but you should) and you may be more inclined to compromise on the Who (and you shouldn't). You won't know What end is up. At 20, you didn't have the experience you have now, so the perfect match for you is based on a relatively small sample size of guys. Now your experience, at least in part, consists of significant failure in a relationship, so perfection is not only fleeting but not to be expected. To the day you say "yes" to a permanent relationship, you may have doubts. Do not over think this as the doubts are much more natural at this age given life experiences than when you were younger. You may never know whether you have made the "best" choice available, but just consider whether it is the "right" choice for you. Consider those things that are truly most important to you and let that lead you.

I wanted a partner who was there for me no matter what, and would allow and welcome me to do the same for her. That was what was truly most important to me. When I thought I may have found her, I hesitated because we had other differences that I had never experienced in a relationship before. They seemed like deal breakers, but only because other relationships didn't have them. There had been other difficulties, which I grew used to and capable of dealing with. But here were new challenges that intimidated me at first. My knee-jerk reaction was why do I have to deal with this? Never had to before. When I really looked at the relationship, it was this partnership that was most important, and she brought that to the relationship unconditionally. And I had never felt that trait as strongly as I did with her. It turned out to be the most important and overriding part of our relationship, so I was able to grow used to and easily deal with the rest because of it.

It can take longer for a woman to find herself after a divorce and then figure out what she wants. You may have "lost yourself" while married, becoming engrossed in the roles you played—cook, housekeeper, mother, wife. Where is "you" in that list? You will figure it out, but it will take time and you may go overboard for a while. My mother got divorced in her 50s. She had been married to a very controlling man (my stepfather) and finally found independence. She took the "now it's time for me" to a new level. She became very self-centered, and for a while, it was all about her. Too much so. Obnoxiously so. She was still finding her way. It was painful to watch and even more painful to experience, but she finally did find her way and had very successful relationships after that.

ON THE DATE

CHAPTER 7: DIARY OF A SERIAL DATER

(WHERE THE EGO MEETS THE WALLET...AND WINS)

Confession: I was an online Serial Dater for a period of time. Actually, I was a serial dater anytime I was not dating someone steadily. Serial dating is the art of having a date every night of the week, sometimes two. Being a serial dater takes several skills. These skills are needed for any attempt at online dating; however, having them honed is mandatory for serial dating. You need to be really good at these skills in order to create enough interest to get enough responses to generate enough dates. If you don't have these skills and just send dumb, poorly worded emails by the thousands, you will fail Serial Dating 101.

You must begin with excellent writing skills. It is your only highway into their lives; you can't be running red lights or getting lost. Reread your email. Make sure it makes sense—to a total stranger. Spell check, punctuation, proper capital letters. We know it's a numbers game, but a well written email increases your chances for a response dramatically. Maybe only from 2% to 4%, but for us serial daters that is dramatic.

Humor is a wonderful asset. I have a knack for clever writing and it has served me well. Don't use dopey humor or clichés. Don't use raunchy humor; leave the sarcasm for friends. Puns are okay if clever. If you are naturally funny, don't be shy showing it off. If you are not, try to be clever but nice. Be conversational, as if you were actually talking to that person. Let your personality come through. Having a genuine personality will help now and even more so once you get her on the phone. And if you are like me, having a good one will compensate for not winning the George Clooney lookalike contest.

Finally, patience and perseverance. Most times when I am just "dating," I need patience and perseverance just to get one date for a Friday night. When I am Serial Dating, it's a whole other level of commitment. I need to spend double or triple the amount of time reading profiles, finding something in common with them, and then creating clever emails. And more time explaining to my shrink why I can't get any work done.

Serial dating became quite my rage. My record was 8 dates in 6 days. On more than one occasion, I actually had two dates the same night, but never managed three. I never had sex with more than one woman in a day, I am sorry to say, but given my age, maybe that's for the best.

While serial dating was quite the ego boost, it was work. You already know that your email will most likely be ignored, no matter how gifted your prose is or how funny you are. Some of my best work has gone without a response. Get out your calculator. Figure that you have to send 10 clever emails to get one back. Then calculate how long it takes to craft the email. Your goal is to get seven dates in seven days. Do the math and you see the time commitment necessary. It is fun in the beginning, but can quickly get tedious.

Everyone has a million stories that they tell. They never change, you just tell them to new people. Internet dating is no different. You are going to send an email to a woman you found interesting. You will find something in her profile you have in common. You may find several women that have the same thing in common with you. For example, maybe you like the Jersey Shore, walking the beach, swimming, pets...whatever. You may find several women in your serial dating quest (remember you are looking at hundreds of profiles) that also like the shore. Your best Jersey Shore story (mine includes Bruce Springsteen as I grew up in Asbury Park, New Jersey) may be worthy of repeating to several of those women. Instead of retyping the same story each time, refine it, save it, and just copy and paste it when you come to an "I like the shore" profile. After a while, you will not have to do any original typing and you can craft your emails in a couple of minutes. As a matter of fact, you can set it up so you only email women who have something in their profile that relates to one of your canned stories. This will increase the number of women you can contact exponentially. This was the number one reason serial dating became easy for me.

I did not purposefully embark on serial dating. I broke up with someone early in my post-marriage dating career and wasted no time reloading. I had to have a date on the weekends, and was immediately relentless. I had refined my cut and pasting prowess. You would be surprised how many women like dogs—and I had a good dog story. And a cat story. And a daughter story.

Most times you don't get a response for several days. This was no different. So every night I sent a couple dozen emails. After a week, a couple of responses trickled in. Hah, I was officially on a roll. I sent more emails and became less discriminate on who I sent them to. It was almost a game. No, it was a game. After a couple of weeks, the responses were flowing, emails were exchanged, and plans were being made. Another week and the dates started lining up. I was Serial Dating.

Of course, more than one of them informed me that they could spot a "cut and paster" a mile away. They didn't. I say go for it anyway.

YOU DON'T NEED A LITERARY DEGREE, BUT...

I have always liked writing. People joke about keeping diaries, but I really did keep them as a kid. I was going through old boxes after a move a few years ago and came across the old diaries. Oh my God, stuff I hadn't thought about in 40 years appeared before my eyes. I realized some things never change. Despite a whole life to write about, my diaries centered around two themes: numbers and girls.

Unsurprisingly, I was the quintessential nerd growing up, which explains the numbers. Of course I liked girls—I just sucked at dating them. Oxymoronically, I was the first in my class to go out on a date. In sixth grade, I took Lori to see *Bambi* one Saturday morning. I don't remember if we had a good time or not, or what *Bambi* is about, but I was proud I had a date. I was the first "stud" of my class before I knew what "stud" meant. Of course, Lori showed up to school on Monday morning with 35 cents. Her mother told her she was too young to go out on a date. Who cares? She could give me my money back, but she couldn't take away that first date.

I used to catalogue in my diary how many book pages I read in a day and how many hours and minutes of sleep I got the previous night. In small print at the bottom of each day: "56 pages, 8:13." There were always sports scores of games and a "Girl of the Day." And a "Girl of the Week." And the top five "Girls of the Month." And the top 10 "Girls of the Year." And the "10 Best Days of the Year" and "10 Worst Days of the Year." It goes on. And on.

I was obsessed with girls, but based on the length of these entries, I had plenty of time on my hands. When I was a junior in high school, the best day of the year was December 18: my first date with Peggy. Unfortunately, the worst day of the year was December 19: Peggy broke up with me. I actually read a couple of entries to my then 17-year-old daughter whose, perhaps expected, reaction was "Ewwwww, Dad!"

But this is a story of serial dating. How I morphed from diary diarrhea into a serial dater is a serious one. My writing skills helped, but I went through much emotional and psychological turmoil. It is a story of coming to grips with who I am and accepting myself, as well as accepting others. I'll begin in the middle.

THANK GOD FOR FREUD

After my first wife and I separated, we agreed to couple's therapy. We saw a psychiatrist who had been recommended to her. While we were in therapy, I was having individual sessions with the same therapist. I wasn't a believer in therapy after seeking help in my 20s, while having difficulty with commitment. I was told that I was like the ocean, the waves approaching the shore were like me becoming involved in a relationship. Then, like the waves, I would retreat out of fear. Thanks, Doc. Descriptive analogy, but I didn't need a fucking analogy, I needed a reason why I couldn't commit. But this time, the therapy ended up doing wonders for me. I guess it is cliché (and when my psychiatrist asked me the question, I did initially say "Ugh!") but he started with, "What was your childhood like?"

So I told him. My father was the strong, overbearing type. He was a large man and had a temper. He was from Europe originally and had been married before, and had a son. Actually, he was my stepfather but had married my mother when I was 4, so for all intents and purposes he was "Dad" and that is what I called him. Well, Dad thought I should do chores and always get As on my report card. And then I should do more chores, and never get Bs on my report card. My parents each had their own car and as early as eight years old, one of my chores was to wax the cars. Yes, like *The Karate Kid*. Wax on, wax off. But I was eight years old and my dad liked big cars. So every fucking Saturday morning, I waxed one of their cars. At eight years old, this took me four hours. Then Dad would come down to inspect my work, inevitably finding a spot I missed. It got to the point where I would painstakingly go over the car before I announced it was ready for inspection. I would be convinced there would be no spots missed, but he *always* found one.

When my report card came out, if I went from a C to an A, it was expected. If I went from an A to a B, I got an earful. When I raked the leaves, there had to be none left in the yard. Not a one. If I did any painting, there could be no spillage or missed spots. When I turned 17, the legal driving age in New Jersey at the time, I was not allowed to get my license because Dad was convinced I would drink and drive because he had as a kid. When I finally found a job in high school, I had to give half my earnings to the house. When I went off to college 45 minutes away, I had to come home every weekend to babysit my younger sister because they did not trust anyone else. And of course I had chores. And I never made a decision on my own. Not what job I would take in high school, when I could get my license, or what I could do socially. Not what college I went to, or what I did when I graduated. The list goes on. This wreaked havoc on my self-esteem.

This helps to lay the ground work for the rest of the story. While my circumstances will differ from yours, I hope you can glean something from this. If something here resonates with you, then this story will have proved even more worthwhile. In any case, back to therapy.

My shrink listened for a long time as I also revealed that I am intimidated by authority. I still run and hide when anyone barks at me. My shrink concluded that I was being "squashed" by my father: controlled and put down, unable to make decisions about my own life or have input into almost anything. Because I only experienced being controlled by him when I was growing up as a child, I felt most comfortable being with people who would control me as an adult. I didn't know how to make decisions and didn't want to learn. This filtered into both my personal life and professional life. As an adult, I had been able to sustain a marriage for some time and was successful in my career, but there continued to be a subconscious need to be controlled. That is all I knew.

So what happened? As I learned, I had slowly begun to overcome the need to be controlled. It was subconscious, but was affecting my behavior and not always in a positive way. I needed to find out why. I had changed and now needed help from my shrink to understand the change and deal with it. My self-esteem was beaten up as a child, and while both my wives propped it up and my career helped, I still had a lot of work to do. I embraced the challenge of working on it and thought I was fixed. That is, until I screwed up with the second wife. Through another round of therapy and many insightful conversations with my mom, I figured out that I seemed to rely too heavily on what others think of me. When folks like me, I feel good. When they don't, I feel bad. Maybe that's normal, but my feelings were too tied up with what others thought about me, especially with what women thought about me.

Rather subconsciously at first, I tended to feel "too good" when a woman responded to me on the internet. This spurred additional advances to get more women to respond and make me feel good.

And because I do seem to have some skill at writing, I was able to get women to respond. It all made me feel enormously good. Since I had this huge void in my life after my second wife left, I wrote to a lot of women and it became easy to line up dates. The more dates I had, the better I felt. Ergo, serial dating arrived.

It became an obsession.

You always start making sure you have the weekend covered. I hated not having a date on Friday or Saturday night. My social choices otherwise were limited. I don't have any single guy friends and I suck in bars. There was this place that sponsored dances and dance lessons on a Friday night. But the crowd was mostly couples and mostly 60s. What single women there were are what you would envision a group of 60-something single women to look like, only worse. The first time I walked in, I looked around and realized I was the best dressed and perhaps most eligible guy there. But for what? The food sucked too. Welcome to my single life! I left and went home to have some fun with new profiles on the internet.

Assuming you don't have to go to "Dancin' with the Seniors" on Friday night and have the weekends spoken for, you then seek to fill out the other days. You will run into women who want to know why you aren't available on a weekend evening. A woman needs to work to become "weekend worthy," it doesn't just happen.

I had an outstanding first date on a Wednesday night. We got along immediately and felt a spark before we felt alcohol. The date went way too late for a week night date and we were planning that I would stay over at her place on the second date. (I love modifying that Three Date Rule.) But the following weekend was spoken for as I was in full Serial Dating mode. I wanted to see her and spend the night, but I had other possibilities and never broke a date with a woman to have a date with a "better" prospect. Not my style—believe it or not. So, we tried to plan our next date and I suggested another midweek rendezvous. She wanted to know why I was not available for the weekend. I had plans. Well, if I didn't want to take her out on a Friday or Saturday night, she wouldn't go out with me.

Wait, I have them lined up out the door and I am going to take shit from this prima donna? Not. We never had that second date.

Meanwhile, the law of averages begins to take hold. You have sent hundreds of emails, had dates with women who responded. So far. What about the ones who haven't? Some of them eventually respond. And you like them. Now Sunday is spoken for. Before you know it, you need a checklist and a secretary. That is how I got to eight dates in six days. I made one of the dates on the way to another. I was going to lunch for a first date and decided to call this lovely woman I had recently met. I wanted to ask her out for Friday as she had become "weekend worthy" quickly. During the conversation, she noted she was free that evening and suddenly I had a doubleheader.

I had had a couple of dates with a woman who loved to dance and was a lot of fun, so I was trying to bed her, utilizing the sacred Three Date Rule. She wasn't buying it. She would not sleep with me unless we were in a committed relationship—hard to do when one is serial dating. It was getting to the point where I needed to move on, but wanted to give it one last chance. We arranged to have drinks on a Monday night. In the meantime, I had met another woman who invited me out for drinks that same night after I accepted the invite from Ginger Rogers. And right before I left to meet Ginger, Girl #3 texted me saying she would be at a local bar later if I wanted to have a drink. When things went as expected with Ginger, we amicably agreed to end it just in time for me to figure out where Girl #2 went for drinks. I met up with her and since we were having a good time, I had to ignore the enormous ego boost of a tripleheader. Girl #2 stopped my serial dating for a few months.

While I have enjoyed my moments as a Serial Dater, I have not taken it seriously. I usually find someone I am interested in and go back to being normal. Plus, it is time-consuming, enormously expensive, and there are a lot of whackos out there. Along the way, I learned a few rules and I feel it's my duty to share them with you.

SERIAL DATING RULES

If you choose to embark on this crusade, there are several rules to keep in mind.

Rule 1— Manage expectations. Literally go up the food chain slowly. It is expensive to take out many women at the same time. Of course, you can pick cheap venues or just meet for a drink. That helps, but the tabs still add up. Also, there will be women, especially some older ones, who will offer to split the tab. I have never been one who can let a woman pay, but there is no reason not to accept if she offers. A good rule is to accept her offer to split the tab if you never want to see her again, but pay if you do. Of course, even if you split it, she will not hold it against you if you want another date. Second dates become problematic because now she is expecting a nicer time. And you to pay.

Rule 2—Keep a list. You will quickly forget who you have talked to about what. You'll see an email on your iPhone and want to respond right away. But you don't remember who the fuck she is. I kept a cheat sheet in my wallet. You can't just keep it at home as one of the entries might call unexpectedly at any time. When Amy from Match calls, and you can't for the life of you remember an Amy, you'll be grateful for the list. Ah, right. The one with the Siamese cat. Just think how impressed she will be if you respond, "Amy. Great to hear from you! How is little Peaches doing?" Her clothes are already half off. Women melt when you remember something from their profile. The more obscure or different, the better. It's not difficult to do: just keep a little spreadsheet with names and a couple of key things from her profile or emails. Golden.

Rule 3—Remember family names. If she talks about her kids, write their names down. This is huge. The last thing you want her to say is, "I told you this already." It's even worse if it's her kids' names. You don't have to remember Aunt Tilly or Cousin Martha, but kids and pets are key. You will be surprised how easily she will tell you a story about Sarah that occurred recently. Listen attentively, perhaps even taking notes. She will expect you to fully understand the relationship between Sarah and herself, and will expect you to respond accordingly. But you have no idea who Sarah is. Sister? Best friend? God forbid, daughter? Can't be the Siamese cat. You can't ask who she is and you better react appropriately. Keep a spreadsheet. And when you text or email her, make sure you get the spelling right. This is not so much a killer if you get it wrong, but you can score big points if you get it right, especially if it's an unusual name. I dated a woman whose daughter's name is Inez, but pronounced "E-nez" not "I-nez" as I would have guessed. When I not only spelled it right, but then even pronounced it right…tons of points.

Rule 4—Never, ever, say the following: "I don't know if I told you the story of…." If you did not tell her that story, it means you did tell it to someone else. So you risk that she thinks the story is making the rounds on Match.com. If you did tell her that story, then she is wondering why you don't remember. How many other people have you told it to? And then she knows for sure the story is making the rounds on Match.com. Get the picture? Just tell her the fucking story and if she says, "You already told me that story," apologize and move on. I can't tell you how many times I have fallen in the trap. Her too. Watch for her making the same mistake. She might also be a Serial Dater. Hey, maybe you could commiserate and write a book together.

Another trap I fall into—asking a question without remembering that the answer has already been disclosed. It could be due to something like the number and sex of her siblings. "Jack, I already told you I have two sisters and a brother." Oops. Now you can challenge her and say something really stupid like, "No, you must have told that to the 'other' guy you are dating." I recommend against that.

Rule 4A—Never refer to the possibility that she may be dating someone else. Even in gest. Especially in gest. You are trying to cover for the fact that you lack those basic spreadsheet skills. Or think you can keep everything straight. Or are cool enough where you can get away with it. You can't and you're not.

Rule 5—Establish your text responding routine early on. Some folks—men, women, children alike—have their cell phone as an extension of their body and never leave it unattended. You will meet women who can't wait to get that text and can't wait to respond. Others are more normal, and respond when they see the message. This may be immediate if the phone is nearby, or it may be later when the phone is checked for messages. It may take some time to get a response since the cell phone does not always go where she goes. You will learn her pattern and come to rely on it.

If she is the "leave the cell phone buried in her purse" type, then you shouldn't get upset if her responses take several hours. If she always has her cell phone in her hand and responds instantly, you will learn to be ready for a conversation when you text her. Don't text her and put your phone away. You texted her, you are now at her mercy. You have been trained, now you need to train her.

This could be the most important rule to serial dating. Inconsistent cell phone etiquette will always get you into trouble. Just like she did, you have to establish your "type" and stick to it. Since you are serial dating, I strongly urge you to be the "oh shit, I left the cell phone in the car/at home/ran out of batteries" type. That is, you never want to establish an expectation that you will respond immediately. Establish a believable reason that you don't respond right away. Perhaps for hours. It is a virtual guarantee that at some point she will text you while you are out with someone else.

A little secret: Whatever strategy you choose, once she knows it, show her how it works when you are together. For example, you establish yourself as the "I never have my cell phone out so I don't always see a text when I get one." But when you see it, you respond and then put your cell phone away. This will come in handy when she texts you when you are out with someone else. She knows you never respond right away because your cell phone is away. You will text her when you see it, and then put the cell phone back away—your "type" does not engage in text conversations. She has been trained. This "type" works well as you can respond to her text while peeing when you are on another date, and she knows not to expect another response anytime soon.

To really make this effective, go out on a date with this woman and arrange to get a text (or wait until you really get one). Randomly take out your phone, respond to the text and put it away again, never to take it out until the date is over. This is gold. You have given your "type" immense credibility. Of course, we know the best dates are the ones where no one looks at their cell phones during the entire date. But remember, you are a serial dater. You cannot afford to wait to respond until the date is over.

Rule 6—When out on a date, feel free to use the following excuse: "I text my daughter each day and therefore, if I see a message and it's from Meghan, I will have to respond." This allows total freedom to respond to someone else's (NOT your daughter's) text while under the pretense of being a great dad. Double fucking bingo.

I was on a date one night with a woman I had dated for a while, broken up with, and now was sort of dating again. We were not sure where we stood, but were fleshing out our feelings. We were not exclusive, but had not disclosed whether we were dating anyone else. I was. Sort of.

Girlfriend #2 and I had also dated for a while and broken up. Seems to be a theme here. We had begun to see each other again, but were not sure where it was heading. We also did not disclose whether we were dating anyone else. I was. Sort of.

I told my date that if my daughter texts, I will need to respond. She totally understood and I was all set. So I get this text that says something like, "I can't believe I dropped my cell phone and broke it." Well it was dark at the bar and I didn't really look to see who sent it, because only my daughter drops her cell phone and breaks it. So I simply assumed it was her and texted back, "Well, at least you didn't drop it in the toilet like last time" which was true—for my daughter.

Unfortunately, "sort of" girlfriend #2, not my daughter, sent that text to explain why she didn't respond to an earlier text of mine for several hours. She needs to read Rule #5. She gives me a "?" response to the toilet reference and I am now confused. I have one semi-drunk woman sitting next to me at the bar and we are enjoying the fleshing of our feelings. I am thinking my "daughter" is being her usual irresponsible self while sipping on my fourth drink. I was about to text, "Honey, I am on a date, can we catch up on your cell phone troubles later?"

Fortunately, I had to pee.

Rule 7—When all else fails, learn how to pee and text at the same time. Whenever someone gets up to go to the bathroom on one of these first few dates, both parties take out their phones. If you get a text and want to respond, you have a very short window to do so. It behooves you to learn how to pee while you text. Be careful not to overestimate your skill. Could get messy.

Rule 8—When you are on a date and don't want to invoke Rule #6, silence your fucking cell phone. You don't want your date to say, "I think that's *your* cell phone ringing." Of course, if you have honed your craft at serial dating, you will simply look in her eyes and say, "When I am with you, you get my undivided attention."

Then go pee.

Ultimately, I do not recommend serial dating. It feels good for about a week. You need money, need to be a good bull-shitter, and need to be able not to care. For me, it kind of fell into my lap when I was at the height of my online dating craze. The dates just appeared simply because I sent enough emails to create enough interest to get enough responses to generate enough dates. I enjoyed it for what it was worth—a good but fleeting time. Enjoy it the same way if you can. If not, monogamy works too. And better.

ON YOUR WAY UP THE RABBIT HOLE

- I embarked on serial dating because of a significant void in my life. Serial dating is only a bandage to the void.
- Serial dating can be fun in the short term providing you can discern a potential relationship and stand down when it appears.
- If you need/want to serial date, learn the rules. Incorporate your own. Do not take it seriously. It is a temporary phenomenon.

- Please be kind to the women who are the subject of your need. You can serial date and be gentle.
- Serial dating will create a void in your wallet.

THE OTHER SIDE

Become weekend worthy quickly. While I may have refused to make the woman who wanted a weekend with me "weekend worthy" soon enough, she had the right mindset. Perhaps you don't have to be as demanding as she was, but she identified someone (me) who was not serious about finding a relationship since I obviously had other plans for the weekend. Don't be shy about doing the same.

Perhaps this chapter speaks to going slow in the early stages of dating; however, I did shut it down quickly once I met someone "weekend worthy" because this was the right direction for the serious commitment I was looking for. A brief interlude of serial dating does not eliminate one from serious contention for a relationship. Okay several brief interludes. But my inclination was driven from self-esteem issues not an inalienable need to always date a lot of women. I calmed down quickly when the right woman came along. You may find the majority of the male dating pool is actually searching for the same thing you are if you only look closely and without prejudice.

Having said all of this, do work on text etiquette and don't be afraid to test his. I may brag about serial dating, but I went on each date hoping for the possibility that it could lead somewhere. I never took advantage of the women I serial dated and did not lead them on if there wasn't a click. Unfortunately, many guys may not be so kind.

SERIAL DATING RULES FOR WOMEN:

- You have a lot more leeway with texting since guys assume all women are serial texters.
- Act aloof. Hell, if you are serial dating, you are aloof.
- Women love confidence, but men can be intimidated by it. Practice yours when you are in preseason so when the

real dating season starts you are in good form and won't intimidate a potential serious date (vs. a serial date). You can be confident without being intimidating.

- Act like the Most Interesting Woman in the World.
- You don't have to learn how to pee and text at the same time; he does.

CHAPTER 8: DATING...THE OLD FASHIONED WAY

(BLIND DATES, CHURCH SOCIALS, AND BARS, OH MY!)

Before the internet, we had to be much more creative in meeting women. There were no winks to send over the internet. We couldn't buy an online rose and send it to someone, or ambiguously "poke" her. We had to date the old fashioned way. Like, go somewhere or do something that did not involve a computer and a mouse. Even in today's world and at my age, leaving the house once in a while can have benefits. One would think. I did venture forth from time to time. Mostly, it was ugly.

I tried the bowling thing and joined a co-ed bowling league. I got put on a team with four women. Holy shit, my lucky day. They were all married but age appropriate and had to have single friends, right? I used to be a pretty good bowler in my day and figured the combination of my athletic abilities on the lanes and fabulous charm on the ladies would lead to a revelation that I should meet one of their single friends. Four women in their forties. They knew I was single and looking. But no, not one single lead from them. What about the rest of the co-ed league? Slim pickin's. Very slim. Talk about "striking" out. Made pool halls seem like a church social by comparison.

Even my best friend's wife couldn't help. They were happily married but she had tons of single girlfriends. I would get together with them with a date from time to time, but she knew my dating status was mostly "available." Maybe since she only saw me with a date, she didn't give it much thought. Until she finally tried to set me up with a neighborhood widow who had just lost her husband and was nowhere near ready to date. Another lucky day.

Given the number of single people in their 50s, there are tons of singles events these days. In New York City, they have Boomer Parties designed for single baby boomers. They are held at a disco and begin at 6 PM, the rationale being that boomers are in bed by 11:00 and the disco could reopen for the younger set after they wheeled the old codgers out. The music was good but the crowd was, shall I say, eclectic. I am being nice. Old is more accurate. If you want to try going somewhere to meet someone and you have anything going on, you could do well here. Most of the men were old or poorly dressed. I went with a date because the music was good, but even I could have scored there.

In New Jersey, they had a social group to facilitate oldies meeting oldies listening to oldies. Really. I remember being on a date one night at a local hotel. There appeared to be music going on in another area of the hotel, so we checked it out. If I thought the boomer crowd was old, "old" was just redefined. When I became dateless yet again, I gave the old age disco a real shot. Actually, I was pleasantly surprised that there were a couple—but only a couple—of women that I found attractive. And it was easy to dance with them since that is why they were there. When you see a 90-year-old asking someone to dance, you lose your inhibitions fast, or you leave. I actually briefly dated a couple of women who I met there. Once again, most of the male crowd was either old, odd, or of rather poor dress. I did not have to do much to make myself look better than the competition.

In both of these places there was a smattering of eligible, attractive women. If you didn't drool, they would probably dance with you. Some might even if you did. These places are the 21st

century equivalent of the church social without the religion. They are in your neighborhood too. Find them.

So how do we find someone the old fashioned way? Imagine this scenario: it's Saturday night, we are not dating anyone, no best friend has set us up with the wife's hot, newly divorced best friend, no Boomer Party, and the internet is down. We can watch porn or go out...or do both. Yes.

You decide to go out. You memorize and execute the section on how to "Dress" (in this chapter) and go to a place where there will be age-appropriate singles. Music is always a good option, although if it's too loud, it is difficult to properly chat. If you like to dance, find a dance club. It helps if you actually can dance—don't be Elaine from *Seinfeld*.

Having a friend along is always helpful. It gives you someone to go back to when you are shot down and you can play off of each other. Unfortunately, often you will have to ride solo and get used to the uncomfortable feeling of being in a bar by yourself. I hate it, but have gotten more used to it over time. Take a deep breath and know that everyone around you is in the same boat.

So you are at the bar and have spotted someone you would like to approach. You will fiercely debate whether you should go say hello or wait for someone better. Like Mother Theresa. Don't waste time and don't overthink it. No one is watching you and no one cares. If you don't hit on her, someone else will. She is expecting it if she has anything going on. I have picked the ugliest woman at the bar so I would not be so nervous approaching her. It has worked on occasion, but not gotten past the brief conversation stage since it was not what I wanted. You are not going to show up on the cover of the *New York Times*. Go for it.

When you finally approach her in a bar, don't do anything funky. Approach her, say hello, and introduce yourself. Be prepared with a question. This is key. She may respond with an indifferent "hello" that indicates lack of interest or her way of feeling you out, but you won't know which it is. In either event, if you give it some thought beforehand, it won't be hard to come up with a question. This can naturally take the "hi" to the next level and show her that you are good at thinking on your feet. She doesn't have to know you have 30 possible questions memorized. Don't be stupid with "Do you come here often?" or "Haven't I seen you somewhere before?" Be original. Anything sincere will do. Comment on her earrings or blouse or name ("Wow, that is my sister's name" but not "That is my ex-wife's name"). Come up with something and figure out the question before you even approach. Feel it. Show it. If she responds, now you have what we call in the dating vernacular "a conversation."

You asked her a question and it worked. You were not given a key to her bedroom. Too many guys think "hi" means "fuck me." It doesn't. You need to get to know her. Observe. And let her lead. You are talking to her. You are happy. No need to push. Read her and follow her body language. Is she a close talker or does she like her space? If she does, give it to her. She will subconsciously notice that and appreciate it. Is she the touchy-feely type? I am, but I never go first. I let her show me she is touchy-feely before I start—then I just go with a light touch on the shoulder or arm. Keep away from the thighs, initially—women can be turned off by being too aggressive too quickly. If she doesn't appear touchy-feely, hold yourself back.

And let her talk. Women love listeners. It may be painful at times, but the rewards are plentiful.

CONFIDENCE

Confidence is the most important trait to exhibit during the introduction and first question. It is the biggest aphrodisiac for a woman—fuck looks, fuck education, fuck clothing, fuck money (okay, maybe not money)—if you are confident, you have your foot half in the door and half her clothes on the floor. It's not easy to self-invent confidence, but you can't be successful without being confident.

How do you become confident? It takes practice. Look in the mirror and act like you are Humphrey Bogart in *Casablanca*. What? Really? C'mon. No, seriously. Practice what you are going to say. It may sound silly and you do not know exactly what words you will use, but if you say something pretending you are talking to a woman and look at yourself in the mirror, it helps. Fake it until you make it, as they say.

When I was a young CPA pup working my way up through the ranks, I knew public speaking would be important to my career. I was painfully shy in front of a group, and always thought I looked nervous. I took a Conference Leaders Workshop where they taught you how to lead a seminar, which doubled as an intro to public speaking. There were 30 or so of us sitting in rows of a small auditorium. We were required to introduce the person sitting next to us as our first taste of speaking in front of a group. This would give everyone 30 seconds or so to begin to experience public speaking. We were all strangers and everyone was nervous, which made it a little bit easier.

In order to introduce the person next to us, we asked each other standard questions. How long have you been with the firm? Hobbies? Married? Kids? Then each person stood up and recapped to the group the answers from the person he/she interviewed. Thirty seconds to break the ice of public speaking. I chose to be a wiseass. I was unmarried at the time and when she asked me whether I had any kids, I replied, "None that I know of." So in front of several superiors and peers, she actually stood up and told everyone that I did not have any kids—at least "None that he knows about." Okay, perhaps memorable now, but it felt like a bad start then.

The story may be that I was a wise-ass, but the point is that the workshop made me comfortable in front of a group. We were each videotaped giving a 3- to 5-minute presentation followed by the group critiquing each video. When I gave my presentation, my heart was pounding so fast that I swore my chest could be seen rising and falling with each beat. I was sweating, every other word was "uh," I jingled change in my pocket, and believed I was completely incoherent.

This scarily mimicked my performance many a night in a bar.

But wait. The magic of video. When I watched myself, it did not look like I was a rambling idiot. I actually looked like I knew what I was talking about. I did jingle my change, but didn't say "uh." By seeing that I looked composed, it was so much easier the next time. The mere fact that I did not look nervous made me calm down and feel even less nervous the next time.

Where were we? As nervous as you think you look, you don't look that nervous to others. Especially that cutie at the bar you want to talk to. You can practice looking confident—no one will know. Just practice in front of a mirror.

Here is another key: You have to say the following to yourself, believe it, and look like you believe it: "If she blows me off, I will be okay." The look on your face will be, "there are a million other women here, I really don't care that you said no—it's your loss—so I am just going to move on." I couldn't do it for the longest time. I was always concerned that if a woman shot me down, the whole bar would know and think I was a loser. In fact, no one at the bar cared and anyone that did was jealous that I had the balls to go up to someone. So don't care. Just smile, say hi, and ask a question to facilitate moving the introduction into a conversation.

You know that there are plenty of women out there and if this one says no, there are a million others. You know that. Act like it. That is called "confidence."

DRESS

Before you venture forth into the offline dating world, you need to address your look. Women spend a lot of time making sure they look good. Shoes match the purse; blouse matches the makeup; accessories match...well, however that works. They spend time on their hair, applying makeup to places that don't need it.

My favorite is when a woman puts on lipstick or lip gloss and then wants to kiss you. It has to be a light kiss because you don't want to screw up the lip gloss. So if you want to make out with her, catch her in the bathroom before she starts the makeup. But really, why do they always wear lip gloss that tastes like lip balm past its expiration date?

And how do we men address our look? We throw on a shirt and a pair of pants, and pretty much don't worry about the rest. At least those of us who haven't dated for a while. We were used to going out with the wife who probably hadn't liked us for the past couple of years and would not have corrected us even if we were completely mismatched. But now you are divorced, and guess what—chicks care about how a man dresses.

I never knew that belts and shoes were supposed to match until my second marriage. Dad never told me, Mom never told me, and I don't have a big sister. But I learned. Then I learned that women check out shoes and watches. God knows why, but they do. I never know what kind of shoes my date is wearing unless it appears that she grew a few inches from the last date. Then I check for high heels. Other than that, I wouldn't have a clue. But then again, I couldn't tell you the color of the ceiling in the office where I work. I would guess white, but I can't say that I ever noticed.

Shoes and watches. By all means, shine those bastards on your feet. And wear your best ones. If you have lousy shoes and are just beginning to date, invest in a new pair. Watches don't have to be expensive, but they should either show class or be interesting. I have been wearing the same watch for 10 years and it is not particularly expensive. I know this because my daughter gave it to me for my birthday when she was nine, which means Meghan picked it out and her mom bought it. It was a Swiss Army watch, but it had a cool face (it's red) with multiple dials, buttons, features, which I have no clue how to work. I have gotten many compliments from both men and women about it. Not expensive, but memorable.

Shoes and watches—hopefully, you got that figured out. What about socks? Socks are optional in the summer, when they need only be worn for work. If the date is casual or it's the summer, sneakers and shorts may be part of your outfit. If so, make sure the socks are short and white. Black socks with sneakers look (insert really ugly fashion word here) and if you are wearing shorts without sneakers, leave the socks at home.

I learned the socks lesson the hard way as I do so many things fashion related. I was the last person in school to buy a pair of bellbottom jeans as a kid. Next week, they went out of fashion. I used to hate wearing ties because they were so tight around my neck. My second wife suggested I buy shirts with a bigger neck. I was 45 fucking years old. I learned about the no-socks look when a guy who worked for me wore no socks in the office on a Saturday. I thought it was inappropriate in the office, no matter when. Little did I know, my boss was also sockless.

I wore long white socks until I realized one day that I was the only one under the age of 80 wearing them. I walked around counting the ratio of long to short white socks. It was low. Very low. Now I have my sock shit together.

Shirt tucked in or out is another fashion statement. For some guys, it's all or nothing. Always tucked or never tucked. It took me awhile to figure out why the untucked look ever came into being. Then I remembered that most things fashion related are created by guys even when it is not in their best interest. But in this case they got it right. I came to the unmistakable conclusion that a guy created the untucked look because it does a very nice job of hiding his huge fucking stomach.

So which look is better? Remember, you are trying to impress with your dress. You can show her how cool you are later. First impression, you want her to think you are classy. It is always safe to keep your shirt tucked in, but when can you feel confident that an untucked shirt will be attractive? Assuming there are no big belly issues, I suggest that a casual meeting outdoors for a drink, coffee, etc., in the summer, would be an appropriate place for the untucked look. I would suggest, however, that you avoid extremely tailored shirts and make sure they have a collar. Don't wear a t-shirt, guys, it's not classy. Women like classy.

Finally, be neat. Clean shaven is good. Save the Fu Manchu for later, or for never. Moustaches should be clean and well-groomed. Wash and comb your hair. Brush your teeth. Use mouthwash. Iron your shirt. Clean your pants. Do I really have to tell you this? It's easy to forget. Be your best.

BODY HAIR

At some point, body hair or the lack of it will become a topic to deal with. There are two parts to this story: "his" and "hers."

I have more body hair than the average size orangutan, so I know from whence I speak. When I was a kid, I never wore shorts. I had the hairiest legs of anyone I knew. I was embarrassed. I was the first kid on the block to have to shave. It was debilitating. Looking back, I should have prepped myself to embrace a "mature" look—perhaps I would have been able to bang high school chicks who thought I was older than I was. But I didn't. I literally never went to the beach because I didn't want to show off my hairy legs. I didn't care how hot it was—no shorts. In high school, my worst nightmare stared straight at me...gym. I did not have a choice but to wear shorts during gym. So, I sucked it up, put on those little short shorts, and went out to play basketball, or dodgeball, or volleyball, or whatever ball was going to distract me from my hair-tastrophe. And it worked. For 50 minutes I didn't even think about my testosterone over-dosed legs. When I went back into the locker room to change, an even worse nightmare was waiting for me. Joe-something cool dude says, "Man, I ain't never seen legs as hairy as yours!" Seriously. Just like that. Fuuuuuuuuuuuck.

If that was not bad enough, I remember walking on the boardwalk at the beach and seeing guys with more hair on their legs than me. Even worse, some of them had hair on their chest and shoulders, and, the worst, their back. I was relieved I only had hair on my legs. Until I started growing hair on my chest and shoulders...and back. I was the hairiest man in the world.

Not helping my hair obsession, later in life, a woman I dated suggested I shave my back. It was the first request of its kind in my life. It just came up one night as we were lying there. Kind of like, "Gee, today was warm outside. Have you ever considered shaving your back?"

"No, do you find it unattractive?"

"Well, uh, you have so much. I was just wondering."

She actually persisted a bit; she was serious. I managed to resist. Never mind that she had the funkiest, frizziest hair herself. I thought about asking her if she ever thought about buying a wig. "I am not saying your hair is unattractive. I was just wondering." We didn't last much longer.

So, how do you deal with body hair? If you are a guy with a lot of it, there is not much you can do. The good thing is that you will find out if she likes you before you show it to her, and once a chick likes you, the body hair won't matter. Chicks are not shallow like guys. Don't sweat it.

Keep in mind, it might be a good thing not to suggest the beach for a first date.

What about baldness? Just my fucking luck, I have tons of experience there also. As much hair as I have everywhere else is as little hair as I have on the top of my head. At least the lack of hair on my head did not crop up until I had just about gotten over the hairy back syndrome. It receded rather quickly beginning in my 30s, but I never went completely bald; I just accumulated some skin on the top of my head in a very odd shape.

I was a financial adviser for several years after my career as a CPA and at one point, I went to visit a new client and his wife for the first time. The goal was to get to know one another and talk about how we wanted the financial relationship to proceed. I drove to their house and met a very large 70-year-old man and his wife. He was the typical older man, but one who had let himself go and had a very large stomach. It was unhealthily large and rather unsightly.

As we chatted, almost randomly and without context he said to me, "You have the most unusually shaped bald spot I have ever seen in my life." Out of nowhere, this fat, old dude decides to rag on me for my look. We just met. And he was fat. My bald spot looked like Australia. His belly looked like Jupiter. I moved on.

I knew that I had an unusually shaped bald spot. I stupidly would keep my eyes open when the barber asked me if my hair cut was okay, and every time, there was Sydney etched over my left ear. But I had come to terms with it. I was married and she didn't give a shit, so why should I worry? Just like the overdose of body hair is not going to turn off a woman once she gets to like you, neither will a bald spot. It is more noticeable, obviously, but there are women who like the bald look. So embrace the bald look. Shave your head if making it appear intentional boosts your confidence. I can't do that because I can't see the top of my head and refuse to run a razor over places I can't see. But lots of guys do it and chicks like it.

Guys, under no circumstances, ever put anything unnatural on your crown. Everyone will always know it's a rug, everyone will always comment under their breath, and every woman will instantly want to call her girlfriend and tell her about this loser date she went on. Then your story will end up in my book.

I was going to work one day and a gentleman in a business suit entered the elevator with a young woman who obviously worked with him. He had done the comb-over thing and his hair was sticking straight up. Think Alfalfa from *The Little Rascals*, but add a fistful of hair. What boggled my mind is that his co-worker did not tell him. The least she could have done is run her fingers through her hair to give him a hint, but they just kept chatting and dildo head never had a clue. So, just don't do it. No comb-overs, no rugs, no implants. Nothing. Ask some women how they think you should wear your hair and follow their advice. I had mine short but not a buzz cut for many years. It looked okay, though the bald spot was quite noticeable (thank you, fat client). Then, I did the buzz cut and now some women think I am "hot." Okay, not hot, but it's no comb-over.

I told my second ex-wife that if I ever decided to do the comb-over thing, she had my permission to cut it all off while I was sleeping. Fortunately, I never went there and who knows what the hell else she might have cut off towards the end of our marriage if I had.

To recap: body hair is okay and won't make or break a relationship. Except for Frizz Queen, a female never mentioned my body hair in any negative way. Bald can be sexy, and women will accept a bald spot or baldness if the personality and connection are working. If you attempt to hide it, beware.

HERS

Women like to mess with their look, including hair, but sometimes the whole system goes haywire when women go for Botox, liposuction, breast implants—the list goes on. I like my women au natural, but there is a limit. Facial hair is not attractive on a woman. I don't mind a little hair on the arms and most women shave their legs, so it is most often never an issue. But there is the stray woman who has a light "moustache" or some other stray hair protruding from someplace that is not expected. So what do we men do? Basically, if you like her and want to be with her...nothing. Don't think she doesn't know about it. Trust me, she has had a lot of conversations with friends and family about it, and made the conscious decision to keep her look the way it is. Don't think you can say something like, "I really like you, but I wonder if you have thought about waxing your face?"

What about hairy nipples? Yikes! When God invented tweezers, he had just this situation in mind. What do you do when you notice a stray hair standing at attention on her nipple? No, saluting will not help. Since this is likely occurring while being intimate, it becomes very delicate. Don't think for a second that by telling her you will be doing her any favors. Again, she knows it's there. That she hasn't plucked it, knowing you were going to see it, is a statement all unto itself. It could be the quintessential "fuck you, take me as I am or leave." Before you leave, remember that if you showed up 50 pounds overweight, you said the same thing.

I knew a woman who put it in plain view to engage in a conversation about it. Talk about confidence. She wanted a guy's opinion. Imagine her cupping her breast, looking down, and saying, "So, Joe do you think this is sexy?" It left me speechless and I only heard the story. Poor Joe.

Most women color their hair at some point in their life. At our age, they are likely taking the grey out. Some may still be coloring it blonde because roots are showing. I am the au natural guy, so I always liked the natural color. I don't care what color it is. Give me the real her. I have to admit, I never really liked roots since it made the color obviously fake. If it wasn't colored to begin with, no roots. But I never liked seeing grey. So coloring then was acceptable. Okay, au natural most of the time. Of all the hair issues, this is the least bothersome to me. I have met women who didn't color the grey in their hair. While it may not be as attractive as if they did color it, it showed a confident attitude which was attractive in and of itself.

We need to be careful suggesting to women how they should change their look, but guys are willing to sport almost any look if our women think it makes us better looking. Women are not the same. She asks you to wear the lavender shirt because you look "hot" in it and you immediately go buy everything lavender at the local men's store. You tell her she looks hot in blue and she wears red anyway. It's in the DNA, let it go.

(WO)MANSCAPING BASICS

Then there is "that" hair. Guys, this is just not about what you like—it is about them too. You may like a landing strip, the 12-year-old look, or the retro 70s full bush. Understand that women also have preferences. If you don't like to have to floss after you "eat" neither does she. You may think that you should have more hair "there" than the top of your head, but she may like you bald both places. If you have a preference for her look, ask her if she has a preference for your look. If you would like your fantasies to be fulfilled, then fulfill hers too.

I never trimmed in my life until after my second marriage when I was with a woman who did. I asked her about what she liked and she gave me the "floss" response, so I bought an electric razor the next day. I now trim and recommend you try it. Or at least talk to your woman and ask her what she would like. It can be foreplay if you trim each other. Steady hands are a must. If it makes her happy, trim. Then tell her what you like. I bet she shows up with a new "do" next time you are together.

Now I don't get going "all the way" with this process, as I do not know how I could possibly remove all my hair without extreme pain or amputation. I have no idea how women can wax, but God bless them for it.

In the absence of a conversation, there are other ways to handle the topic. I like the subtle approach. If she gives you an opening, then you are free to walk in the door. If she comments on the subject, you can go there. Don't do what happened to my sister. She always likes to "interview" guys on the first date. Subtle questions that aim to discover certain important facts about his life. It was a typical first date and she was making her mental notes. Imagine her surprise when he had something important to discover. "So, do you have a landing strip?"

I always believe the way to make someone open up about a subject that you want her perspective on is to give yours first. She will be more amenable to telling you about her "landing strip" if you tell her you trim. If this is a terribly important topic for you to find out right away like it was for my sister's date, you have issues. But with patience, you can find an opening. Maybe you are talking about vacation and lying on the beach in a bathing suit. "I have a very hairy back. Someone actually asked me if I would ever consider waxing my back. Never gonna happen. You ever wax?" See, you are there, but do not mention what you like. She will clam up if she doesn't do it that way. Ask her what she likes or how she does it. Or if she ever thought of doing it differently. Express no preference and no judgment, and make sure it doesn't really matter. Because if the size of her landing strip is important to you, you are going to have to find another spot to land your plane.

BEDROOM TIPS

We have talked about the Three Date Rule and some other sexual tips and observations. I recently read an article from a prominent men's magazine that gave the results of several interviews with women regarding sex. Of course, every picture in this magazine is of a gorgeous man and the articles are about how you can have great abs or dress like Justin Timberlake or nail women. This one was of the latter variety. I found it interesting and it inspired comment. I took the comments from the interviews with a grain of salt as it was clear they were designed to be provocative. Or some guy just made this shit up. Anyway, here are some general ideas from the article and my views on them.

According to this article, women want sex as much as men, but the man is almost always the pursuer. The following pointers may assist in getting her in the mood:

- *Ask her to pose naked*. What, for pictures I will take with my iPhone and send all over the internet the minute she breaks up with me? I think not. Asking her to pose naked will certainly get *me* in the mood. Perhaps if we are sleeping together, I could suggest it, but the risks are really great in this day. I have to admit however, that back in the 70s, I did take a picture of my girlfriend in college in the nude. You know, with a real camera and film. It turned into a traumatic experience getting the picture developed. I had to take a roll of film with 12 pictures on it, including one of her spread-eagled naked on the bed, to a local camera development place (I can't even remember what they used to call them). I was nervous as hell thinking he would make some copies for himself and his buddies. God knows what they were going to do with the picture. But since I wanted that picture of her, I had no choice. If I wasn't embarrassed enough taking the roll of film there, I was even more embarrassed picking it up. It was kind of like buying condoms back then. Of course, the guy behind the counter didn't develop the film and had no idea there was a naked picture in the package. Or did he? When we broke up, she made me give back the picture along with the negative. But I still remember that pose.

- *Read up on sex—many men do not know how to please a woman properly.* There is a thing called the clitoris that needs to be stimulated. There are a lot of guys who don't know this. I was dating my first love and still a virgin. She was religious and wanted to wait until marriage. We would fool around and do everything but have sex. Our specialty came in the movie theater, where we would get a seat in the back row and begin making out, letting one hand lead to another. She was good at finding my spot and I thought I had found hers. There was a "happy ending" for me at least. When I was done, I would stop and she would be fine. Now I had no idea what I was doing and had never heard of the word "clit." But one day I told this story to a guy I worked with who knew a little something about this. I described what I did to her and he told me what I was doing wrong, or better yet, what I was not doing. He offered me a visual with the middle finger moving in and out and the thumb gently going around in circles. At the time, I was clueless, but the next time I was with my girlfriend, I employed my new technique. As usual, when I finished I stopped. Not this time, buddy boy. She grabbed my hand and commanded, "Don't you dare stop!" That is how I learned to please a woman.

- *Talk dirty.* It took me some time to embrace the dirty talk thing. I thought it would make her feel like I was just fucking her instead of making love, but sometimes women just want to be fucked. I was with a very hot girlfriend one night, and in the middle of it, she let out an "oh, fuck me, baby!" Once I got over the initial shock, I was glad to oblige. Point is that some women do like it. If she finds it a turn on, I am happy to multi-task. Just be careful using it before you know if she likes it. This is a fairly easy question to ask if you are already intimate. I do suggest you gauge how she will react before you lay too crazy a line on her.

- *Treat sex like a buffet.* Bring on the strawberries and whipped cream. Women love foreplay. And for foreplay, food fits in nicely. Literally. I have done both strawberries and whipped cream, but my favorite story had to do with a grape. One night I snuck a cold grape into the bedroom. I inserted it and twirled it around a bit. She tensed up at first because it was cold, but then relaxed at the feeling of it. She was clearly getting turned on when all of a sudden...I lost the fucking grape! I could no longer find it no matter where I probed. She had no idea and was moaning. I was in a panic. I don't know enough about a woman's body. For all I know, that sucker was swimming upstream faster than sperm and who the hell knows where it was going to end up? It's like the story of the guy who went to the hospital because a coke bottle was stuck in his ass. I was going to have to bring my girlfriend to the hospital to extract a grape from her vagina. Yikes. I didn't know I didn't need to panic. I did. I officially deemed this an emergency, but I couldn't call 911. Could I? I managed to compose myself and finally found the grape. Intact. I ate it. All the while, my girlfriend was thoroughly enjoying this food experience. I wanted to tell her what happened, but didn't have the heart to tell her that while she was moaning, I was worrying about surgery.

- *Kiss her in front of friends.* I am very comfortable making out in public. Bars, restaurants, street corners, trains, taxis, and the list goes on. This is a little like dirty talk, but not as risky. Some women don't like it and you have to be ready for a rejection. Some think it's hot. Kissing in front of friends, however, should be left to the younger set.

- *Share a sexual fantasy of yours.* Best to tell her this in the context of a dream. "Honey, I had this nice dream last night where you and I did...." Don't tell her you did this with a hooker one time, long ago, and want to reenact it with her. And keep it a bit tame at first to test her reaction. Then she should be more comfortable telling you one of her fantasies. If you are like me, there is nothing hotter than satisfying your partner's sexual fantasy—it's like magic to your sex life. So go ahead and give her a light fantasy—you know, sexy lingerie or maybe doing it in the kitchen. Delay the mile-high club or swinging until you are sure she can handle it. By the way, I never went swinging, but I was in a situation once where another couple got really friendly with me and my girlfriend. Over the course of a few months, we went out regularly and ended up at one of our places getting totally trashed with loud music and tons of jokes and laughter. They were both good-looking, and we would dance with each other's partner and then flirt and slow dance. One night, we played strip poker and got down to our underwear. Another night, we told hot stories from our pasts and had a group make out session. I never wanted to have sex with anyone but my girlfriend (and we never got there with this couple), but after hours of flirting and titillation, the sex when we got home was off the charts.

- *Ambush her in the shower*. Make sure certain spots are well cleansed. Clean them again. Aim that shower massager right at that place you now know about. Let the ambush begin.

- *Shower before bed*. I am sure she can picture you walking out of a steamy shower with droplets of water dripping from your biceps. She won't be able to resist licking those droplets off and letting things go from there. Unfortunately, I don't have biceps worth licking and water doesn't cling to them like I am 25 and buffed. But the idea of coming into bed naked and smelling clean certainly has its upside. That also means that sex will be a surprise and there is nothing wrong with that. Then again, she could be asleep by then. I prefer to invite her into the shower with my newfound shower massager.

That's a smorgasbord of advice.

ON YOUR WAY UP THE RABBIT HOLE

- Find a place or an activity you are comfortable with and use that as a venue to meet women. Remember the other men (and women) there are in the same boat.
- Confidence can be a learned trait—practice to increase yours. Remember to have a question ready when you say "hi."
- You may not care how you dress, but she does. Watches and shoes are telltale signs to women.
- She doesn't really care about your body hair or lack thereof. Don't worry about it, but also don't make hers an issue.
- Go buy some grapes.

THE OTHER SIDE

First of all, it's okay to go somewhere with the express hope that you might meet someone. Don't feel that you are less or lacking because you have to go to a bar to meet someone. You don't *have* to, you *choose* to. If you go somewhere to meet someone, have a plan. Have a 'kick off the conversation' story. Maybe a funny "he tried to pick me up story." Not an intimidating one, but a friendly humorous one.

Play neither too coy nor too interested. How do you do that? Beats the shit out of me. I was always too interested.

Don't overdo appearance. Think about the personality of your date. You don't really know him, but have gained some knowledge of who he is and what he likes. Consider the venue and how he will dress, assuming he will dress appropriately—if this ends up being a bad assumption, well, that's a clue. He will be doing the same as he prepares for the date, so hopefully you meet somewhere between cocktail dress and t-shirt.

What should you take from the way he dresses? Your instincts will guide you. You can give him a break on the first meet as long as he is somewhat near appropriate. You can choose to make his dress a deal breaker or look to other qualities. Plus, lots of guys don't mind women telling them what to wear so you may have an opportunity to mold his look later.

If the guy is wearing a rug, you have my permission to do the "L" thing: Laugh and Leave.

It's scary to be getting older, especially when single. Physical appearances take on more importance than they should. Unfortunate but true. What can you do?

- Hide your grey.
- Get that new makeup.
- Show some cleavage.

Sorry if it sounds chauvinistic, but the point is to either not be self-conscious about your flaws or do something about them. If you have a light moustache, accept it or get out the make-up. Don't be afraid to make him feel at ease about his flaws and he may surprise you with the same consideration.

Confidence. Maximize yours. How? Do something to give you confidence. My sister took Texas line dancing lessons. She could get out there on the dance floor and enjoy herself. As she got good at it, guys noticed. She just showed up and guys were interested.

Smile and show off your fun personality. That shows confidence. Some women will sleep with men to gain confidence, but that is just loosely covering a wound.

Do let the man do something for you—it does not mean we don't think you can do it yourself. Wait for him to hold the door for you, not obnoxiously, but certainly give him the opportunity. Same with the coat and chair thing. Be yourself, but be soft about it so he can be himself also.

When you get to the bedroom, talk about what you like. Men generally want to please and will be nervous the first time. You can defuse this by talking about sex.

Some women carry condoms. I suggest grapes.

CHAPTER 9:
TO V OR NOT TO V

(WHERE NOT ENOUGH MEN HAVE GONE BEFORE)

Here you are, 50 and single, wondering not when you will get laid next but if you ever will again. You pick yourself up, look around, find the computer, and start putting yourself out there. You follow all the advice in this book and finally meet someone. She may not be your type, but at this point you don't care so you give it a shot. You go out a couple of times and have fun, but are somewhat of an emotional mess so you don't know up from down. You can't figure out if she likes you because she doesn't respond to your texts instantly. And of course, you begin to play *that* game—when she texts you, you do not respond instantly on purpose. She is busy Friday night going out with her girlfriends, but you wonder if she really has a date with someone else. Should you keep pursuing those other women you have contacted on the internet or concentrate on just this one? What is she doing? Do you stalk her to see if she was "Active within the last 24 hours" on the dating site where you met? Is she stalking you? You don't know if you should be pushy or back off. Should you call every day or skip a couple? Do you play "hard to get" or act like you are really into her? You haven't dated in 30 fucking years and your head is about to explode.

By some miracle, you get through those first couple of dates and she seems to like you too. You begin to think about sex. A lot depends on her and how much you like her, but you know it's getting close and begin to get anxious. Yes, it's been 25-30 years and you were nervous back then when sex was imminent. Now you get nervous just meeting someone while you have your clothes on. What's it gonna be like when they come off?

Well, I can tell you I was an emotional train wreck after my second divorce. I started dating someone for the first time before I was emotionally ready. She was aloof and never responded to my texts on a timely basis. I thought she wasn't into me. She still had a flip phone and hated having to hit the 7 key four times just to type a fucking "s." I didn't know that at the time. She would disappear for a couple of days without any contact. She was just busy and had a life. I did not. And I was clueless.

Back then, there was no such thing as a Three Date Rule. We were having fun and I finally thought it might lead there. A woman will never tell you that *this* is the night. They may think they are ready and this will be the night, but they won't give you a hint. Unfair, but we have to deal with it.

Well, of course, that night I was hoping but not expecting. We liked to party and I did not think far enough ahead. I drank a bit too much. At 25, alcohol doesn't matter. At 35, alcohol actually makes it better as it slows you down. At 45, we realize that maybe we need to plan sex if the plan includes drinking. And at 55, you have a built in excuse in case the nerves get the better of you. I needed one. Between the emotional stress of being "out there" for the first time in forever and the natural stress of having to perform, my best efforts were not forthcoming.

I had actually asked the second wife if I should engage in some stamina enhancements—not size wise—although I could use help there too. Little did I know that she wasn't having a particularly grand time in bed with me, anyway, as we were on the way out of our relationship. We didn't go there, but I never had an issue with the concept. Now, times were different.

I PROMISE I WON'T OPERATE HEAVY MACHINERY

I went to my doctor and told him I was having emotional difficulties that were affecting my ability to engage in sex with my new girlfriend. Just like that, a prescription. I thought I would have to make a medical case to get a prescription, but my mental disabilities were sufficient. "Doc, I have a problem. I have a new girlfriend and…" He had his prescription pad out before I finished the sentence.

"Wanna try some?" He winked.

I nodded.

10 pills, 100 milligrams each. Done.

Little did I know I had just come in contact with my new best friend. And as such, I had to give it a name. Having nothing to do on this particular night, I thought long and hard. Something with the right combination of strength, length, and worth. I went through the alphabet, looking for something that did not favor one gender over the other. Something that had iterations that connoted all the amazing things it could do. Something that would be worthy of the reverence I would soon come to bestow upon it.

VAL

It can be both male and female (see Val Kilmer and Valerie Harper).

It may not turn you into Rudolph VALentino but will bring some VALidity to your manhood.

It will definitely come in handy if you have a date on VALentine's Day.

If you forget it at home, you will need some VALium.

If there was a school for limp dicks, it would be VALedicktorian.

VAL

Next time I had a date with the girlfriend, the first crisis of taking Val came up. Do I take one tonight? Will we have sex? I hate to waste this shit; it's fucking expensive. I rolled the dice. And being the basket case that I was, I took a rather large dose. The pressure to perform became nearly overwhelming. If I couldn't get it up now, I really had a problem. I kept the alcohol to a minimum, just in case. I have not often found reasons not to drink, but this was one of them. I was nervous as hell as we started making out and it seemed like she was ready. I felt like a 17-year-old. Well, not to worry, the stuff is amazing. She looked at me cross-eyed and I was the Rock of Gibraltar. The shit really works. As a matter of fact, you can't help yourself. I began carrying around a small dose of Val like I used to carry around a condom. I soon realized that I did not need to take a 100 milligram dose, so I would cut up the pill into several smaller pieces. I carried them around with me in one of those little contact lens cases. That worked for an overnight bag or even a briefcase, but was not going to work for spur of the moment needs. So I began taking one of the pieces, wrapping it in plastic wrap, and hiding it deep in my wallet. Problem solved.

Except I would have to find a private place to go into my wallet, find the little devil, unwrap it without dropping it, and pop it in my mouth. Since it had a weird taste, I needed to rinse my mouth so she would not taste anything so a bathroom was preferable, but not always available. One night I was walking with a date to my car knowing that this could be the night. We were going back to my place. I figured I could always excuse myself to go to the bathroom, but then again, that may give her time for second thoughts. Or perhaps clothes are on their way off and it does not look good taking your wallet with you to go pee. Waiting was not an option. I had to take action sooner than later. So there I was. I opened the passenger door for her to get into my car. On the way around the back of the car, I ripped out my wallet and dug my finger into its inner crevices searching for my life line. And searched. And found it. And dropped it. Thank God for plastic wrap.

It wasn't always a circus show. Once I got my confidence back, I would use it for those evenings when things were going to get wild. One night, my girlfriend wanted to take me back to her place after dinner. It was my birthday and she had an idea for a nice present. I had my usual stash and time to take it without incident. She knew I used it from time to time and had no issue with it. She thought this would be a good night for it to really come in handy. See, she had a Jacuzzi. And a floor. And a bed. Man, did that do the trick. I was 25 again. Triple overtime.

I did some research on my new favorite recreational drug, having first heard of how it came into being on an episode of *Law and Order SVU*. For you fans out there, Belzer is talking about something and he goes, "yeah, they thought they had found this heart medication, but guys kept getting a woody" or something to that effect. In reality, a group of chemists in England initially thought it could be used for hypertension, but it didn't work very well for that. A major side effect among participants was increased erections.

Val pulverizes some enzyme that is trying to stymie the blood flow to the penis. More blood flow, more penis. It leads to easier arousal and a more enhanced erection. Val can also diminish recovery time, meaning that after an orgasm, a man can more quickly get an erection again. Double fucking benefit. Val was patented in 1996 and approved by the FDA in 1998 (ironically, on my mother's birthday). Other brands came on the market in 2007, creating "stiff" competition.

Supposedly, you should take it 30-60 minutes before engaging in sex and it lasts up to 4—6 hours (there are "weekender" pills, which apparently last longer). I have taken Val in the evening and woken up the next morning with more than just your average erection, so there may be some lingering effects. But Val doesn't give you an erection just because you take it. It is not an aphrodisiac. There must be some sexual stimulation. One of the first treatments for erectile dysfunction did give patients an automatic erection. As the story goes, a urologist by the name of Dr. Giles Brindley injected his penis with a drug called phentolamine. To prove to the world that it worked, he went on stage at a urologist's conference after injecting himself and dropped his pants in front of everyone, showing off his rather large erect penis. Talk about proving a point.

My doctor told me the story of a guy who took it expecting an instant erection. Not only did that not happen, but his wife decided to go to the mall. He was too embarrassed to tell her that he took something and the mall would still be open in half an hour. He didn't know that he needed some form of stimulation and it would also last a few hours, so he called his doctor in a panic on a Saturday to ask what he should do. Unnecessary worry. There would be plenty of pulverizing activity left when she got back from shopping.

Val can't create an erection, but it sure can enhance it.

AND I'LL REPORT THOSE FOUR HOUR ERECTIONS

How do the ladies deal with it? Some are thankful their man can participate again and it is a wonderful addition to their lives. Some women think that the erection is caused by a drug, making them feel inadequate, or less sexy and romantic. It is important to discuss this together so she feels part of the miracle.

Love making lasts longer and there is a measure of enhancement. Is she happy with this? Sometimes yes, sometimes no. And now he can get it back up in record time. Is she happy with this? Sometimes yes, but at this age, she's probably asleep.

I have had mixed reactions. On the plus side, I had one woman who encouraged me to take large doses and we would have off-the-charts sex. She had no psychological hang ups that it wasn't her making it all work. She just really liked that it worked. Others encouraged it or were ambivalent. A couple of women were bothered by it from a medical standpoint, like potential side effects. They preferred that I not use it. I also thought that a woman would be able to tell when I was on and when I wasn't—I could feel the difference, surely she could too—but no one ever mentioned a difference. I did not always tell a woman that I was using and I have had several ask me if I did. I have always been very open about it, especially once I got my wings flying again. It has become my recreational drug of choice, but I am careful not to overuse it.

One bad side effect of Val is that it does not turn you into an Adonis. Just because you can get an erection (or a bigger one) does not make you instantly attractive or necessarily improve your relationship. Just because you are "packing," as I call it, you can't forget to brush your teeth or decide to wear your 1960s tie-dyed tee shirt on the first date. Remember, you need to be stimulated, and to get her to want to stimulate you, you need to put your best foot forward.

Now for some good news. It is not addictive. Well, it is not physically addictive, but could become psychologically addictive. The effect it has on performance is real, especially at this age. And it is tempting to try to recapture being 25 again. This drug can do that. You can't help yourself. She winks at you and bam! You have an erection. She brushes up against you and bam! You have an erection.

AN ALTERNATE REALITY

Some interesting Val stories.

Val has been shown useful for the prevention and treatment of high-altitude pulmonary edema, a life-threatening condition of fluid accumulation on the lungs associated with altitude sickness. Talk about losing the mood. This can affect mountain climbers. So you take Val to avoid altitude sickness so you can climb some stupid mountain. Imagine climbing the side of that mountain and you get a hard-on because the broad climbing above you has a great ass. Unfortunately, the erection is useless even if it is as big as your ice axe.

Israeli and Australian researchers discovered that a very small dose of Val dissolved in a vase of water can extend the shelf life of cut flowers, making them stand up straight for up to a week beyond their natural life span. If it can make flowers get an erection, what *can't* it do? So scrape a little dusting of your newest best friend into a vase that you bring over to your new girlfriend. She will totally love how long the flowers last and may begin to wonder how long you can last.

In 2007, the Ig Nobel Prize in Aviation went to a trio of Argentinian researchers for their discovery that Val aids jet lag recovery in hamsters. Really. Two articles I found on this were titled "Sildenafil accelerates reentrainment of circadian rhythms after advancing light schedules"[1] and "Extracellular nitric oxide signaling in the hamster biological clock."[2]

Other than "hamster," I have no idea what any of the other words mean.

By the way, the Ig Nobel Prizes are an American parody of the Nobel Prizes, given each year in early October for ten unusual or trivial achievements in scientific research. The aim of the prizes is to make people laugh, as well as make them think. It's a fun list to go through. Some of my favorite studies that won an Ig Nobel Prize include the 2003 Biology award that went to a study documenting the first scientifically recorded case of homosexual necrophilia in the mallard duck. In 2013, the Peace award went to the president of Belarus for making it illegal to applaud in public and to the Belarus State Police, for arresting a one-armed man for applauding. The Medicine award in 2012 was for advising doctors who perform colonoscopies how to minimize the chance that their patients will explode. Finally, the 2011 Peace award went for a study demonstrating that the problem of illegally parked luxury cars can be solved by running them over with a tank.

You can't make this shit up!

Ultimately, it all comes down to this: To V or Not to V? I say V. If you don't need it, good for you. Fortunately, most of us don't. Even if you don't need it, it can enhance both your erection and stamina. Consult your doctor and make sure it is medically safe for you to

---

1   Agostino, Patricia V, Santiago A Plano, and Diego A Golombek. "Sildenafil accelerates reentrainment of circadian rhythms after advancing light schedules". Proc Natl Acad Sci U S A. 2007 Jun 5;104(23):9837-9839. Epub 2007 May 22. http://www.ncbi.nlm.nih.gov/pubmed/17519328

2   Plano, Santiago A, Patricia V Agostino, and Diego A Golombek. "Extracellular nitric oxide signaling in the hamster biological clock". FEBS Lett. 2007 Nov 27:581(28):5500-5504. Epub 2007 Nov 6. http://www.ncbi.nlm.nih.gov/pubmed/17991439

engage in sex. And remember, I am not a doctor and do not provide medical advice. I don't use Val all the time, but when I do, I take very small doses and the effect is worth it.

Viva La Val!

ON YOUR WAY UP THE RABBIT HOLE

- Make sure you consult a doctor before trying Val or any ED medication.
- You need to be stimulated for Val to work. It has a lingering effect, so it does not have to be taken the moment before the stimulation.
- Some women will like that you are taking Val, others will not. I'm guessing you will.
- Val does not make you more appealing to women. It won't cure asshole-ness, won't make you good-looking, and won't give you a better personality. You still have to work to make her want you.
- Don't take up mountain climbing.

THE OTHER SIDE

Think about how you might need additional stimulation at this age so you can appreciate how Val can help. You won't have to work so hard. Blow jobs become just fun instead of a necessary evil. Hell, you won't have to work at all. Just show up and wink.

The effect of Val is significant enough that it can literally take performance anxiety out of the equation. It can't *not* work if there is even just a little stimulation. Your partner will no longer worry about performing, and you can both relax and enjoy the build-up.

Avoid dating mallards.

CHAPTER 10: THE APPROACH

(HOW TO MAXIMIZE YOUR VERY MINIMAL CHANCE TO GET A RESPONSE)

We have talked about how to approach women on the internet. You need to be somewhat creative, tailor it to their profile, and be witty. Women love humor. But even on your best days, you will get very few responses. This chapter will offer some examples of actual emails sent. The emails matched something from a woman's profile, and in some instances, an easy, random item in her profile was chosen to make things quick and simple. In others, I actually found something unique and had fun. I have sent many notes where I was the only one who got the joke and knew it when I sent it. I couldn't resist, but they did.

Always remember that no matter how clever you are, or how good-looking you think you are, or how well-crafted you profile is, you will get a very small percentage of responses. Face it, she may not have a sense of humor, she may not think you're attractive, she may not like your profile, or she may have met someone already. There are tons of reasons why you may not get a response beyond there being anything wrong with you.

Most dating sites also show the last time a person visited their site. It ranges from "last visit within 24 hours" to "has been active within the past three months." Spend more time and effort on those that have been active recently. If she is only on the site once every three weeks or perhaps has found someone, your efforts are better spent elsewhere. In any event, patience is important while you wait for a response. I have had responses 4-6 weeks after I sent the initial email, by which point I had forgotten her and was dating someone else.

And for God's sake, spell-check your emails.

I've referenced a portion of a profile and noted what I wrote in the initial email approach for you. Some approaches are serious attempts to make a connection, others are lighthearted barbs just to have fun. All are self-indulgent, and if not at least somewhat helpful, hopefully somewhat entertaining. No response was ever expected. Also, it is good to have a catchy "Subject Line" as that is the first thing they see. Try to avoid just a "Hi." I have included the Subject Line for some. For virtually all of them, despite some of my best work, I received no response. The biggest correlation to getting a response is luck, timing, and sending a shitload of emails. Cleverness only increases your odds from very, very low to very low.

EMAIL APPROACHES

She talked in her profile about how her children meant the world to her; enjoyed cooking, dining out, gardening, traveling, the beach, and wine tasting. There's a lot of material there that I sincerely related to. I like to pick something that I can be sincere about. It plays well and sincerity will help if she ever responds. It may be something I love and will tell her we share it, or something I hate, which I will have fun with. My initial email to her had both.

> "Hi, (insert name here if discernible)! We seem to have some things in common. You like the beach, traveling, and dining out, as do I. I have spent most of the last 15 years near the Jersey shore and want to travel the world. I have been all over the US a couple of times, but only to France overseas. Italy, Alaska, and Australia top my bucket list, but I want to see it all. And I love dining outdoors in the summer, especially with a view of the water.

But all is not rosy. I do not like gardening (will encourage you from the back deck with a glass of wine in hand...), but I do like wine tasting (chardonnay here) and I make a great sous chef. And you must tell me about your children. I have an 18-year-old daughter."

See, that was not so difficult. I referenced several things from her profile that were also parts of my life and made fun of the things that were not. Make sure there is something you can share; do not force it. If she loves hiking every weekend and you hate the woods, don't bother. In the beginning, anything cute will create a desire to contact. You can always go back to the cute hiker, but move on for now. When you find someone with something in common, spend a little time and give it a little thought. It will be easy to create a nice first email.

In part, her profile read: "I tend to find the joy and fun in just about any situation. Or really, it seems that the joy and fun find me! I try to balance my *I Love Lucy* streak with an equal part Audrey Hepburn...." She also noted that she was a lawyer, but had transitioned to her own business, had a daughter, wanted to win *Dancing with the Stars* someday, and enjoyed dining out. By the way, you will begin to see that a lot of the profiles look alike. It's finding the difference in them that will help you find a topic for your note.

Of course, a subject line should always try to grab their attention, so I tried: "Lucy, You Got Some 'Splainin To Do." Certainly not original, but at least she knew I read her profile. And then the body of the email:

"Hi there, I couldn't resist... :)

How nice that you have transformed from a lawyer to your other job of bonding with your daughter. I have an 18-year-old daughter and her mother is a lawyer—I could be the only person to divorce a divorce attorney and

> survive…but she is my shining light and has grown into a wonderful young lady (my daughter, not the ex-wife).
>
> There is so much in your profile to chat about, including winning *Dancing with the Stars*—can I be your partner? I love to dance and can do the Deney Terrio thing, but not quite like he could—though I promise not to drop you!"

This was clearly corny, but so was her profile. Try to feel the mood she felt when she was writing her profile. If she seems playful, be playful back. If she is serious, just the facts, ma'am. You are trying to connect to a total stranger. Odds are long to begin with. Remember to always have fun. And if you don't know who Deney Terrio is, go buy a Bee Gees album and watch a rerun of *Saturday Night Fever*. He was host of *Dance Fever* and coached John Travolta who played Tony Manero in *Saturday Night Fever*. I was hoping to at least get a "Who is Deney Terrio?" response. No such luck.

This next profile was seeking a meaningful relationship, but noted she wanted to have fun along the way. She had a 16-year-old daughter who played tennis and basketball, and she loved the beach. I love the daughter themes because it makes me look like a good, cool dad. Not that I'm not, but if I can toot my own horn without it sounding forced, all the better. This one was more business-like and serious, which many will be.

I tried to be clever with the Subject Line and came up with "I love your profile and attitude. I also have …"

And the body of the email:

> "…a daughter. She is 19 and soon to be a sophomore in college. I am a Jersey shore guy and love walking the beach at night when it is empty, especially with a partner. My daughter was a very good softball pitcher and I coached many of her teams, so I know how you feel about your daughter's tennis matches and basketball games.

Fun is important, but only once you are grounded. I am. You seem to be, as well."

She seemed to have her shit together. I wanted to sound like I had mine. It didn't matter whether I did or not—I would cross the bridge of proving it when I had too. The connection of coaching your kid's teams is a powerful one. There is nothing like it. If you have been there, you know the feeling. I love talking about the times when I coached her teams, and having someone listen who feels the same way was great. I found something profoundly personal here and tapped into it.

In addition, a Subject Line with a "..." can create curiosity so she will actually open your email.

This woman actually liked bald men, spent most of her adult life in Denver, was well-traveled, and had a son who was a professional golfer. Since I am clearly hair-challenged, I loved this one. The Subject Line was easy: "I'm Bald." The rest (which was not particularly relevant) went like this:

> "Hey! Now I have a reason to live...ha ha! So what brought you to New York after a lifetime all over the country? You must be loving Peyton Manning these days. And just who is you son? So much to chat about, so little time."

When you find something she likes that few do, pounce on it. Baldness fit here. The more obscure the connection, the better. Look for the unusual. If she mentions tofu and you like tofu, you have a connection. If she is a democrat and you are a democrat, you have the same connection half the population has. Nothing special. But tofu makes you special. Exploit it. In a good way. (By the way, Peyton Manning had just been signed by the Denver Broncos at the time of this note.)

I can't paraphrase this one, so I will quote a part of her profile: "I fancy language and provocative, unexpected words and ideas that can be re-assembled into a dazzling new array of various sorts. I'm always looking for what's different, or better yet, that rare show stopping ability—even better when it comes with an interesting twist – in ideas, things, or people…. What makes me respond to someone's message is a highly complicated algorithm that changes by the hour (hour, in this case, is a synonym for mood)—kinda like the Google search mystery, only far less fathomable :)"

I had no fucking idea what she was talking about, but I was intrigued and inspired so I responded with:

Subject Line: "Math."

The rest of it went:

"+rel.}s3r*7&Q@=

That's an algorithm for 'you're cute and I would like to hear from you."

When you see a profile like this, there is a risk that it was created by a woman just to see who would respond. Or a crazy woman. That's okay, just understand it. Actually, accept that most profiles are designed to be self-indulgent. When a woman writes a profile like this, she is writing it to make herself feel good, not to attract a man. The end result may be the same—the motivation is very different. If she is on the wrong side of the motivation, you will want to steer clear. This will be almost impossible to recognize initially, but knowing it exists can help you screen her out more efficiently. Be wary of funky profiles. I just had fun with this one and tried to come up with a clever response. Always keep expectations near zero.

She liked tennis, and my pathetically corny side came up with:

"Hi there. You seem to be an ace of a person, serving up a nice profile to set the table to find your match…."

That was fucking horrible.

She tried to be cute herself by noting she loves all that New York City has to offer…everything from "A"rt exhibits to the Bronx "Z"oo (from A to Z, get it?). She also mentioned that she plays softball and recognizes the need to compromise in a relationship.

Never to be outdone, I tried:

> Subject line was: From "A"djusting to meet a partner halfway
>
> "To wanting a partner who is just a little bit "Z"any…. Hi! I see you play softball. I coached a coed team at my former employer for 15 years. Never had so much fun! And I so agree with the need to compromise to make a relationship work. We seem to think alike and I can still play 3B!"

I touched on fun and serious. Did any of it resonate? I have no idea because I did not hear back. Don't ever take that personally. She could love your email and still never respond. I have spoken to many women who told stories about great emails they received and never responded to. When I asked why, there was usually something in the profile that turned them off or they were already dating someone. Women are very selective online. They get hundreds of emails and will respond to one or two. They know this and look for the perfect profile, the perfect look. They have that luxury. We do not. Just keep plugging along. Put your best foot forward at all times. It will hardly ever matter, except for the time that it does. Don't lose that opportunity because of laziness. Be happy you took the time.

I had a *M*A*S*H* lover on my hands who was also a medic, and her nickname was, of course, "Hotlips." She also noted a zest for life, and her bucket list included a Safari and staying in tents. If you really think I want to sleep in a tent at my age, you are out of your mind. But this one was really cute, and you can take a little poetic license with that first email. I could not resist the "Hotlips" possibilities.

"Major Burns here. Ready for that safari under the tent and in the woods when that jerk Hawkeye goes to town….

Bet you haven't heard that one before :)

I wanted to say hi because I love your profile and your zest for life. I want to travel the world and no place is NOT on my bucket list. The safari sounds great and I want to do Alaska and Australia and everywhere in between."

If it walks like corny and looks like corny and quacks like corny, it is *corny*. Corny doesn't necessarily work, but since hardly anything does, practice your writing skills. Take a chance and don't worry about being corny. In this case, you have a major *M*A*S*H* fan on your hands who is corny herself. If you like *M*A*S*H*, bring up your favorite episode and ask her for hers. If you were not into *M*A*S*H* but are a doctor, make up some shit. Worry about reality later—it is fucking internet dating.

Sometimes you just have to say "What the Fuck" like Tom Cruise in *Risky Business*. This lady was smoking hot in a bikini in one of her pictures and loved dogs.

Subject Line: "Is that You? …"

"…or Bo Derek lying on the beach?

Hi. I have a cute dog story for you. When I was a kid, my Dad almost ran over this dog on the Belt Parkway in Brooklyn. He finally stopped the car, opened the door, and Skipper jumped in. He was my first dog and while quite the schizophrenic (who wouldn't be after being chased down the highway by Mack trucks), he was my favorite (had two others growing up)."

Of course, you know that the dog story was a cut and paste for any cute chick that loved dogs. That and my real favorite—the daughter/Katy Perry story—were my most popular cut and paste sections to use. Women seem to dig guys who are close to their children and like dogs. Find your best story and tell it. If you have a teenage daughter, you know you can alternately go from a large nerd to a pain in the ass in her eyes. "Cool" and "Dad" are oxymorons in her vocabulary. For me, finding the one moment that I suddenly seemed cool was my best story. Cool was fleeting for sure, but it created a story I can share forever.

The Katy Perry story goes like this: "My daughter thinks I am really cool when I put the convertible top down when it's snowing, or play a Katy Perry song on my radio and know the lyrics. If I start singing them, nerdhood resumes immediately. Once I sang the words to a new Train song before she knew them. Me knowing a song before she did. That was cool. Next thing I know, she has the song on constant replay on her computer. That was priceless."

Don't think it will be easy to replicate that father-daughter moment, I was just lucky. But use those canned stories as much as possible. It does not take away from your sincerity and a cut-and-paster is not lazy. You are responding specifically to something you have in common with the woman. You are just telling a story you have told before. She may actually give you points for being clever.

She likes auto racing and dogs (love those dog lovers!!).

I jumped in with:

"So do you like to race/ride in race cars, or just watch? I once rode with a pro driver—quite fun! My dad was a stock car driver in the day.

And I see you have a dog. I have a dog story. (Insert dog story here)

I have cat stories too, but I don't want to scare you off."

See, it's easy. There are a couple of iterations of the dog story and there are a couple of daughter stories. Sometimes it depends on what is in her profile, sometimes the stories are saved in different places in my computer. I use the first one I come to. I know, it's cheesy, but when you get 24 matches a day and are not particularly choosey on who you date, you do have to sacrifice originality at times for proficiency.

Here's another whacky profile that may not be designed by someone serious about meeting someone, but I simply couldn't resist responding. I'm just going to repeat her profile verbatim—another one too good to paraphrase:

> "Hi there…. The way I describe myself is simple I've got a Ford body (built to last) A Mercedes Engine (smooth and classy) A Lamborghini Personality (Flamboyant and sexy). Upbeat.
>
> I have modeled all over the world, traveled and I have a winning Personality
>
> I'm a down to earth chick who cares about the person she's with. I like sweet things little flowers and kittens and homemade romance…."

Now this I like! She is fun and irreverent (a word I can spell but never pronounce). As you may guess, the Subject Line is simply: "Vrooom!"

The rest goes like this:

> "I have the energy of a 280Z, the fun of a BMW 325 convertible, and the class of a Porsche. The body—well, let's call it sleek like a Jaguar and finely aged like a mint T-Bird.
>
> The mind—that's another story completely.
>
> Wanna drag?"

I have wondered if some of these profiles are created by men who load up any picture they can find. Now there must be something psychotic about being a man pretending to be a woman just to fuck with people, but it happens. You will come across psychos of both sexes in the online world. Don't give it too much thought and don't lose sleep if you happen upon one of them. I remember back in the dawn of AOL and chat rooms, there were many stories about people pretending to be something or someone they were not. It was not to meet anyone; it was just to screw around. How do I know this to be true…?

All of the above profiles were true. You will shake your head at a lot of what you see, but they are shaking their heads at some of the crazy shit they see, as well. Keep yours somewhere in the middle. Fun and real, but not crazy enough to show up in a book.

A final thought. When emailing someone, don't abbreviate like you are texting. Spell everything out. Remember you are talking to 50-somethings, not 20-somethings.

ON YOUR WAY UP THE RABBIT HOLE

- Be creative. The good news is it does not take too much work to be creative online. You don't have to be silly or make stuff up, just find something in her profile and mention it.
- If you can't find anything, move on to the next profile—there are thousands.
- Most women write way too much about themselves, so there certainly won't be a lack of material to choose from. Experiment with different approaches and don't be shy.
- Remember, no matter how clever (or dull) you are, the response rate will be miniscule. And I am not sure it increases dramatically if you write like a poet. Just fucking write.
- Go buy a dog.

THE OTHER SIDE

Guys are going to look at your pic and act on their initial impression of how you look first. If they like it they may proceed, if not, they will move on. What you write will have no consequence. If you choose to make the approach, make sure you have a good pic up. Assuming that is in order, do something unusual. Guys are not used to getting approached, so this will be new and an opportunity that will not be passed up. Assuming you pass the look test, he will read your email with vigor. Do something interesting and he will be hooked.

Don't think your wacky profile will garner a response because it's wacky. Spend time on your presentation, but know what guys look for. Looks first, then funny, then unusual. Be real, but focus on these items.

Experiment with different profiles if you are on multiple dating sites. Experiment with different approaches if you are comfortable making the first contact. Experiment with different responses, especially to those you are not particularly interested in. Yes, to those you do not care about. That is how you learn. Feed off the responses for those you do care about, but always keep in mind that this is a numbers game and your best efforts will likely go unrewarded most of the time. Do not be deterred.

Don't make too much of his profile. You spent more time trying to figure out whether the blonde you or the brunette you is better for your profile than he spent putting together his entire profile.

Do not be self-indulgent—be real.

"Cool" dad works with women, but "cool" mom will not work with guys. Leading with your kids or talking about them often while getting to know someone new can make a guy think the kids are likely to get in the way of dating. They want a relationship with you first. Don't flaunt that they are *always* by your side. If they are, don't date.

Cut and paste away—we will never figure it out.

CHAPTER 11:
AFTER THE FIRST DATE

(DO I REALLY HAVE TO LEARN HOW TO MAKE HOSPITAL CORNERS?)

Wow, that was fun. She turned out to be cute, fun, and totally real. She didn't mind that I was a little chubby and had lost some hair. We hit it off great. She even likes the Knicks. I think she likes me too. She laughed at my dog stories. I couldn't have asked for a better result.

Now what?

Uh oh. She looked cute in her pic, but something was different. We had a nice time, she had a great personality. She is such a good mom and was totally screwed over by her ex. I like her, but didn't feel that connection I was looking for. I would still like to see her again and explore if we can get some chemistry going.

Now what?

What a great make-out session to say goodnight. She was totally hot and I was surprised she accepted my advances at her car. It didn't seem like she was into me most of the night. She had her phone handy and must have checked her texts five or six times. She went to the bathroom three times. Is she playing the field or playing me?

Now what?

These are only three out of the thousands of results and feelings you may get after a first date. What do you do with them? Regardless of which you experienced, the first thing to remember is that she is likely wondering what to do also. After that, remember first dates are intoxicating. The longer it's been since you had one, the bigger the high.

Don't do anything rash. I have gotten the midnight text after a first date where she was ready to move in with me. I have sent the midnight text after a first date where I was ready to move in with her. A midnight text is not a good answer to "now what?" unless it just says "good night" or "thanks, I had fun." The first thing you should do is go to sleep. Whatever euphoria or depression you felt after the date will be lessened with a good night's sleep. Then wake up, make some coffee, and go about your normal routine. Run. Read the newspaper. Watch CNN. Whatever it is that gets you grounded. Then, send her a text.

This isn't a game. If she sent you one first, answer it as soon as you can. If she hasn't, don't wait thinking it's high school again. Send her one. Be real, be honest. If you like her and want to see her again, tell her just that. If she feels the same way, ask her what she would like to do. Cede control of the second date to her. She will appreciate it. If you feel compelled to offer a second date suggestion, keep it generic and easy to accept. Don't go for the romantic candle-lit dinner at your place unless you are sure she will accept. And don't think that your read of her is accurate. She will be loath to expose her desires to you, whatever they may be. She may want to sleep with you, but will not let you know. Arouse all the patience skills you have.

So one of you will be the first to send that "after the first date" text. Don't stress out based on how she reacts to you if you send it and don't try to interpret her texts. You have yet to learn her text etiquette and she doesn't know yours. You won't know whether she still thinks you are a serial killer or wants to fuck your brains out. She is not ready to tell you and may not be for a long period of time. If she blows you off, move on.

According to staticbrain.com, there are 41.2 million people in the US who have tried online dating. 48% are women. That's 19.8 million women. Think there might be someone else out there who will like you? If you can send a "wink" every 10 seconds, you can contact every single one of them in a mere 55,000 hours. Or 6.3 years. Trust me. I did the math.

DÉJÀ VU ALL OVER AGAIN

First dates are tense, make second dates fun. Take it to the next level, gently. If you met for coffee, suggest a drink. If you met for drinks, maybe dinner. If you hit it off great, plan an entire evening. Come up with the plan, she will love that you gave it thought. Create the plan with flexibility so she still feels she has control. Take her likes into consideration. If she mentioned she likes Thai food (or it's on her profile), find the best Thai restaurant in the neighborhood. If you don't like Thai food, suffer for the night. And you will score big points if you can let her know your sacrifice without being obvious. If she likes walks in the park, suggest a picnic. If she likes romantic movies, suck it up and find the best tear-jerker at the local theater. Dinner, then a movie or dancing is a great recipe.

If you are not sure how much she likes you or how much you like her, keep it simple with mutual escape plans. Lunch works. Or the movie. You can go home after a movie. Movies are also great because you don't have to talk during it. You can then have a good time talking about the movie afterwards.

Pick bars and restaurants carefully. You want to be able to hear each other. You are still getting to know one another and the purpose of the date is to gain knowledge. If the music is too loud or the restaurant too noisy, you may find that opportunity fleeting.

How ever you appeared in the first date, look better for the second. Never take a backward step with your look. Don't think because you looked good in a conservative business shirt on the first date that you have carte blanche to wear the Grateful Dead t-shirt to the second date. Yes, it does happen. You need to dress for the occasion. Look good no matter what that occasion is.

Do you bring a gift to the second date? I like to. Something small and inexpensive but that shows you listen or are thoughtful. If she likes chocolates, no need to buy the six-foot chocolate bear. Just a small package will do. Women completely embrace the "it's the thought that counts" concept. I like the two non-red roses signifying our second date. Listen to her, you will figure it out.

If you have any secrets that you didn't disclose on the first date, you might want to take this opportunity to fess up. What are the things I am talking about? You already know the answer. Something you are hesitant to tell her, but is not a fatal character flaw. Something she will have to find out sooner or later. You will know if you have one of these. You will feel it. Maybe it's a parent or child issue. Maybe it's financial or an issue with your ex. Perhaps an addiction you are recovering from, a medical issue. A legal issue. The list of possibilities has no end.

Why do you need to fess up now? To you it is life, and no big deal. To her it may be a deal breaker. It should not be a deal breaker, but that is her decision, not yours. You are not a bad person, but she may not want to deal with whatever it is. Maybe she has her own secrets that do not allow her to tolerate your issue. Better to find out now rather than after you fall in love with her.

"Oh, by the way, honey, my dad died just before we started dating and Mom will be moving in with me."

"Just so you know, I go to AA meetings every Wednesday night. I lost my license because of a DUI."

Do you really want to have this conversation after you fall in love? And what about the stress of not telling her in the interim. Do it now before it becomes an emotional albatross. These are "Whoa" moments that could break relationships apart. And there are a lot more of them when you are in your 50s. Better they occur on date two rather than date 20.

Keep in mind one more thing. Do you think she won't find out? You don't think she will Google you? If it is in the public domain, she will find out on her own at some point. Many a first date has confessed to Googling me before the date. At 20, the only pre-date requirement is a pulse. At our age, she is worried. About what? Crazy shit. Stuff that doesn't really matter, but she thinks it does, and that is what is important. That is what you have to deal with. Like, what would Mom think? Or her friends? Or her kids? So what if you got arrested for peeing in public? We all could have. But if she discovers this out of context, you are finished.

Some don't want to put it all on the table this early—I say it's the best time to do it. You have little emotional capital invested. If it is a deal breaker, it will likely be one later on when you are more involved. Find out if it matters to her before you care too much. Don't think she will be more accepting just because she thinks she loves you. "Whoa" moments can trump love.

So if there is an issue, it is either not so bad and would never matter, or so bad, she would leave you no matter what, even if she is in love with you. Better to find out before half your assets are at risk. Or your heart. I am not suggesting that you stand up and make an announcement that you are a convicted but rehabilitated felon on the second date, but you may be able to find a way to work whatever it is you need to tell her into the conversation. Don't be afraid. Your innate goodness will show through. The honesty will be huge.

What will you learn from that second date? Only what she wants you to know. There will be things she is not ready to disclose. She has secrets too. Those things are not likely to be a big deal to you, but she may feel they could be. Just like you feel yours will be to her. But if you take my advice, she will be more ready to disclose her issues. Women love men who acknowledge their faults and take responsibility. It will make it easier for her to tell you her secrets sooner than later, just in case you can't live with them.

Realizing that you only know what she is willing to tell you, how do you proceed? If you are really into her and she seems into you, and you have an honest relationship, congratulations, you are dating. If you have lingering doubts or sense some from her, then you need to decide whether you want to have a serious discussion or let things proceed naturally. Two dates does not a relationship make, but the online dating scene is very much about getting involved quickly or moving on. Lots of fish in the sea and it's a big fucking ocean. Find out if it is a good match today, not tomorrow.

I dated a woman who wanted to see me as much as possible right from the start of the relationship. She wanted to find out as soon as possible if we were compatible. She figured why do it only on Saturday night? If a woman meets someone she likes, she often becomes exclusive pretty quickly. It may not be spoken, but the X chromosome works this way. Also, being in your 50s works this way. We do not want to waste time chasing things that are not meant to be.

But it's only two dates. If, despite my advice, you haven't told her that your ex is a total freak or that you absolutely have to golf both days on the weekend, or whatever you are afraid to tell her, that's your bad. Expect the same lack of disclosure from her. Where does that leave you? Golfing on weekends, dealing with your ex.

DON'T TELL HER IT'S A RULE

Date #3. There are too many variables by now to really have a coherent discussion on what occurs on the third date. Suffice it to say, you had two dates and you still like each other. Promising. If you do execute the Three Date Rule, keep in mind it might be a sleepover at her place. If not planned for, it could be awkward. What, no condoms? Finding her bathroom in the middle of the night might be problematic. If you have to fart...Christ, it's so much easier being single.

The first sleepover is a whole new dimension. If it's at your place, it is a little bit easier. It begins with who sleeps on which side of the bed? I had a girlfriend with whom this was a major issue. We slept on the same side, and when she slept over the first time, I reluctantly gave up my side to her. The problem was that she noticed my reluctance. My bad. She was way too hot for me to be splitting hairs about who slept where. I would have slept in the fucking garage after a night in the sack with her. Don't be like me. Who cares?

Toothbrushes. She will kiss you. She will stick her tongue deep inside your mouth. She will eat half your appetizer using your fork after she said she didn't want any of it. But she will not use your toothbrush. Nor will she let you use hers. I hope I am not the only guy who doesn't give a shit about this. I kiss you, I can use your toothbrush. If you are anticipating she might sleep over, get her a toothbrush. You have no idea how impressed she will be. I had a first sleepover and was prepared. I put a fresh toothbrush in the bathroom for her. Unfortunately, it was light green and my toothbrush was dark green. I knew the difference—I lived there. Every time she came over, she asked which one was hers lest she use mine. I got smart and bought her an orange one.

Please have a hair dryer. If not, she will ask you to go to the local drug store at 9 AM on Sunday to get her one. A nice bathrobe is a plus. Fresh towels just for her are a must. Don't give her yours even if they are dry and clean. Pull something out of the drawer while she is watching so she knows they are fresh. This stuff is important to women. You have been married. It's not different now, she just hasn't moved in yet.

Another way to impress her is to have some of her food handy. This is tough to do for an impulsive sleepover since you are not going to buy her favorite pickles without knowing if you even want to invite her in. If it is a possibility and you know she loves half and half with her coffee in the morning, go pick up a pint. I still have a bottle of red wine I bought because a newbie date loved it and there was that chance she could come over. And I can't tell you how many jars of olives, soy milk, and mixed nuts I have bought trying to be prepared for when she might come over. Sometimes she never did, sometimes we just never got to the anointed food (or used it for other purposes). But when she shows up and you have her favorite cheese, she will be very impressed.

Make her feel at home. You do things a certain way. Your way. How you make your bed or how you stack the dishes in the dishwasher. How you hang the bath towels. Are you an "over" or "under" with your toilet paper? These things have become very important to you as a single male. They define you and demonstrate your independence. Then she comes along and fucks it all up. She makes the bed her way. She likes hospital corners and tucks everything in. You never tuck anything anywhere. She loads the forks face down in the dishwasher. You load those prongs up, so you recognize them when you remove them from the dishwasher. She is fucking with your manhood. What the hell do you do?

If you've been paying attention, you should know the answer to this. Nothing.

I had a first sleepover and she put the glasses in the lower rack. I moved them to the upper rack. She made the bed a certain way. I fixed it. Only once. After I got an earful from her, I never did that again. It was not so much her being mad, but I had made her feel like a guest. If you want her to come over again, make her feel at home. Do it her way. If she asks how you like stuff done, fine, but don't correct anything she does. Do you really care about hospital corners? Christ, she made the bed.

Another one was being such a good guest, she was going to do the laundry. Her stuff was included too, so this was not the second or third date, but it was a relatively new "sleeping over at my place" scene. She had an armful of clothes she was about to dump into the washing machine. Dry. As in, before the washing machine was turned on. Anyone who has ever done wash knows you don't put clothes in before you turn on the machine, let the water fill up at least partially and mix the laundry detergent in so it doesn't just go on the top two items and never soak into the rest of the clothes. Everyone knows this. Except her.

Okay, maybe I'm anal. So I did what I thought the good host should do. "No, no, honey, you shouldn't do laundry, let me take care of this." I took the clothes out of her arms and dropped them on the floor. Bad move. Anything short of putting them in the dry washing machine was a big mistake. I turned on the water, let it fill a bit, and put in the detergent. Ahh, now this is the way to do laundry. All the while with her watching, arms folded. You are beginning to get the picture. Once I put the clothes properly in the half-full washing machine, I turned triumphantly towards her, ready to move on and enjoy the rest of the morning. Not yet. I got an earful about how I invited her over to my place and told her to make herself at home, but then made her feel like a guest since laundry had to be done "my" way because it was "my" place. And if she was going to be treated like a guest, she would act like a guest. She proceeded to sit down and told me I had to take care of all of her "guest" needs. Of course, I made matters worse by laughing. That was my last bad move. Her look straightened me out. I realized she really was uneasy at my place. Even though I thought I was making her comfortable, my own little trivial habits were making her feel bad. I gave her the remote, the keys to the car, and let her fold my underwear any way she wanted. We survived the day.

Speaking of laundry, don't do hers unless you know the rules. Colors, fabric, shrinkage all come into play with women's clothing. We don't give a shit as long as it's clean and dry. If our undies turn blue because they are washed with our jeans, so be it. If the Meatloaf Hang Ten Tour t-shirt turns green because it was washed with the new Gang Green Jets t-shirt, we think it adds character. I learned this, as with many things in my dating career, the hard way, so you don't have to. On this occasion, I was being the good guest and helping with the laundry. I knew to counsel with her to help separate the colors from the whites. It's not that easy. Sometimes the black panties can be washed with the whites, but sometimes the white shirt with the yellow pattern has to be washed with the colors. Don't ask why. Just make sure you ask what goes with what.

So, a successful wash! No issues with putting the clothes in before the washer was full. I am an experienced clothes washer. I wanted to surprise her with my thoughtfulness, so I took everything out of the washer when it was done and put it all in the dryer. I didn't have to tell her. The best acts of charity are done anonymously. I was proud of myself. Until she said the most horrible words I could think of hearing.

"You didn't put my brand-new jeans in the dryer, did you?"

Fuck.

I did the laughing thing again, and again, it did not work. I have now learned the laughing lesson. Don't laugh in the middle of a fight unless you want it to escalate. If you are looking to piss her off, laugh like you're watching George Carlin's best routine. I laughed, she got pissed. After sparring for a bit, we went to the dryer to examine the results of my stupidity. Not good. She took out the almost dry and two sizes smaller brand new jeans. Oh well, I guess no sex tonight. Or so I thought, because I would never say it out loud. If you think laughing about her being pissed off is bad, make a joke like "well, I guess there will be no blow job tonight" and see what happens. She won't necessarily hold out any longer, she will just make your life really miserable while you wait.

In the meantime, my jean-less girlfriend was no longer at all concerned that I would not feel like a guest. She ripped me a new one. Over a pair of jeans. She was really mad. Finally, I offered to buy her a new pair of jeans as I literally flung the shrunk ones out the front door and onto the street. Luckily, as the jeans landed in the street, she realized she was overreacting a tad and began to laugh. The whole scene became a memory we could laugh about.

Moral of the story is—take out the trash, let her do the fucking laundry.

Remember she has been the caretaker of the home for a lot longer than you have. Her ways began to set from her first day of marriage. Yours from the first day of your divorce. Her habits run deeper and mean more. Go with her flow and give her some control at your place.

And never, ever be afraid to treat a woman like royalty. Make her feel like a queen. It could be the first date or the millionth date. If it is date two or three, you will score big points.

ON YOUR WAY UP THE RABBIT HOLE

- Don't get carried away if you think you fell in love on the first date—you didn't. Don't get depressed if you don't hear from her right away—you will eventually. But you *can* go first.

- Pick a second date with her likes in mind. Bring a thoughtful, inexpensive gift, but not too romantic.
- Don't be afraid to tell her those little truths that make you wonder if she will accept. Better she find out early, before it will hurt when she finds out later.
- Prepare for that first sleepover—have food she has mentioned, fresh towels, a hair dryer, and her own toothbrush.
- Don't put her jeans in the dryer.

THE OTHER SIDE

Women are more intuitive. It is more likely that you will have a better read on him than he on you after the first date. Don't overuse the advantage. Use it to determine how to proceed, not to play games. I have read the first date wrong many times, but quickly learned to temper expectations.

Find out why he is divorced. Don't ask outright, just observe. It is likely that past patterns will continue and because you are more intuitive by nature, you'll identify them.

How does his apartment look? Don't buy "guys will be guys." Messy is messy.

Has he shut down his dating web site? Or is he maybe still trolling? I got into trouble because of the dreaded "online in the last 24 hours" notation by my profile.

What about prior relationships? Were there lots of short-term ones? Listen. Judge the type and length of those relationships to gauge his readiness for you.

Remember, no interviews. Sharing is a more effective path to open communication.

Your place or mine? He won't care about his own toothbrush, but if you don't want him using yours, getting him his own may not matter. Better to hide yours. I would use yours just so when we are dating five months later, I can tell you I used it.

Let him help with cleaning, straightening up, etc. Don't feel you need to do everything. Better yet, see if he offers to help. Does he ask or just do it? What does that mean? If he asks, do decisions come difficult to him or is he just being considerate? If he just does it, is he a control freak or just nice. Don't worry, you will get the answer soon enough. Enjoy the help.

It is okay for him to do it his way, especially at his place. He has not been alone as long as you or perhaps just never did that stuff before he got divorced, so he may not be the most efficient, or may not do it the right (your) way, or may not know there is an app for that. Give him some leeway. Just like you needed to get some "living alone" wings, he does too. Your instinct may be to correct (control), but he may feel really good about just doing it, the right way be damned. Of course, he may be happy to just dump the clothes in your arms and let you do the laundry any way you want. Be open to discussion and compromise.

What do you do if:

- he looks in the mirror to fix his hair too often?
- he spends more time in the bathroom getting ready to go out than you do?
- he spends too much time working out?

In a word, lookout.

If a sleepover is near, wear clothes that don't shrink.

THE NEXT LEVEL

CHAPTER 12: SO NOW YOU'RE DATING

(SOMEWHERE BETWEEN A ROCK AND A HARD PLACE...AND HEAVEN)

Okay, you have had a couple of dates and maybe a sleepover. Maybe you ceded her your side of the bed, maybe not. Now it's time to figure out just what the hell is going on. For purposes of this chapter, let's leave sex out of it. It doesn't matter whether you incorporated the Three Date Rule or waived it. This is about handling a new relationship.

By now you have learned some stuff about her and begun to gauge whether or not you have something that can build into a long-term relationship. You have also learned about some habits and ways of living. Does she call or text? What's her relationship with her kids/family? How has she emotionally handled being divorced/widowed, and where is she in the evolution of trying to find a new mate? Does she like to cook? What does she like about you? And so on and so on. Remember, she is learning similar things about you.

You have discovered some little things you have done that she likes (or perhaps doesn't like). Does she like flowers, and what kind? I dated a woman whose favorite was pink carnations—I smiled every time I paid $10 for a dozen pink carnations while the guy next on line was paying $50 for a dozen roses. Chocolate? Gluten? Meat? You will know if she likes a morning text from you or a good night text from you. Or both. Keep in mind, you are setting the standard. If you do something she likes and she tells you, you will feel obliged to continue doing that.

I dated a woman for a few months and once I became enamored with her, I began to send her a morning text. Just your typical sweet nothings. The kind of stuff women love. It was sincere, but it was also just a couple of months. I may have overplayed my hand. She told me she loved getting up in the morning and seeing she had a text from me. I thought that was kind of cool, so it was an incentive for me to be clever in the morning. But it became pressure—I didn't always feel clever in the morning. Sometimes I just wanted to read the paper and enjoy my daily constitutional. If you start a pattern, keep in mind that it may become expected. Tread softly with patterns that are not sustainable.

You may resort to flowers to impress her early on. I noted earlier that I like to bring two non-red roses to the second date, but then what do you do for the third date—three roses? And the fourth? You get the picture. Carefully choose your methods of impressing her and showing you care. Make them easy to replicate and inexpensive. Random is good. It keeps expectations in check.

If you write well, send emails or texts. Poems are another great way to make her smile. Piece together a few words that rhyme and she will get weak kneed very quickly. Don't fret if you are not feeling like Edgar Allen Poe. Go find a book of poems and pick out one that fits. Tell her you "scoured the poetic landscape to find the perfect poem for her." There go the knees.

I have done song parodies using her name as the basis for a poem. Like Debbie.

D is for the Day we first met

E is for Everything about you I get

B...

This does take some writing talent, and if you don't think you have a lot of it, keep it simple and sincere. "Roses are red" poems are perfect for this.

Roses are red, violets are blue,

I always love cuddling with you.

Roses are red violets are blue

My lips are ready to be kissing you

Roses are red violets are blue

My door is open, I am waiting for you

Roses are red violets are blue

There is no one around quite like you

It's not hard to come up with a "roses are red" poem. If you are struggling with finding words that rhyme with blue, go to RhymeZone.com or Rhymer.com (or a million other web sites, I am sure). You can also be a little creative, use some poetic license, and rhyme with words that are almost "blue" like "food" and "use."

Now, you are not stuck with "roses are red, violets are blue." "Violets are blue" can be replaced by virtually anything, just keep the cadence (or most of it). Again, it is not how clever, funny, cute, or romantic you are. It's just the thought. You have no idea how powerful a simple poem can be.

I once had a girlfriend send me an email that blew me away. We had only been dating a few weeks. It was titled "20 Things I Like About You." Wow! I figured she found a poem or a passage in a book that listed 20 nice things about a potential relationship or man, or something similar to that. I did not expect that she had created this list from scratch, but as I read through it, each of the 20 items were clearly specific to things we had done together or said to each other. Wow! Now listen, I cry over *Star Trek* episodes (especially when Spock gets emotional), so I am the emotional sort. Imagine the tears that were welling up as I read all these lovely things she thought about me.

So I would recommend sending something like that to your new girlfriend. I am sure you can come up with your own list of 20 things you like about her (make it 10 things if you can't, but then you may want to reconsider why you are dating her). Just in case,

I have canvassed hundreds of women to find out what they would like to hear about in those 20 things a guy likes about them. Okay, I interviewed my sister and her best friend and then made up a bunch of shit.

THINGS I LIKE ABOUT YOU

Here is a list of my 40 favorite things women like to hear. Feel free to pick among them if you desire, but again, being creative and making your own list is so much more preferable.

1. I like your honesty.
2. I like that you are a lady.
3. I like how your kisses make me weak in the knees.
4. I like the way you look at me.
5. I like falling asleep in your arms.
6. I like waking up next to you.
7. I like our similarities.
8. I like our differences.
9. I like how smart you are.
10. I like your sense of humor.
11. I like how it makes me smile whenever I think of you.
12. I like that you hold my hand wherever we go.
13. I like that you acknowledge the importance of communication in a relationship.
14. I like how comfortable we are around each other.
15. I like that you challenge me to be a better person.
16. I like your confidence.
17. I like that you are beautiful.
18. I like the way you feel when I touch you.
19. I like the way I feel when you touch me.

20. I like that we can talk about anything.
21. I like that we have so much fun together.
22. I like that you are thoughtful and kind.
23. I like when you call me out on my bullshit.
24. I like that you make me feel alive again.
25. I like feeling that I want to fall in love with you.
26. I like that you're sexy and classy.
27. I like that you like *Star Trek* and *Survivor*.
28. I like that you want to spend weekends with me.
29. I like that you are a schoolteacher/prostitute/other profession.
30. I like that you accept me for who I am.
31. I like that you ski/hike/sky dive/etc.
32. I like that we never go to bed mad at each other.
33. I like that we can be silent together, yet still be communicating!
34. I like that when I am with you, I never want to leave.
35. I like that when I'm not with you, I can't wait until I am again!
36. I like that you have already created moments in my life that I will never forget.
37. I like all the little things that you do.
38. I like that all my fantasies include you.
39. I like even more that all my realities include you!!
40. I like that I am nowhere near being done counting the reasons I like you!

Hopefully, you can come up with your own, but if you are lazy, word-challenged, or just want to get in her pants and not spend too much time, use the above to select your ten or twenty. Adjust the number (e.g., 10 Things I Like About You), the title (e.g., 20 Things I Love About You), or make up a different one (I can't help you with everything). Seriously, though, getting this list from someone I was just beginning to build a solid relationship with made me feel wonderful. I sent a similar list back and it made her feel great. Try it. You will not be disappointed.

IF SHE HAS A SENSE OF HUMOR…OR YOU NEVER WANT TO HEAR FROM HER AGAIN

Now if you have a different kind of relationship or she is someone so special, you feel you can have some fun with her, then you can try including one or more of the following:

1. I like that you have a GREAT ass.
2. I like kissing you in public.
3. I like having sex with you in public.
4. I like your body just the way it is (or I really like your boob job).
5. I like that you have all your teeth.
6. I like that your ex- is not a relative of mine (or yours).
7. I like it when you go commando.
8. I like that I know you're a natural blonde and no one else does.
9. I like that your breasts look as good on Skype as in person.
10. I like that once we started dating, Tinder became something you start a fire with.

If you are still dating after that list, then you have a keeper.

HMMMM

As you continue to get to know each other, you will come up with some things that make you say "Hmmmm," as in, "I'm not really sure I like that." Some may be serious, but others will be more about a lifestyle you (or she) has developed over the years of being single. A lot of them are minor but seem major because it's how you do things these days. When you were married, these didn't matter at all, but because you are alone now, certain things take on added importance simply because you don't have someone in your life to replace their importance.

You are a night person; she is a morning person. (Fuck, I have to turn the lights off or watch *Seinfeld* reruns in the living room.)

She likes to read the *New York Times* over coffee on Sunday morning for an hour; you like to go for a walk. (It would be nice to finally have company. And exercising is good.)

You let mail accumulate and open it once a month; she pays her bills the day they arrive in the mail. You don't mind, but she thinks you are a deadbeat for waiting. (Just leave me alone, please.)

She likes to garden; you don't even have a thumb, no less a green one. (Do I really have to get a pair of *those* gloves?)

She likes all sorts of ethnic food; you are a meat and potatoes guy. (Just my luck, there is an Indian restaurant in the neighborhood.)

Maybe you are thinking that these are deal breakers, but they are not. If the connection is there and you really like each other, those little things, which you can't imagine giving up or compromising about, should melt away. Do not worry about those things, though it will be a struggle to let go. And she will be struggling with her stuff too.

You will find that the walk you went for on a Sunday morning to clear your mind and make you feel better was necessary because you didn't have someone you loved waking up next to you. If you have some patience and take a deep breath, maybe she will like you enough to want to go on that walk with you. See, she only found it so important to read the *New York Times* on Sunday morning because she didn't have someone she loved waking up next to her. And later on Sunday, when she wants to garden, bring your mail to the back deck and pay your bills so you can be together even though you are each doing different things. She won't want to garden as much as she used to, just like you don't need that Sunday morning walk as much as you used to. And you will find that you don't mind helping her garden (okay, that might be stretching it) just like she found that she likes to walk with you in the morning.

The relationship and love and caring that you build together will trump those "things" you each did independently and the "way" you did them. They were important when you didn't have someone in your life. Now that you have someone, they are not as important. It won't feel that way at first, and if they remain as important, then perhaps you don't have the right person. You need to rank your priorities and ask yourself how important they really are. Is playing softball four nights a week really that important? Maybe you can compromise.

Aha! The magic word for sustaining any relationship at any age. Compromise—do it early and do it often.

Compromise means communicating. One of the most important aspects of any relationship is open and honest communication. I have seen many relationships sustain themselves without this kind of communication, but there was always something lacking. If you can establish open and honest communication early on, it can go a long way. You can't assume your partner will be able to read your mind. If something is bothering you and you say nothing, it may very well build over time into something much bigger than it was originally, and then explode when you reach some trigger point that may have nothing to do with what was bothering you. Self-sabotaging recipe for disaster.

One of my first relationships after my second marriage was with a woman who liked certain things her way. 95% of the time, she was easy going. Whatever I wanted to do or wherever I wanted to go was fine with her. But that other 5%—oh my, she was the indomitable drill sergeant. For example, she was the quintessential back seat driver and always knew the best lane to travel in, who to pass, when, and which route was the best. It was important to her that I follow her instructions. More so than you can imagine. I didn't know why—it must have been some kind of control thing—but, I have to admit that this was pretty early after my split with the second wife, so I needed *a* relationship more than I needed *this* relationship. She filled a void and I wanted to keep it filled, so I put up with her 5% without ever saying a word because I didn't want to piss her off even if it pissed me off. So much for communication.

After several months of dating, we went to a party with a bunch of her friends in northern New Jersey. We had to drive a ways to get there and I was not familiar with the route. She gave directions, which I dutifully followed. I discovered a shortcut for the trip back home, but she told me to go home the same way we came. I wanted her to be able to sleep on the ride home and not bother her with asking where to turn, so I decided to take my shortcut. As I was about to veer onto a highway that led to my shortcut, she shouted, "No, not that way," and grabbed the steering wheel to turn the car off the entrance ramp. Had I let her control the wheel, we would have ended up in a ditch. I was stronger than she, so we avoided an accident. And all my repressed feelings came to the surface, all at once. I lost it. I pulled over to the side of the road and started yelling at her.

Later on, I realized that the 5% was building up over time and since I never addressed it with her, I was a ticking time bomb. All I did was yell, but boy did I yell. And that was the end of that relationship.

Moral of the story: communicate, communicate, communicate.

LOVE VS. INFATUATION

My therapist sends out a quarterly newsletter on various psychological topics. He sent me one recently on love, which included a section on love versus infatuation. Since I have always fallen in love (I thought) hard and fast, I was curious as to whether I was typically falling in love or simply infatuated. I realized there were many (maybe most) times that I was merely infatuated.

Now that you are dating someone and perhaps still feeling your way around the new dating scene, it can be easy to fall hard and fast. It should prove helpful to look at the below definitions of love versus infatuation and determine whether you are infatuated or truly in love. The first time I took this "test," I was in a relatively new relationship (six weeks), but was falling hard and fast. I went through the differences and realized that while I still had a ways to go to feel love, that I was not headed down the path of infatuation. It gave some credibility to my feelings, as it should yours. And if you come to the conclusion that it is indeed infatuation, it doesn't mean it can't grow into love. You just have to acknowledge where you are now and where you have to go to make it real. You might also pass this on to whomever you are dating and have her compare her feelings to the list of criteria.

Here is what my therapist's newsletter said.

Infatuation is one set of glands calling to another.

Love is friendship that has caught fire—it grows one day at a time.

Infatuation is an artificial love based on appearance, status, and sexual passion.

Love goes much deeper, to include companionship, friendship, and commitment.

Infatuation is insecure—it's exciting, but there are nagging doubts, annoying habits that you can't examine too closely for fear of destroying the dream.

Love is quiet understanding and mature acceptance of imperfections.

Infatuation says, "We must get married right away—I can't risk losing him/her."

Love says, "Don't panic; s/he's yours. Plan your future with confidence."

Infatuation breeds jealousy and possessiveness. When you're apart, you wonder if your lover is cheating—sometimes you even check.

Love is trusting.

Infatuation leads us to do things we later regret.

Love never will.

ON YOUR WAY UP THE RABBIT HOLE

- Learn her likes and dislikes. Cater to her.
- Write her a poem or tell her the things you like about her. Keep it light but make it real.
- Remember why those little things that seemed so important to you were so important—you didn't have anybody. Let go and compromise. Don't play the "control" game.
- Learn the difference between love and infatuation.
- Infatuate with some 30-somethings along the way.

THE OTHER SIDE

W is for Worldly, we would like him to imitate
    Woeful is often the result at the end of the date

O is for the Orgasm that becomes more fleeting at this age
    Read the next chapter 'cause toys are all the rage

M is for Making the Hmmms go away
    M is the Migraine you get if they stay

E is for infatuation breeding Excitement
    E is for Ending infatuation with true love Enlightenment

N is for Nauseous, a feeling you may get
    If I don't end this poem in the next nanosec

Poems are fun and not mutually exclusive to male authors.

It is more important early on to express yourself. While you may be reticent to derail a burgeoning relationship by bringing up things that bother you, they are important to express. Make sure, however, they truly are worthy of a "bother you" tag, and are not just a product of you being alone or your inner need to have things your way driven by insecurity, anger, or whatever else Freud might put on the therapeutic table.

If he is a sports nut, introduce him to DVR. This has helped me tremendously as I can now do things on Sunday afternoons in the fall. Some guys will need to watch the game live, but most will be willing to compromise, if you matter. I have found it a challenge not to hear the score somewhere along the way before getting to watch the recorded game. Watching it is no fun if you already know the result. Work with him on this.

One Sunday afternoon in the 80s when VCRs were brand new, some important event to her was trumping football. Ugh! I implanted the cassette firmly in the Betamax (ask your mother) and triple-checked the timer. All parties I might run into were on alert not to divulge any details on pain of death. The car radio was set to a music station. We went to whatever the event was that was so important I had to miss the Jets game and everything went smoothly. Until I entered my car to go home. I knew there was a chance—an infinitesimal chance—that someone could mention the game on a music station, so my plan was to turn the radio off as soon as I turned on the car. Damn, I planned this well. The stars were aligned, the gods in tow, just needed two seconds when I turned the car on. Don't ask me why I didn't do that when I turned off the car—I just forgot. Of course you know what happened. Literally the first and only words heard when I revved up the engine were "Dolphins 17, Jets 14."

He knows it's not as important as Granny's 70th birthday party, but to him, it is still very important. Viva la DVR!

If he says he's not getting married again, listen. Just how important is that? He may change as the relationship develops. You may change as the relationship develops. The need to be married at 50 is very different than the need to be married at 25. I have been married twice. I have no need to marry again. At my age, it serves very little purpose. If you are heading towards permanency, would a living will and some jointly held assets satisfy your need? Or maybe marriage represents financial security. There are more ways to execute that result besides marriage, so look into this before considering it a deal breaker. It remains a very personal decision that you and your partner will figure out. Or not be together, which would be a shame if communication and compromise could avoid that.

IF YOU NEVER WANT TO HEAR FROM HIM AGAIN…OR HE HAS A REALLY, REALLY GOOD SENSE OF HUMOR:

1. I like that you are balder "there" than "there."
2. I like that the picture of your penis I saw on "hookmeup.com" is actually smaller than in real life.
3. I love that you are willing to spend every Sunday afternoon in the fall at my parents with me and my kids, looking at photo albums, listening to my niece play the flute, and not drinking.
4. I *love* that your bank account has a *lot* of zeros in it.
5. I *really love* that your kids are all grown and have been written out of the will.

CHAPTER 13: TOYS

(NOT YOUR GRANDFATHER'S CHOO-CHOO TRAIN)

Whether it's love or infatuation, whether it's a long-term relationship or just a fuck buddy, once you are intimate and comfortable with that intimacy, it is not unreasonable to expect the subject of sex toys to come up. Even if you are not so inclined to bring it up first, do not be surprised if she does. I was pleasantly surprised when women spoke about sex toys easily and were not concerned what I might think. Most already had their own.

Why are toys important? I never heard of/used/felt the need to go to a sex shop when I was young. Yes, the proliferation of the internet and loosening of societal mores have made toys more accessible, but why the need now? Quite frankly, we are older and things don't work quite as well as they used to. And men are not alone in that. Women don't get excited as easily and may need extra stimulation. Also keep in mind that many of them have been alone for the first time in their lives and may not have been with a man in a while. They may not admit it, but are "taking care of themselves." They are likely more comfortable "with" themselves than you remember when you were younger. And some of the toys are amazing. They have been using toys and just need to feel comfortable with you to discuss it, then perhaps you can use them together.

Masturbation is not a topic to be ignored either. Howard Stern got that topic started on his radio show in the 80s when he freely admitted to doing it and challenged others to do the same. It may not have been the only impetus to a more open dialogue on the subject, but it certainly helped. Masturbation is natural and while everyone will admit to themselves that they do it, most will not acknowledge that others do it, stifling any hint of conversation on the topic. Masturbation may actually be an easier topic to approach than toys. If you believe it is and you wish to bring toys into the relationship, then start with a conversation about masturbation.

What about porn? Porn is a more difficult topic than masturbation and toys. Society has made it "dirty" for a woman to enjoy watching others making love and being turned on by it. Unfortunately, I have found that for the most part, society wins. It is a rare woman who will agree to watch porn with you. It is a rarer woman who will enjoy it. I recommend leaving this topic alone.

How do you start these conversations? Gently. You may be surprised how open she is, but she also may be hesitant at first. Once you are intimate, it will be easier to talk about sex, which will ultimately lead to opportunities to broach these topics. Use them.

LET'S GET DOWN TO BUSINESS

But alas! Men have been in charge of society since Adam and Eve and have created our own sexual apocalypse, telling women they shouldn't have sex without love or a ring. Are we out of our fucking minds? And we made it even worse by ultimately creating a world where toys were designed for women and not for men. Why? Because men will go to the sex shop or internet sex toy site and buy shit for their woman. The woman isn't going there. "Oh my God, Jocelyn, my neighbor might see the mailman deliver that huge dildo to my door!" No, they won't do it. This has led to a proliferation of sex toys for women and blow up dolls for men. Men will do anything to enhance the sexual experience for their woman (as long as it doesn't affect their manhood), but women draw the line at the entrance to sex toy shops. At least at this age. At least by themselves. A birthday blow job—yeah, a shower fantasy—no problem, maybe even the mile high club, but they ain't going shopping to buy you a toy. Here's the rub. If she isn't going to shop for them, no one is going to research how to make really good ones.

So, where does that leave us men? Without any good toys to speak of. As much as I am searching the world for the best veal parmesan, I am also searching the world for a toy that comes anywhere close to doing for a man what those vibrating things do for women. I do not think it exists.

Let's concentrate on what we as men can do to facilitate enjoyment for our women. As Americans, we have certain inalienable rights. Unfortunately, one of them is *not* a vibrating penis. Female toys vibrate. Men do not vibrate. I don't care how expert your tongue is, it cannot vibrate. Rubbing is one thing, vibration is a whole other one. The first thing you will have to do is get over your lack of vibration. Yes, you can be replaced by something that can do something you cannot. Kind of like the George Carlin joke about dogs. He noted with an amazing amount of logic that dogs can lick their balls, and if he could do the same, he would never leave home. Touché. But we can't lick our balls and we can't vibrate. That's what toys are for.

While we cannot vibrate, most women prefer a live man over a machine. While we cannot vibrate, women are emotional creatures and dildos have never been known to cuddle after sex. Rest assured you are not really in competition with an inanimate object. If you can't get over that, I hope your hand is in good shape.

ADAMANDEVE.COM

That is all you need to know. Go check it out. Toys, videos, games, they have it all. Toys for men and toys for women and toys for ferrets and...okay, not ferrets. (Who wants a ferret as a pet, anyway? That would be kind of like having Borat as your etiquette instructor.) I think they make a fortune since the stuff they have seems so cheap—they get $34.95 for a piece of rubber with a battery, and you have to buy the battery separately.

They have thought of everything. Their web site has a link to "Popular Categories," which includes: Sex Toys, Vibrators, Women Sex Toys, Men Sex Toys, Adult Movies, Lingerie, Lube, Extras, and my favorite, Clearance Sex Toys. The Clearance section includes a bunch of marked down DVDs and a whole bunch of other stuff that looks like the non-clearance stuff. I think they rotate things from "New and Improved" to "Clearance" and charge the same outrageous price for all of it. Although, there was a dolphin vibrator in the Clearance section, which even I found a little distasteful. Where are the animal activists when you need them? With a billion things to choose from, even I can stay away from a vibrating dolphin. No wonder it's in the "Clearance" section.

You really do have to check it out (or other similar web sites, there are tons) or even go to a local sex shop. That's a gas. I have done that a couple of times with a woman. The employees can share expert knowledge about how to use each device, complete with unabashed references to the places they stimulate. It is difficult to figure out how some of the items work, so their expertise becomes necessary. I think they must have all tried them as a prerequisite for hiring since they know so much about them. Now that's a nice job for my retirement.

TOYS FOR BOYS

Alas, a very short topic for effective toys. Among the categories are cock rings, pussy strokers, penis pumps, anal sex toys, and love dolls. Several porn stars have put their names to certain devices (I can't imagine that "Lexi Belle's Pussy Stroker" was named after somebody's cat) in an effort to make you think that the toy will be like the real Lexi Belle. Yes, it does work. Well, at least the marketing. Others have very clever names like Hammerhead Vibrating Stroker. Just the visual I want—a fucking shark gripping me. They are all pieces of rubber shaped like a vagina, or some facsimile thereof, and some of them vibrate.

Let's start with cock rings. They slide onto you and vibrate as you have intercourse. Some have a little extension that looks like a small finger to stimulate her and it vibrates along with the ring. The vibration feels good and the extension, properly placed, will stimulate her a bit more. While this can be a slight enhancement, it can also get in the way unless you have room to spare down there. I don't.

The pussy stroker can be manual or automatic. It's a piece of rubber shaped like a vagina and you simply "slip it on." For the manual flavor, you simply grab a handle or the whole device and move it yourself. It is not much different from using your hand, but a rubber vagina is tight. The automatic variety comes with a "bullet" that (with batteries) provides vibrating stimulation at various speeds. The bullet is a small oval shaped metal device. You insert it into the rubber vagina and it creates a vibrating sensation. You can also manually intervene as well. This is the closest thing to a hands-free device that I have found. I always like the option of being able to do other things while having fun, but it is awkward and usually requires some attention.

Penis vacuum pumps are used to create a vacuum around the penis, encouraging an erection by increasing blood flow into the penis. Insert yourself inside the cylinder and begin pumping. Since the cylinder is clear, you can see your progress. There are even measuring lines to note your length as visions of porn star size dance in your head. If you had a head start, the pump can enhance you all the more. You are cautioned, however, that after 10 minutes of vacuum packing, it is advisable to reduce or eliminate the pressure. More than 10 minutes at a time can be dangerous. It's like the four-hour erection.

According to the ad, you can use a penis pump for your own simple pleasure or for foreplay with your partner. Not. If you want to have fun with your partner, bringing out a device that looks more like a blender will induce laughter rather than excitement. Strictly in the interest of research, I tried it. There I was in the blender, feeling like I was watching someone else's. Did it work? Sort of. But it also hurt and extrication was not comfortable. It was a waste of $29.95. Honestly, I prefer Val.

You will want to start with the small version of anal beads. Lube is a must. Gentle helps, as well. I suggest playing with the area first before inserting anything. Make sure you and your partner are comfortable with stimulation there. There are multiple sizes, lengths, and shapes that can be experimented with. Take care not to lose anything in there. Most anal beads come with something to assist in their removal. If you are germ phobic, you can always put a condom on the beads before inserting. (That sounds a little anal.)

Don't forget the vibrating version. It comes with adjustable speeds and is quieter than your average toy. Perfect for those long train commutes.

Here's a great ad: "Name your Temptress, then have her as you please! She's 5 feet tall with a pretty face that's ready to swallow you whole, anytime, anywhere you want! Her pretty kitty's ready for lovin' and she will spread her 33" long legs or bend over for it in her tight behind!" Damn, sounds like a hooker ad, but then this is in fine print: "Durable, inflatable PVC; supports up to 250 pounds."

Love dolls. The ad even suggests that you can use "her" alone or with a partner. I hope you don't desire a woman who wants a love doll to participate in the bedroom with you. Not my idea of a threesome. When I mentioned love dolls to my girlfriend, she laughed. When I told her I bought one and wanted to try it in the interest of research, she almost had a heart attack. She got mad at me for wanting to fuck a rubber woman and turned ice cold on me for a week. When I said it was only for research for my book, she asked if she could fuck a guy in the interest of "research." I told her it was okay if it was a rubber guy.

After she calmed down and we talked about it further, she insisted on being with me when I opened the package. There "she" was. Unfurled from her plastic bag and ready to be blown up. Complete with rubber nipples, a painted face, and slots for insertion. This was going to take some blowing up, so we deferred on the experiment at first. Next time I saw her, she asked me if I had "done" the doll. I told her no, but we decided that if we were going to continue to talk about this, we should give her a name. So Candy was born. However, despite my overwhelming devotion to science, experimentation, and to you, the reader, Candy remains a virgin.

IF IT VIBRATES, SHE WILL COME

Ah, the ladies have it made. The dildo came first. It started out with hard plastic, straight, some contour, good for insertion. Rubber ones were better. Firm, yet soft. They come in various sizes, shapes, and colors. Physically correct with head, shaft, and even veins. Some are even curved. Firm grip at the end of the shaft allows manipulation in any way she chooses. But then someone invented batteries and a whole new world lit up.

After the dildo came the original Venus Butterfly. It looks like a butterfly and moves like a butterfly. It is a simple little device that fits snugly where it should and vibrates at different levels. Every woman I have shared toys with has found this the best. It may not give as strong a sensation as others, but it is small, soft, and cute. It can also be used during sex. You can experiment with this in various positions and find what works best for you. Try it with oral sex, as well. It has an added feature that others do not. It comes with straps and can be worn under clothing for hands-free stimulation. You women have it made. Take it with you when you walk the dog. Plane delayed? Who cares? Grocery shopping takes on new meaning. Those fucking string beans have never looked greener before. I will stand here and check out every one. This is my dream sex toy. It makes me yearn for my own hands-free device.

The Rabbit Vibrator appears to be the next most popular item. It combines a dildo that can penetrate along with a "finger" that stimulates a separate area. Both vibrate. The dildo portion is shaped like a penis—a large penis, with a head. You can rotate and vibrate each part independently or all at once. One version has 16 functions. It even has independent light-up controls. Who needs video games?

Far from dainty, this is strictly for business. It is a rather intimidating contraption akin to the penis pump. Perhaps good for going solo, but it may be a little much for use with a partner. However, I do know women who swear by it.

Another item of interest is called a Wand Massager. It has a long handle with a large massager at the end. It is not for insertion, rather for outside stimulation. It is rather large and looks like a back massager, which makes it easy to camouflage from the kids and other relatives. It appears to work wonders and has different intensity levels. One drawback is the power cord instead of batteries. One woman I dated kept the massager under her bed, plugged in, and frequently had middle of the night excursions to orgasm land. I have seen some of the most intense orgasms by women using this massager.

While the Butterfly can provide a nice, easy, flowing vibrating experience that can be coupled with foreplay and even intercourse, when the Wand Massager comes out from under the bed, it's time to find ESPN. She has had enough of you, but not of it. Never take it personally if she wants more after you are done or even after she is done (initially). And if she wants to have fun by herself for a bit, know that you are the one that made her this horny. Keep in mind one thing with the Wand Massager: you can probably get the functional equivalent of it from any department store at half the price.

In the interest of sexual equality, the Vagina Pump is similar to the penis pump in that it uses a vacuum to increase the size of the excitement. Put on vagina and squeeze. There was no warning for overuse, but your feeling will tell you when you have had enough. It stimulates sensitivity in the area and readies a woman for the next level, whether it be solo stimulation or with a partner. In either event, the sensations are elevated.

Now there are many other types and kinds of sex toys, and some of them are wildly ridiculous and incredibly large, but there are also a ton of funny things. Well, I think they are funny—perhaps others swear by them. There is the Amazing Fellatio Kit and its brother, the Amazing Cunnilingus Kit. If you are lucky, you can find a two for one deal and get both. The fellatio kit includes a DVD on how to give the best blow jobs, sex spray to make him taste better, playing cards with additional instructions, penis ring, and a rubber vibrating mouth simulator in case hers gets tired. The cunnilingus kit comes with its own set of DVD instructions and playing cards, some flavored spray and a vibrating tongue in case his gets tired. And get this—it comes with batteries included, something toys typically do not come with.

The Evolved Romance Collection was on sale as I wrote this and may end up in the Clearance section soon. It includes a grab bag surprise bundle of stimulating things. Buy it before they run out. Then there is the 18" dildo, along with others that come in assorted sizes. There is even a 5" version (for those of you who want to remember me). Of course, an assortment of strap-ons, ben wa balls, edible underwear, games, and stuff you can't even imagine.

They actually have sex *furniture*.

The Hot Seat Vibrator Sex Toy is a blow-up seat that inflates just like a typical pool toy. Or Candy. It comes with a special appendage to enhance her experience—a vibrating dildo that sticks up from the seat, perfectly placed for her to squat and smile. It comes with built-in handles on the side to assist her in balancing herself as she goes up and down, and is able to hold up to 300 pounds. The vibrating dildo has different speeds and the control can be used by her partner if she wishes to relinquish control over her pleasure. It is a plug-in toy.

My favorite could be the Fifty Shades of Grey Submit to Me Beginners Bondage Kit complete with blindfolds, satin restraints, and a paddle. Now, did adamandeve.com have to pay royalties to E. L. James to use the name? It does say she approved it. Hmmmm, I wonder if anyone will want to use my name for some kinky stuff….

Different web sites will call these lovely creatures by different names. So you may have to go by the description or just use your imagination. It will be easy once you see them.

GOOD VIBRATIONS

So how do we take all this and put it to use? Once you have been intimate, the subject of masturbation and toys is likely to come up. I have had women initiate the conversation. When I have brought it up, I have never upset anyone. She may not have used any, but was comfortable talking about it and asked about my experiences. If they haven't used toys, they have thought about it and might embrace the opportunity to explore. You should feel comfortable bringing it up—we are all here trying to be happy and feel good—and don't take offense if she prefers not to talk about it. Perhaps, she is not ready, perhaps she never will be. It's not about you.

I have found the Butterfly to be the best way to introduce the topic. Make sure you have talked about it, otherwise expect some hesitancy. If she's a rookie, she may only be willing to use it on "low" for a few seconds the first time, but once she gets that feel, she always comes back for more. Make sure you do not recycle the Butterfly or any sex toy. You will find that since you used it on someone else, she will be adamant that you need to get one special for her. It's like the toothbrush thing, only worse. And understandable. Just buy the woman her own.

How ever you start, start small. I would not start with anything that is intimidating, too big, too weird, too anything. A small dildo is a potential alternative to the Butterfly as it is more main stream and thus may be something she is familiar seeing. If she is initially embarrassed talking about toys and masturbation and you make her feel comfortable, then she may very well respond positively. From my perspective, the introduction of toys into the bedroom has only enhanced the experience.

If she is experienced, she has her own. Get her one for your place. Better yet, take her to the local sex shop for a special outing and let her pick out what she wants. If she's too reserved for the adventure, have her wait in the car and think about what you're doing as that will contribute to her arousal later.

ON YOUR WAY UP THE RABBIT HOLE

- Women are more comfortable talking about sex toys and masturbation than you might think.
- Porn is another thing altogether.
- Toys can enhance the experience and, since we are older, may make it easier to get ready. Start small and be gentle. Experiment. Have fun.
- Some toys do appear hazardous to your health, so don't go overboard and understand what you are getting yourself "into."
- Candy is available on eBay.

THE OTHER SIDE

If you can find your way to a sex shop, go—it's a pisser! In the meantime, if you are a *Jeopardy!* fan:

Dildos for 200, Alex.

Answer - 13 inches.

What is something the author dreams about?

Let's try Good Vibrations for 400, Alex.

Answer - $34.95

What is the amount of money you are glad you did not spend on this book?

Umm, Choo Choo Trains for 600, Alex.

Answer - The Double Penetrating Smoke Stack Orient Express.

What replaced the Hot Seat Vibrator Sex Toy when it went to Clearance?

Butterflies for 800 please Alex.

Answer - Lepidopterists.

What happens when my zeal for finding vibrating butterfly analogies runs into the internet? (You are going to have to look that up.)

———

Wand Massagers for 1,000, Alex.

********Daily Double*********

I'll bet it all, Alex.

Answer - World peace.

What happens when Kim Jong Un buys Candy?

CHAPTER 14: DATING TIPS FOR WOMEN FROM A MAN'S POINT OF VIEW

(WE DO LOVE YOU LADIES, EVEN IF YOUR PROFILES ARE TOO LONG)

While there has been an "Other Side" to each chapter with some thoughts for women on that chapter's topics, I wanted to include some matters that are specific only to women and expound upon some earlier items.

THE ONLINE DATING DIFFERENCE

Ladies, first of all, kudos to you as you take a bigger risk than men when putting your picture and life story on the internet. More women are serious about their attempts to engage in internet dating to find a relationship than men, putting a lot of effort into writing their profile and providing multiple pictures of yourself. You probably spend more time reading a man's profile than he spent writing it, and you take it seriously. First mistake.

If you think about what you wrote in your profile, you will realize that you put your best foot forward. You did not talk about your issues or bad habits or bisexual fantasies (although that will be a turn on to many men) and focused only on the good things about you. Your counterparts did the same. Men will keep hidden things that would make you instantly move on. As will you. I believe that guys are more likely to lie in their profiles than women because of insecurity. So take what you read with a grain of salt, especially if his profile sounds like all the others.

Try to find someone with a different spin to his profile. It may be a sign that he is more honest, but don't completely discount the ordinary run-of-the mill profile. Just because it doesn't appear that he spent a lot of time creating it or just talked about the good stuff, doesn't mean he isn't a good guy. Maybe even a potential mate. It may not be robust because he's a rookie. Maybe he is hesitant to disclose too much. Or just testing the internet dating waters. Keep in mind that no one profile will make or break a real relationship. Think about what is and is not in yours, and you will understand.

I would evaluate the "approach email" more than the profile. If a man took the time to read your profile and it is obvious, that is a good first sign. If he sent you an email only talking about himself, you can feel more comfortable moving on.

I have learned to keep my evaluation of a profile simple. If she is cute, geographically desirable, and doesn't have kids living at home, I give her a shot. Even if she lives on tofu and bean sprouts. But I am sifting through hundreds of profiles to decide who to contact. I need some kind of screening mechanism. You are only responding to emails. You will come up with your own criteria.

Women have it easier dating on the internet. Most guys make the first move, so you just have to sit back and wait for the winks, pokes, and smiles. Guys have to pursue. Ladies, remember this rule—guys like aggressive women. We like it if you send us an email. If you are not ready for that, a smile is welcome. Most women don't like the smile thing since it seems like a lazy way to say hello, but guys know the female is hesitant to make the first move, so a smile is a great start. Wink and smile away.

When you get an email, I suggest you respond with equal vigor. If someone smiles, it's okay to just smile back. But if he takes the time to write a nice email, don't send a smile back or say "thanks, nice to meet you." If you are interested, at least match his effort. If you are not interested, there is a "delete" button. Remember, guys are sending out dozens of emails to women they might consider having a date with. They will follow up with the same vigor that you replied with. If you are interested but do not give an effort, you may lose him. Just like you want him to read your profile and act like he gets you just a little bit, we men appreciate a matching response.

I know you get a lot of emails. You must; someone is getting the dozens that I and all the other guys are sending. So I know you have a lot of reading to do and have to determine based on a few words whether or not you might be interested in a date. But we made the first move and already invested time, so it's not an excuse that you don't have time to respond to all the emails. Don't respond to all of them, just respond appropriately to those that interest you.

Internet dating is extremely fast paced. You can be in and out of a relationship in between responding to emails. You get 20 emails. You answer three. You arrange one date. This repeats itself…daily. You may get an email from someone who you find interesting, but he does not respond to your email for a week. Meanwhile, you have had two dates with another guy who you also like. Now Guy #1 is stuck on the sidelines until you figure out if Guy #2 is worth it. Don't feel bad. In the meantime, Guy #1 sent out 20 emails, got three responses, and arranged for one date. Daily. When Guy #2 doesn't work out, oops, Guy #1 is now serial dating. Don't feel bad. You have 75 emails to go through. It can become dizzying.

It is natural and understandable for women to want to go slow, perhaps several emails and multiple phone conversations before an actual meeting. For the most part, guys get this and are willing to go at your pace, but do not draw this out. I went out with a woman who until we met, did not give me her phone number. She really was afraid I might be a criminal. We even joked about how I was getting out on parole just to meet her. She turned out to be a normal, fun woman, but admitted she really was scared that a guy she meets might be a serial killer.

Most guys understand going slow but also want to move more quickly. If you get comfortable, just go ahead and chat, then meet.

Take control of where and when you meet so you feel safe. Any guy worth meeting will encourage and support that, and you can always bring the appropriate bodyguards if necessary. He will appreciate moving at faster than a snail's pace.

Okay, now it's the first date and you meet for a drink. Who pays? Most guys will automatically offer to pay. If he doesn't or suggests splitting it, what does that mean? He may have decided that he no longer needs to impress you because he doesn't want to have another date with you. Or maybe it's his way of showing you he respects equality between the sexes? Or maybe he is poor. Or that is just his nature. Don't read too much into it. If you like him, a second date will disclose the answer. Honestly, if I were poor, I would rather suggest a free/cheap date that is still nice and classy rather than suggest we split the tab. You will probably be able to tell the difference between cheap and poor.

I have always been impressed when a woman offers to pay, although I have yet to accept. I suggest that you offer to split the bill on the first date, then offer to occasionally pick up the tab or take him out to drinks/dinner. A lot depends on your financial situation, and neither will know the specifics of the other early on. Play this by ear and do what feels natural. If you are financial equals, you may wish to treat half of the time. If he is in much better shape than you, then an occasional offer will be very much appreciated. It is not so much the dollar value of the offer, just an acknowledgement of the situation. Feel comfortable saying, "I would love to pay, but I cannot. Can I cook your favorite meal instead?"

But by all means, never—and I mean, never—tell a man that you expect him to pay every time you go out or that you expect him to pay for vacations. You can have the expectation, and if you fall in love or he is wealthy, it may never be an issue. But if you tell him you "expect" him to pay for everything, you look like a moocher. Feel free to be honest and say something like, "I'm sorry, but I can't really afford to take vacations." If you tell him a week later you're going to Florida with your girlfriends, don't expect roses anytime soon, though. The point is normal, financially stable guys are more than willing to spring for dinners and shows and the like, but no one wants to be taken advantage of.

WHO ARE THESE GUYS?

Just like you have been putting up with your asshole husband for all these years, he has been putting up with his asshole wife. There are two ends to every asshole. Do not expect that your new guy will have the same bad habits as your ex or that he wants to be treated the same way your ex did. Don't expect him to treat you the same way your ex did, either. It's a brand new ballgame. The date you have tonight is completely different from any date you had before you were married. You are both older and, while you think you and he are the same, you are not. Now that could be a good or a bad thing. Only time and that date will tell.

As you begin dating again, I would like to share a few things that bother me. I think many of my male brethren would agree. These are things that can come up early in a relationship or even within just a couple of dates. I know there are similar things that bother you about us. Maybe more, maybe worse. And by all means, please share them with us. But I thought it would be helpful to put a couple of things on the table that some men do not react kindly to. If you can avoid these things early on, the man will appreciate it.

I do not like it when a woman tells me that she is going to do something or not do something because she thinks it's best for me. For example:

"I don't think it's a good idea that we spend the day together. I know you need time for yourself."

It may sound right to you, but subconsciously, it's masking the real issue. Maybe you are not into him or maybe you have things to do and need time for *yourself*. I have had this happen to me more than once, and guess what...she was not into me. It sounds condescending. It's better to be honest. I would rather know where I stand than forced into trying to interpret what you mean.

This next one can be a relationship killer. Don't expect men to read your mind. "Well, he knows I like chick flicks, why did he suggest the new James Bond movie?" "He knows I like him to text me at least once a day." Talk to him. Tell him what you like, what you want, and encourage him to do the same. If you don't tell someone what you want, it is very likely you will not get it. Look at it this way. If you are afraid to tell him what you want because he might react negatively, then you will have to accept living without it. And if you do that long enough, you will eventually decide you can't live without it and leave. If you tell him what you want, he may say "no" and you will leave him, but that was going to happen anyway, and now at least it will happen sooner. If, on the other hand, he says "yes," you have the best of both worlds: what you want and him.

Here's another one, and guys "should" listen too. Please stuff those "shoulds" deep in your pocketbook. Like "I think you should drive slower" or "You should be nice to your mother." Or think of it in the context of yourself. "I should have gone to the gym today" or "I should have called Mom." The use of the word "should" sucks. It's judgmental. If you "should" do something, and you don't, you failed. If you tell someone that they "should" do something and they don't, they disappointed you. Don't do it.

Instead of saying "should," say "want." "I want you to drive slower" or "I want you to be nice to your mother." Now there is no judgment. You are expressing a desire and if doesn't happen, you may be unhappy that your desire was not met, but you have not made a judgment on the second party. You can even say, "I wanted to go to the gym, but didn't." Now you haven't failed, you just put off something you should, oops, want to do. The use of "should" happens without thought and if you are going to try this, you will have to concentrate. Give it a shot.

OLD HABITS DIE HARD

As a single woman in your 50s or so, you have been living on your own for a while and have a new single life. You have taken up new activities and feel like it's your turn now, especially if you spent many years raising kids (even more so if one of the kids was your ex-husband). You have become fiercely independent, engaged in a lifestyle that has become important to you, and have found things to occupy your time that do not include a man. One thing you *must* remember is that dating takes time out of your day. *Your* day. All those things that occupy your time. Something's going to have to give. Are you ready for that? Can you give up that cappuccino you have at the local coffee house every Thursday night with Martha to have a date? Can you go to the gym on Sunday morning instead of Saturday morning so you can stay out late with a date you are enjoying Friday night? Then there is all the little stuff in your life that you don't consciously think is important. Until some guy interferes with it. Then you realize it's a deal breaker. Or is it? Putting the cap on the toothpaste. That fucking toilet seat. Watching Fox News. Chill out and let it go.

As you begin to date, you are naturally going to look for someone to fit into your life, at first unwilling to compromise. ("I would never watch Fox News.") But if you are serious about meeting someone and creating a mutually wonderful relationship, you will need to compromise. Just as you would like to meet someone who "fits" into your life, so would he. But the odds of you finding someone who fits into your life perfectly is zero. You will both need to change at least a little.

So take that list of 35 items you created of things that a man MUST have for you to be with him—maybe you even wrote them down like my sister did—and look hard at the things that really matter. You shouldn't (oops)—you won't want to compromise on the first date, or on everything, but find the real deal breakers. Put everything else (which should be—or you will "want" to be—most of the items) on the "I'm willing to compromise" page.

MAMA'S BOYS

This is a touchy subject. Let's face it: no one wants to be with a Mama's Boy. You will always play second fiddle and his relationship with her will piss you off more than you can deal with. Even more importantly, he will never love you the way you want to be loved because of the emotional stronghold his mother holds over him. I think you know enough to steer clear, but the real question is how do you identify a Mama's Boy before you are in too deep?

It won't be easy at first. There is no sign tattooed to his forehead, although if Mom could swing it, there would be. He may be very charming and successful, like dating, and may be good at it. Marriage? Another thing completely. When you begin to suspect that he is a Mama's Boy, your first inclination will be that you can change him. But the change thing is a dangerous one. Women always want to change men, and think they can. It must be that mutant X chromosome or something. You will cling to the belief that you can change him for a long time. You may even marry him and bear his children. I caution you with a big red flag: you won't change him.

Honestly, if you have to change someone, is he really worth it? You will either have to accept him and Mama (and do so unconditionally) or leave him. Neither is easy.

What are the signs? An obvious one is when he's never been married. My aunt was a Mama's Girl. She lived at home her entire life, taking care of her parents. Whenever she dated and brought home a guy, he was never good enough. My grandparents laid the guilt trip on her and she ended up, as she would proudly say, "a 78-year-old virgin." Now, guys she dated really never had the chance to figure out whether she was a Mama's Girl because Mama would not let anyone get that close. You may not have that luxury.

Meet Dan. My girlfriend and I met him in Aruba. He was traveling with his business partner, a female. We struck up a conversation over lunch and hung out for a couple of days. He was 55, a good-looking doctor, financially stable, and had a charming personality. Never married. She was in her late 40s, also a doctor, decent-looking, and totally into him. It was obvious and she even admitted it when he wasn't around. He couldn't have cared less. I talked to him privately and he told me she was just a friend, oblivious to her flirtatiousness. He called it Jeannie being Jeannie.

Dan had been engaged, but it didn't "work out." He had no other long-term relationships to speak of. He was controlling, making all the plans for him and Jeannie, including where and when they would go for dinner, what beach to hang out on, and what she should wear. He talked about his mother frequently, but not in the best of tones. They clearly still had a very close relationship, though the undercurrent of his comments was not very positive. It was the tone of his voice. Even when he said nice things about her, there was resentment there. He seemed to treat Jeannie the way he wanted to treat his mother but could not. He tried to control Jeannie and likely most things in his life as a way to combat his inability to overcome his mother's control of him.

I didn't get to know Dan that well, but I would clearly label him a "Mama's Boy." If he wasn't still overly controlled by his mother, then his mother had an undue influence on him that made him unable to commit to a woman. Certainly his attitude toward women made him an undesirable long-term mate.

If you are dating someone, you will begin to get a sense of what is going on if you are watching. Are dates broken because Mom suddenly needed something? (Is what Mom needed really a need?) Is he bitter towards his mother because he subconsciously recognizes he is a Mama's Boy, but can't do anything about it? How does Mama react when you meet her? How is the dialogue between her and her son? If she is cool to you and appears to be controlling of your boyfriend, you could have a Mama's Boy on your hands. Does he still live at home? If yes, death knell, sure sign, 100%, get the hell out. Don't take any, "well, I am out of a job and it's just temporary" bullshit. He's 50 freaking years old—if he hasn't figured out how to save enough in the past to get through a tough time without running to Mama, you don't want to be there.

Is he willing to commit to you? Maybe he says yes, but when is the wedding or when will you be moving in with him (or vice versa)? Does he keep promising to set a date but then puts it off again and again? Does he buy you a ring and then take no further action? I was with a woman who had dated a man for 10 years, engaged for five of them. He never pursued setting a date, changing the subject when she brought it up. They had a lot of fun during the week, but he went to visit his Mama every weekend. Every single weekend. Mama's boy.

If you find yourself with a Mama's Boy, the relationship is doomed. You cannot change him. Run for the hills.

THE CHANGE

I've done some research on the effects of menopause and I hope, through personal experience, have gained enough knowledge and have enough compassion to be appropriately respectful of the subject. I have personally experienced it with my second wife as well as with a couple of girlfriends who were going through it. Although their bad moods might have been correlated to me being an asshole. Guys don't deal with the Change very well. They don't understand it, can't possibly experience it, and often misinterpret it. Guys take stuff like mood swings personally. We take everything personally.

For example, when my ex-wife was pregnant with our daughter, there was one morning when she woke up before me. Well, most mornings she woke up before me so this really wasn't much different, except she was pregnant. When I got up and greeted her in the kitchen with a completely innocuous and sincere "good morning," she burst into tears. Initially, I took it seriously, like she was mad at me or something. But all I did was wake up.

Little did I know that her hormones were screaming at her—and me. It wasn't menopause, but it was hormones. More importantly, I took it personally. Guys always think it's about them. Especially when they are in their 50s, divorced, insecure, needy, and generally an emotional mess. So when you get moody, they are going to wonder what they did.

I will never diminish or trivialize the effects of menopause. Most guys have no clue. If you can help them get a clue, it will make life easier for you both. Try to understand how they might react to your moods. This is merely a plea to help these dimwits understand what you are going through. If they choose to still take it personally or get mad at you, then move on. But don't let a good one get away just because they don't *understand* your hormones. And if he is a good one, he will do his best to understand once you help him.

If you can recognize that you are in a mood and it's not because of him, let him know. Maybe you don't know what is causing it, but you know your man has done nothing wrong. If you are in that kind of mood and don't give a shit (which may be frequent or always), you won't be able to tell him at that moment that it's just the hormones. But when you are feeling better let him know that it was the hormones talking. We will interpret the moods as though you are pissed at us and react accordingly, so it will be easy to tell that your man needs this gift from you. If we know it's not about us, we have a chance to just deal with it. And quite frankly, it is in our best interests to just deal with it. Would we like to trade places with you? Fuck no.

You can try something that I did with a girlfriend. At times, we had a rather tumultuous relationship because we were both going through some emotional shit. We would get mad at each other for no apparent reason. With the help of the world's greatest shrink, we realized that we both had a "Schtick." A Schtick is something from the past, probably our childhood, that would crop up from time to time and overtake any sense of reality. It would turn a seemingly rational conversation into insanity at the drop of a hat. Some innocuous comment would cause all hell to break loose. We could not recognize it when it was happening and could not stop it from escalating. I, from tons of therapy, had learned what my Schtick was, but was not always able to recognize it. She, on the other hand, had little idea of what hers was. Neither of us could deal with it effectively when a Schtick appeared. One thing we both knew was that I recognized when her Schtick appeared, even though she could not, and she recognized when mine did, even though I could not. So we agreed on two things: 1) we would tell the other person when her/his Schtick appeared and 2) we would not take the other person's Schtick personally. To make it easier to bring up, we even decided to give our Schticks a name. Hers was William and mine was Elizabeth.

William came from a young boy we met at a restaurant one night. My girlfriend was particularly hungry and service was slow. We were sitting at the bar next to a man and his son. The son was around 8-years-old. He was finishing up his French fries when his dad got up to go to the bathroom (I presume). My girlfriend was spying the leftover fries (there were three uneaten and he seemed done) and jokingly asked me to ask him if she could finish them if he was not going to. I didn't want to seem like a pedophile, but apparently he overheard her. Next thing we know, he was sliding his plate of three French fries to my girlfriend. We laughed and started chatting with him as his dad came back. His name was William.

Elizabeth is much more boring. My daughter's and mother's middle name.

While we were at it, we also named other things. Actually, I named mine when I was a youngster. The disc jockey for a local radio station where I grew up referred to himself as "World Famous." In an obvious moment of pure adolescent fantasy, I decided to refer to mine as "World Famous." It had some panache and was a good story. I had never shared that with anyone before her and since I had named mine, we had to name hers. World Famous aside, she liked the trend of royal names, so she settled on Victoria for hers. Not Vicki, Victoria. And one day, in a moment where World Famous was in total control, I asked her if Victoria was keeping herself a secret. That took a minute.

Back to Schticks. When I saw she was getting into a mood, I would say something like, "I think William has walked in the door." This helped her realize what was going on and frequently, was actually able to defuse what in the past had escalated into bad feelings. Of course, she did the same when Elizabeth made an appearance. We would actually joke that when things were particularly good, William and Elizabeth were on vacation together.

Moral of the story: try the same thing with your man when you are going through menopause. You can really use this tool anytime, but it could be particularly effective when your moods are caused by hormones. Talk to him and have him pick a name for your "mood" when a menopause moment occurs. He can tell you that your

"Joseph" or "Richard" just appeared and maybe it will help lighten the mood. If nothing else, it will help him deal. Of course, this should not be just about you, so pick a name for his mood when it is caused by something other than you.

BO-TOXIC

Okay, ladies, I understand that you are 50-something and looking in the mirror, you see evidence that you aren't 25 anymore. To top it off, you are single at an age when you thought you wouldn't have to deal with being single. Suddenly, you notice a bunch of flaws and panic. You think the best course of action is to get some "work" done. Those that do this kind of work call it enhancements, I call it mutations.

When I became suddenly and unexpectedly single, I looked in my mirror and said, "Yikes!" I was losing my hair at a record pace, had a nose you could ski down and a mouth like Snaggletooth. Well, at least that was my oh-my-God-I-am-now-alone and how-do-I-find-another-woman state of mind. I probably looked no worse than my competition, but I didn't know that. I thought I would be unable to attract anything, much less a woman I'd find attractive.

I made the world's most unusual bald spot barely noticeable by getting a "buzz" cut. I had a cap fixed on my upper tooth from an accident when I was a teenager. I had some unsightly mutant tooth cropping up out of my lower mouth shaved down so I didn't look like a vampire. I had my teeth whitened. Previous to my divorce, I never gave my odd bald spot or teeth issues a thought. Now all of a sudden, I am an ogre. I took action.

The nose issue was relatively minor, but I could have made it a big issue. Which Olympic event was it best suited for? Could I really obscure the Statue of Liberty with my profile? My best friend had one even worse than mine and he didn't care. I could have made a big deal out of it, but I didn't.

The action I took was rather natural. I just shortened my hair and had some work done on my teeth. I was never really bothered by the nose, so that was not too hard to let go of. You ladies tend to get a bit more dramatic. I didn't go for penile implants or extensions, or hair implants, or even a nose job.

I encourage you ladies to do the same. Which is nothing. Especially when it comes to your breasts. My sister told me of a guy she dated briefly who told her she should get implants. I, being the older brother, but more importantly, thinking that I know everything, told her to dump his ass. Her breasts were fine. She thought they might help her in business. She was the CFO and office manager for a small law firm. Her current boss did not hide his preference for cup sizes at the other end of the alphabet. I asked her if she really wanted to work for someone who hired her because she had big breasts. I have never been a woman, so I cannot fully understand the discrimination towards women in the workplace, thus won't get on too high a horse here, but I will say that from this man's point of view, go *au naturale*!

I once dated a woman with implants. She was short and thin and had perfect breasts. I don't know what they looked like before the implants; I can only imagine that they were fine. But now she had implants. Which were hard as a rock. Her nipples were not as sensitive as they used to be. She was tiny. She should have small breasts. I like proportion, damnit. Sure, she looked fabulous in a bikini, but I bet she would have looked just as fabulous without implants. And those breasts would have been much more enjoyable for both of us.

If you want do something that has very little risk, then fine, but I encourage you to discuss it with your man. Not to cede him control, but find out if he thinks you need it. If I am any proxy for the average dude looking for someone at this age, he won't care. At this stage of our lives, we do not care about big lips, big breasts, tight faces, and so on, and so on, and so on. We just want to find someone we can be happy with. Just like you. And you probably couldn't care less about the amount of hair on our heads, whether we have an overbite, or the size of our penis. If you find someone who cares about the voluptuousness of your lips, how tight your skin is, or the size of your breasts, tell him to go fuck off.

Please, if it isn't medically needed, don't do it. We love you just the way you are.

SEX

Most men in their 50s can't perform like they did in their 20s, so they are not in as much of a hurry to get there. If they are fresh off a divorce, there may be performance anxiety. This could either delay the event because they are avoiding it or make it awkward the first time (it's always awkward the first time, at any age). In addition, some men have performance issues simply because of their age. Many will be using performance enhancements. And by the way, do not feel bad about that. Val only enhances the excitement; it does not create it. You still have to turn him on for him to get excited.

Most men do not want to use condoms after not using them in decades. I took a blood test so I wouldn't have to use them and gave the clean results to my new girlfriend at the time. Of course, it was too late by then as she couldn't wait for the results. My offer may have led to it happening more quickly than it might have otherwise. If you are concerned about whether your man is clean, talk to him. He will probably take it personally, but you know that now and are prepared. At least give him the option of a blood test or a condom. Condoms, yuck.

Rule of thumb: sex can naturally occur on the third date if there is a connection building. You won't have a third date if there is not at least *something* there. Guys will be patient if they like you. I dated a woman who had not had sex in 10 years. She had taken care of her sick husband and was just getting her life back together. When I found this out, I knew I had to be patient with her. Unbeknownst to me, she had gone to her gynecologist to make sure all her relevant parts were in good working order. They were.

Just because she hadn't sailed in a while, didn't mean she wasn't seaworthy.

And here's a novel idea—talk about sex. I have found most women talk about sex easily at this age. Don't be shy. We are adults. Talk to him about how you feel about sex; what you expect; what you want. Give him a clear sign that will tell him you are ready, but don't expect him to read your mind. Ask him how he feels and what he wants.

Surprise, it may not be the first date. Don't fear game playing. The older you are, the fewer the games. Make the first couple of dates easier and more comfortable. Imagine how much more relaxed the nightcap at your place and good make out session will be if he knows tonight's not the night.

I LOVE YOU

Who says it first? It becomes a game almost. I always believed that I said "I love you" when saying "I *really, really* like you" was no longer adequate. I also firmly believe that everyone's definition of love is different and everyone is at a different place on the love scale that goes from like to love. And we all have our own love scale that defines our feelings. I might say "I love you" when how I feel is the equivalent of how you feel when you say "I really like you." In other words, I am closer to "like" on your love scale but have reached "love" on mine. Conversely, I might say "I really like you" when the feeling I have is your equivalent of "love." I am now closer to the love end of your scale even though I am not ready to express it.

We are just different in terms of expressing our feelings and interpreting our emotions. How many times have you heard/said, "If you really love me, you would (could never have)…?" What is being said is that *you* would do "(whatever)" if you loved someone, but that is your definition of love. His is different.

Neither of us really knows how strongly the other is feeling when the words are spoken and can only interpret the words as how we would feel if we said them. This inconsistent application and interpretation makes it difficult to say how we feel at first.

Once I feel I am in love with someone, I want her to know. Being in love is the greatest feeling in the world, and I don't want to be hemming and hawing with myself about whether I should tell her. I want to tell her; I want to feel it.

What is the worst that could happen to you if you go first? He doesn't say it back? Who cares? If you really do love him, you will show him and he will know it whether you say it or not. Someone has to go first. We are way too old to be losing sleep over this. The last time I said "I love you" for the first time, it became a whole discussion. "What do you mean by that?" "Are you just saying it to play games with me?" "How do you really know?" Shit, honey, I just said the three most amazing words a man can say to a woman. Let them sink in and smile.

Just say it!

FINALLY...

In the end, it's up to you to believe what you want and act in a way to feel comfortable. Never sacrifice who you are or your morals and beliefs. Figure out what you want in a relationship or from a man, and go for it. Just like you hate men who play games, they hate women who play games. We are as emotionally scarred, as scared to be out there, and ultimately looking for happiness and a partner in life, as you are. Be honest, be open, and most importantly, communicate.

Good luck, ladies.

ON YOUR WAY UP THE RABBIT HOLE

- Discerning the potential gems from the riff raff online is not easy. Don't get too carried away with the content of the profile and respond with equal vigor if interested.
- You "should" take that list of 35 "must haves" and figure out which ones really matter. Very few.
- Be wary of Mama's Boys or any kind of man you think you have to change. Move on.
- If he doesn't love you the way you are, he won't love you the way you want.
- Forget looks, fuck money—if you want a man to fall in love with you, put the toilet seat *up*.

CHAPTER 15:
YOU CAN'T MAKE THIS SHIT UP

(DATING STORIES FROM THE FRONT LINES)

The stories below are all true. They manifest the real emotion, hesitancy, trepidation, and downright fear that first dates can evoke. These emotions, in hindsight, are usually unnecessary as your date feels the same way. Unfortunately, you don't know that at the time. If you can laugh at these stories, all of which happened to someone other than yourself, then you can approach your date knowing that it could be a lot worse.

Most of the stories are from a woman's perspective. Don't be the guy she dated. The advice, however, is bisexual. The names have been changed.

WE'VE ALL BEEN HERE

Pic was nice, profile was reasonable (not that it ever mattered to me), and she spoke English without a Lithuanian accent. So far so good. I agreed to meet her, but there was some distance between us. I, as the gentleman, offered to drive, but she said she didn't mind driving and we could meet near me. Even better.

As I got ready for the date, I went through her profile one more time and admired her very pretty picture. I wanted to recognize her and key in on something in her profile to impress her that I had done my homework. I did notice that the picture looked staged and was only a head shot. I wondered why no full body picture, but let it slip my mind quickly. Of course, this would be the one and only time I did that.

I arranged to meet her outside a nice bar for a late afternoon drink in the summer. It was light out and warm. I arrived early as I am supposed to and basked in the sunshine awaiting the arrival of this delicious blonde. I looked around from time to time, trying to spot her first. This is the typical game. Not that I will run away if I don't like what I see. I just want to be prepared for it. I don't want my jaw to drop when she shows up looking completely different than her picture. I failed to spot her. My jaw dropped. Obviously, her picture was air-brushed, or taken when she was in her 20s. Or she was just someone totally fucking different, because there was virtually no resemblance.

Moral of the story: Air-brushed head shots. You would think the king of internet dating would know better. This was early on. Very early.

THE EARLY MORNING PHONE CALL

Andreas was a good-looking man and he came from a different land. He had just recently come to the States at the behest of a friend. He had been a mine worker in South Africa, and was looking for work in the US while staying at his friend's place. In his spare time, he was online dating.

Andreas and Eileen met online and, after a brief virtual courtship, agreed to meet. He was going back to South Africa for a few weeks to take care of some business so they settled on his return for the first date. She didn't mind waiting, but wasn't going to be sitting home, either. This is internet dating. She had 100 other emails to go through. You snooze, you lose.

Just before Andreas left for South Africa, he called Eileen…at 3:00 AM. "Eileen, while I am away the next couple of weeks, I would like you to promise me that you won't go out with anyone else."

Eileen, now wide awake, responded, "Excuse me?"

"I would like you not to see anyone else before we get a chance to meet."

Eileen was the feisty type and took shit from no one. Here a guy she never met was asking her to be celibate until they get a chance to meet. As she so eloquently put it, "Are you kidding me?"

Apparently not. While he was new to online dating, he was not new to being a conceited pig. He insisted. She resisted. He went so far as to now say he owned his own mine in South Africa.

The conversation finally ended with Eileen uttering a rather loud "You're a dick!"

Moral of the story: If you want celibacy before the first date, your look, last name, or bank account better resemble "Kennedy."

BAND-AGE MAN

Steve wasn't a bad-looking man and the conversations were fine, but there wasn't exactly an instantaneous spark over the phone. If Lori had a better option for Friday night, she would have taken it, but was new to online dating and figured it would at least give her some experience. As any normal person would, she wanted to look her best on their first date. She needed practice. So, she put on her best outfit and dolled herself up. She looked in the mirror at this stunning blonde looking back at her and said, "Now, why the fuck am I single?"

Fully flushed from the exhilaration of getting ready for a date, Lori became excited at the prospect of a date, not necessarily at the prospect of a date with Steve.

Steve was also new to online dating and apparently missed the chapter on "Put your best foot forward" and "You never get a second chance to make a first impression."

Of course, Lori didn't know this. Her absolute best foot was forward. And hair. And cleavage. And she was expecting the picture she saw on the internet. Well, she got what she expected. Sort of. Lori showed up and looked around, wondering if Steve was there already.

She laughed for a moment when she spied some fellow sitting at the bar...with a bandage on his nose. Must be here to watch a ballgame, she thought. "Thank God, that's not my date."

Dread began to overcome her as she heard "Lori?" coming from the approximate area of Bandage Man. And yes, he was not a bad looking man...for someone with a piece of vinyl glued to his nostril. As you might expect, she could not take her eyes off the bandage and it prevented her from ever really engaging in the conversation. The injury was never discussed and there was never a second date.

Moral of the story: Feel free to use the "multiples stitches, head bandage, I saved an old lady from a speeding car" excuse, but a no-explanation bandage is a no-no.

BAND-AGE MAN II

Joe was a very good-looking guy and Melissa liked him from the start. The emails had just the right touch of flirtatiousness and phone conversations were articulate and fun. She was excited to meet him when they finally agreed to a date. In her previous dates, she would meet the guy somewhere safe for a drink or cup of coffee. She made the same plans with Joe, but was feeling pretty comfortable with him already and would be agreeable to going somewhere else if they were getting along. She had been here before, so she didn't get her hopes too high. Nice-looking guy, good conversation on the phone, but then a dud in person. So she was excited but cautious.

When they met, Melissa was relieved to see that he was what he represented. Even more handsome in person. A good start. And he made her feel comfortable immediately. He was easy going, personable, even helped take her coat off. He had a sexy twinkle in his eye. She was now officially excited. So when Joe told her about this place that he would love to take her, she quickly agreed.

They got into Joe's car and drove to a nice lounge. They walked inside, sat down at the bar, and ordered drinks. The bar seemed age appropriate for them with plenty of attractive couples. There was going to be music in a bit, so maybe they could even dance. Melissa had not danced in ages.

Wow, she thought, *this is going to be my best internet date yet.*

As they sipped their drinks, Joe pulled two bandages out of his pocket. Melissa was instantly quizzical, but figured Joe would explain. Joe proceeded to tell her that the lounge they were in was a meeting place for a Swingers Club but also open to the general public. So, to let others know which genre you belonged to while in the lounge, one put on a bandage if one was swinging. Melissa began to laugh hysterically, thinking Joe was making all this up. Then Joe opened a bandage, put it on his pinky, and offered her the other one. She then began to look more closely at the good-looking, age-appropriate crowd. To her astonishment, there were several couples there with bandages. And not one of them was on their nose.

Moral of the story: Okay, maybe Mr. Vinyl Nose was not so bad after all. Be wary of dating someone who gets a lot of paper cuts.

I LOVE MY DAUGHTER

Millie hadn't been on a date in a while and finally came across a reasonable fellow on the internet. They emailed and even chatted briefly, then decided to meet. Millie was excited and told her 20-year-old daughter that she had a date. Bless her soul, her daughter bought her a pedicure and manicure. Millie got all primped up. She looked better than she had in years. She tried to temper her enthusiasm and picked a local chain restaurant as a casual, no frills place for the first meet. He agreed.

Millie showed up early and got a chance to look around at the guys at the bar. But this wasn't on anyone's five-star restaurant list. She was not thinking there would be any single doctors there trying to meet a cute 53-year-old. Anyway, the guy she was meeting would be better than any single doctor she could think of. She ordered a glass of wine, took a sip, and waited for that awkward first hello.

When Joe showed up, she quickly recognized his face from his picture. Nice. But wait. She then eyed the rest of him. Joe was wearing a man purse and his nails looked better than Millie's. He hadn't even taken a sip of his Tequila Sunrise before he began bragging about getting his own pedicure and manicure. Millie gagged on her wine. She got through an hour and then excused herself. Forever. As she was leaving, she said to herself, "At least he didn't have man boobs."

Moral of the story: Somewhere, someplace, there is a person with nicer nails than you. Just hope it's not tonight's date.

SPEAKING OF MAN BOOBS

Lisa was a cute 50-year-old, short, nicely shaped, former TV newswoman. She could still pull off looking good on camera and was looking for a fun, outgoing, good-looking man around her age. She was online looking over the tons of emails she got, using her own screening mechanism to make what could be days of work into minutes. She was busy and not looking for bullshit, but did want to meet someone. She came across a nice looking photo, tall thin handsome man with a decent profile and a reasonable first "hello" email. She replied and they began to correspond. He was a no-nonsense type as well and she found their ADD similarities too strong to resist. The sex would be good but quick and she could get back to work. Perfect!

They finally agreed to meet. Lisa was the "get there first" type and showed up early. She hoped he was too. She had things to do. She could usually tell within minutes if she was going to be compatible with someone. This one took seconds.

They made eye contact and she realized that his photos were at least 100 pounds old. He had to weigh 350. Guys make this mistake too. Lisa, being a lady, greeted Mike and they sat down and ordered a drink. He noticed she was a bit startled, but was apparently used to that reaction. He began with the obligatory, "I know I wasn't honest in my profile, but…" story. He went on to say that he had a Jaguar, his own very lucrative business, and a private jet. He explained in a very endearing way that he had a lot to offer a woman and just wanted a chance to tell his story, but was afraid no one would meet him if he put his real picture out there. He hoped he would get a chance like he was having with Lisa to tell his story and see if something clicked.

Unfortunately for Mike, Lisa wasn't much into money; she had plenty of her own, and she sure as hell wasn't into plus-sized men. They parted soon thereafter, with Lisa shaking her head.

Lisa did not give up. She took a quick deep breath and went back to work. Juggling the hundreds of emails she gets from her public relations firm with the hundreds she gets from Match.com was one of her joys. She continued to have fun with the guys and responded to more emails than the average woman. Sometimes she was playful, sometimes serious, but she was always something. She found another attractive man with a nice profile and a good introductory email, but had learned her lesson. This one had multiple pictures, including body shots, but no close ups. She cleverly got the needed information out of him without asking him directly. He was slender. They agreed to meet. She felt good about this one and picked the same place. Lisa, of course, was early and perkier than usual. *Thin and good-looking—my kind of guy.* But she did decide to order a drink this time before he got there. Just in case. Good move.

She looked around the bar and recognized him as he walked in. He was perfectly svelte and quite handsome...for a 72-year-old. Lisa took a deep breath and ordered another wine. This guy was also engaging but his story was the same. He was looking for a younger woman and was fabulously wealthy. If he told the truth, most women would not meet him. If he lied to get the first date, he hoped his personality and money would overcome the lie. Lisa wasn't interested in men old enough to be her father any more than she was interested in men with bigger boobs than hers. But he was nice and fun, and she actually enjoyed the date. She decided to give him some advice. "Be honest in your profile. Brutally." She had an idea about what he should do. He was all ears. The first thing she suggested was the headline to his profile should read "Gold-diggers *Please* Apply." While this was obviously tongue in cheek (although not totally), it was cute and, more importantly, accurate. He realized that a younger "trophy" wife was more important to him than finding true love with a 70-year-old. To each his own. They worked on his profile on a cocktail napkin, had a few laughs, and parted friends.

Moral of the story: Lisa did not succumb to these disappointments. Some might call her a two-time loser. I call her twice as smart. She was determined to overcome her new form of ADD (Always Dating Duds).

WE GOTTA GET OUT OF THIS PLACE

Martha had recently divorced and was just getting her act together. She was still stinging from the break-up with her husband, who left her for another woman. It had taken a long time, but she thought she was finally ready and signed up for one of the online dating services. She had always poo-poo'ed dating services and was not particularly comfortable putting her story on the internet. Forget about posting a picture. But one night she took the plunge and instantly became addicted.

Her first "meet and greet," as she called them, was to be with a nice, seemingly grounded guy with whom she had quite a few chats before agreeing to meet. He suggested coffee and she agreed. It seemed easy to agree to a date, quite another to execute it. As the time approached, she began to feel the nervousness first meets often cause. And this was her first date since her divorce. With a guy from the fucking internet. As she got in her car to drive to meet him, she almost called it off. *Am I out of my mind?* she asked herself.

She managed to get to the coffee shop and was shaking with nerves as he spotted her and said hello. He was quite handsome and quickly admitted he was as nervous as she was. His honesty and shyness actually calmed her down. Two lost fish in a very big pond. They laughed about their mutual dating haplessness. At least, they had one thing in common. When they began to chat, she found him endearing and funny. Soon they were officially hitting it off. After they finished their coffee, Phil suggested a nice restaurant in town for drinks and perhaps dinner. Uh-oh. Martha knew the restaurant and knew that her ex-husband went there frequently. To make matters worse, it was near where she worked, and if someone from work saw that she was out on an internet date (like we wear hats that say "Match.com Loser Here"), she would be embarrassed. Now she was nervous again, but she asked Phil if it would be okay if they went to a different restaurant. She didn't explain, but he had no issue. Phew.

Newly relaxed and smiling, Martha was actually fine with going to Restaurant #2 in Phil's car. The chat in the car was even better and she was feeling good that she had the courage to ask that they switch the restaurant. "How mature am I?" she mused to herself. Communication, communication, communication.

Martha and her date showed up in Restaurant #2. It was actually nicer than the first choice, and quiet, so they could talk and get to know one another. And no wait. Perfect. Until...she saw her ex-husband, his current girlfriend, and her ex-in laws all staring right at her and her date as they walked to their table. Martha was excruciatingly embarrassed, but had enough strength to walk up and say hi. That was not easy then, but how good did she feel later that she had shown off a new beau to the asshole ex? Very. Martha and Phil decided to leave, though, and ended up at Restaurant #1. No co-workers showed up. This dating shit sucks.

Moral of the story: Stop obsessing over exes. Or go on a picnic.

AND THIS LITTLE PIGGY...

Ellie met Dave online and they agreed to meet. On the first date, he was nice and fun, though she was not sure there was a connection. She always looked for that spark—the sign of excitement. He seemed really into her. She knew to take a step back if someone appeared too eager, and Ellie got that feeling, but was really busy with life. She didn't have time to pursue a whole lot of dating options and agreed to go out with him again. It was better than staying at home and watching *Dr. Phil* reruns.

She had a much nicer time on the second date. Maybe there was something here. And then there was that kiss goodnight. It was a knee buckler. She was looking for "pitter-patter" and she just felt it. It had been decades since she felt "pitter-patter." She was surprised and excited, and wondered what she should do. Was she ready to sleep with him? Not after two dates. But damn, it had been awhile. Mom would even approve and she could bring him to all the family events. *Does he like to dance? He can't be that good? And I was not even sure I wanted a second date with him. Does a good kiss have that much effect on me?* Her mind was afire with both euphoria and questions.

As she debated what to do, she got an email from Dave. The email said, "Hi, Ellie. I would like to buy you something from the web site below. It is my favorite web site and I hope you like it too." *How sweet*, Ellie thought. Then she clicked on the link to the web site. A very large picture of five huge toes and a large foot appeared, which morphed into a picture of a scantily clad man rubbing the foot of a woman in a bathrobe. The web site was a foot fetish web site. With pictures of feet doing things you can't imagine. And gizmos stimulating things you didn't think you had. And a gift offer. She never got to what it was for. Click.

Moral of the story: Beware of geeks bearing gifts.

WHERE IS THE NEAREST ATM MACHINE?

Maryann had just met Connor who seemed a good egg, but loath to disclose too many personal things about his life. He would tell funny stories that made her laugh. She loved a sense of humor and he was such a gentleman, and cute. But when she asked questions about him, he seemed evasive. They had only been on two dates, but she didn't really know where he lived or what he did for a living. They split the bill for the first meeting and he paid for the second one, although it was an inexpensive venue. She was completely willing to be thrifty and even willing to share the dating costs. She was into him. *But why the elusiveness*, she wondered.

He was not aggressive physically, with just a light kiss on the lips after the second date. Maryann would not have minded a little more aggression. Again, aloof. She decided to be patient with his seeming insecurity about self-disclosure and sex. She would become the aggressor on their next date.

Then she didn't hear from him for a couple of days. She figured it was Connor being insecure. She did not get upset and just sent him a text, but there was no response. A phone call only got her an unreturned voice mail message. When two days became a week, she began to wonder. As she was about to give up on him, she got a call. From Connor. Finally. He was back. She promised herself she would not let this happen again. She would sleep with him, if need be. She did not want to go back to dating purgatory again. She would go over to his home right now and seduce him.

But he was not home. He was not at work. He was calling Maryann from somewhere else. Jail. Needing bail money. Enough said.

Moral of the story: Figure out a way to bang him *before* he gets arrested.

THE STALKER

Lauren liked to meet guys on her turf, in public places, so she typically picked a food establishment at the local mall as a place to meet. Public, crowded, easy getaway. She arranged to meet Scott and showed up on time, but no Scott. She looked around the bar and decided to give him a few minutes. She ordered a glass of wine and wondered what the date would be like. Her experiences had run the gamut, but they had always shown up. Until now.

She finished her wine and invoked her 15-minute rule. She did not like sitting at the bar by herself, in the fucking mall, no less, so she decided to leave. When she walked outside, she finally saw what was going on. Scott had taken up residence three stores down so he could get a peek at her before he had to commit to a drink, but was late and missed her entrance. Scott figured if he saw an unattractive woman, he could just leave. He was still standing there 15 minutes later. Loser! Lauren left and beeped him as she drove by.

Moral of the story: Have a getaway plan or show up in a bandage disguise, but show up. Dumb Scott—Lauren was pretty hot.

WHERE IS THE NEAREST ATM MACHINE, PART 2?

Amy responded to Pete's email and phone numbers were quickly exchanged. Pete was pleasantly surprised she was willing to share her phone number so quickly. She actually called first but had to leave a message. "Hi, I wanted to talk to you because I was just laid off at work. I am not sure what I am going to do now. And I lost electricity during the storm." Pete thought Amy was trying to call her friend or sister or mother with this news, not a complete stranger. It wouldn't have been the first time someone dialed the wrong number and left an inadvertent message.

He called back, but got her voice mail. He simply said, "Hi, sorry I missed your call." Her response was an unintelligible voice message referring to being sick and not being able to sleep. Completely different downer message. She could not have dialed the wrong number twice, could she? She didn't say his name, so he was confused.

Not ten minutes later, she left another message: "Hey, Pete, sorry I missed your call but I just got laid off and lost electricity." *Who is this whacko?* He totally wrote her off at that point, but it did not deter her from one last call. This one he answered. "Did I tell you I lost electricity during the storm? And I just lost my job. I sure wish I could meet someone who could lend me a thousand dollars to tide me over."

Click.

"Pete, you there?"

Moral of the story: *The Biggest Loser* has taken on new meaning.

CATCHING FLIES

Colleen met Joe, an EMS technician who worked crazy hours. That made sense. Availability might be random and cancellations would have to be accepted. But the first couple of dates went fine, so she was willing to deal with that. He did however, seem a little aloof.

She found out that his father, for whom he was the primary care giver, lived in a trailer in his backyard. Wow, what a great guy. Colleen was totally family focused and wanted to meet a guy who felt the same. She knew that there could come a time when she had to provide care to her mother or father. Maybe she found someone who understood this. She would certainly support him.

For the third date, he invited her over for dinner and a movie. Nice. He cooks too. Maybe she would meet Dad. He put the lasagna in the oven and they went into the living room for a glass of wine. She wasn't quite sure what it was that was hanging from the ceiling fan. Was that fly tape? To avoid accidental entanglement with humans, fly tape was typically hung in relatively inaccessible spaces. The ceiling fan is rather accessible. Joe explained that Dad had seen a rodent and asked that he put fly tape on the ceiling fan to capture any of those rodents that might be crawling. Or flying. She didn't question how a rodent would find its way to a ceiling fan. Worse, she didn't run for the hills right then and there.

The front door was open to let a breeze in. Colleen stood in the middle of the room. Under the ceiling fan. Under the rodent snatcher. The wind kicked up. No. This can't be the worst date ever. George Carlin once said that someone, somewhere, has an appointment tomorrow with the world's worst doctor. Someone, someplace. Well, somewhere, someplace, someone has to be on the worst date ever. Hi, Colleen. The fly tape above her head detached from the ceiling fan and affixed to her hair. And neck. And arms. And hands. With the flies. It was four feet long. "Gross" is a totally inadequate description.

Moral of the story: Beware of dads in trailers, rodents that fly, and going out on a date without a wig.

NOT THAT THERE'S ANYTHING WRONG WITH IT

Erica was set up by a friend, with Keith. He seemed normal enough on the phone and they agreed to meet for drinks and dinner. This was not an internet date so she was not sure what he looked like. Only how her friend described him, which was nice, but when is a friend going to describe a blind date as an ogre?

When she walked into the bar, she knew to look for a dark-haired man with a blue sports jacket and goatee. She spotted him sitting at the bar. Wow. She loved the goatee. She looked around the bar to make sure there weren't two goateed, blue jacket adorned men present. It would be just her luck to meet the ugly goateed dude. But no, today was her lucky day. Only Keith.

She noticed that Keith had been chatting with the gentleman sitting next to him and thought they might have known each other. They were quite animated in their discussion and she became concerned that she might be on the outside looking in on a heated sports debate. Sports was not her cup of tea and she began to question the sanity of her decision to accept a blind date. But she went up to Keith and introduced herself anyway. He greeted her with a warm hug and light kiss on the cheek. Much better. Then he turned and introduced the man he had been talking to, but since his attention was now focused on her, she presumed that they had just met and were chatting while awaiting her arrival. Until it was time for dinner. Keith ordered a table…for three. He invited his new found friend to join Erica and him for dinner. Whoa. This was supposed to be a date, not a reunion of old friends. They suddenly seemed to know each other better than if they had just met, and sat down next to each other, with Erica across the table. Just what the fuck was going on here? Like Jesus coming down to answer a prayer, she got her answer. She dropped her napkin on the floor and went to pick it up. She gasped as she saw Keith's hand firmly planted on his friend's thigh.

Moral of the story: Even I could not believe this story. Maybe the internet is the way to go. And dump your friend who set you up.

JUST DON'T BRING A DATE TO THE FUNERAL

Sue, 48 years old, made up a rule that she would not date anyone more than 5 years older or younger than her. She might have some leeway, but did not want to be a cougar or date old guys. Of course, as soon as she made this rule, along came Dan, 64. She initially said no because he was too old, but ended up going out with him a couple of times because he was alarmingly attractive. So much for rules.

Then she met Mr. 71-year-old, who was from a very famous family that was always in the society pages. His dating exploits were known to the public. She was actually intrigued by his fame and when a common acquaintance suggested they meet, she agreed. It was not too soon into that first date when he looked at her somewhat quizzically. He put his hand under her chin, turned her head side to side, and said, "It's remarkable a woman your age hasn't had any work done." She was shocked, but then realized that she should not have been. It was Mr. 71-year-old society dude, after all. At least he didn't ask about a boob job (she certainly didn't need one of those).

During dinner, he told her all these stories about women he had been dating in the past. Seriously? He turned out to be quite charming, handsome, and was very rich. After dinner, he invited her back to his apartment to see his collection of paintings. All of us guys have used the "do you want to come up and see my etchings" line, but this guy really had some etchings, a world-class collection of crafts and paintings. She declined but agreed to a second date.

On the second date, he picked a restaurant right around the corner from where he lived. He was once again very charming and she sensed he was going for the kill. It was hard not to like him, yet she could not put her finger on why. He invited her up again and she agreed.

Jim was a widower—this is important to the story—and he started showing her around his apartment. Indeed, he did have this incredible collection of paintings. Then he made a move on her. She didn't want to go all the way, but was not averse to some nice kissing. So they made out. Nice! Maybe too nice. Was this guy really 71?

She had already broken the age rule. Was she now thinking that she might break her two date rule—never sleep with a guy on the second date? She became torn as his kisses wobbled her knees. He took her by the hand and led her to the door of the bedroom. Game time. Now what? She had prepared herself for this moment all night, had prepared her speech and was ready to deflect his best shots. But words were not forthcoming as he opened the bedroom door....

There, sitting on the dresser, and the night stand, and hanging from the wall, were what must have been a dozen pictures of his dead wife. No way.

Moral of the story: Keep pictures of your dead wife as far the fuck away from any place where you might wish for another woman to get naked. Did I really have to write that down?

GOING DOWN

A concept with many connotations, one of which Doug eagerly embraced on most nights, but this date gave it new meaning. Doug had started communicating with Lori. They hit it off and agreed to meet. Her picture was nice, she spoke without a lisp and didn't mention any blood relatives that were married to each other. How refreshing. You may think this is tongue in cheek, but Doug had a lot of bad experiences with women on the internet. His expectations were at an all-time low, for good reason. Expect nothing and you can't be disappointed. Not a recipe to create good karma for a first date, but he was almost numb to the experience.

Just in case you might be thinking there was a glimmer of hope for Doug, when he arrived, lo and behold...she had committed the cardinal sin of internet dating: real life and her profile picture came from different parents. Or so it seemed. Doug took a deep breath and thought, *what the hell, let's make the best of it*.

They sat down and had a drink. She was funny, personable, and smart, but we all know that regardless of which side of the chromosome pool you come from, there has to be some level of physical attractiveness for a first date to have a chance for a second.

Doug knew from the moment he saw her that anything short of Paris Hilton's bank account would preclude a chance for a second date. He was just not attracted to her. She on the other hand, was *really* enjoying his company. I couldn't blame her, Doug was good-looking and a professional. She ended up getting quite drunk and he became worried about her ability to get home. He couldn't stop her from drinking and couldn't let her drive.

At this point, he wanted to say, "Beam her the fuck up, Scotty," but Scotty was out chasing Klingon tail himself. Doug was stuck. She began to slur her speech and became unsteady on her feet. Doug finally decided to do what he knew he needed to do—take her to his place for the night and get her to her car in the morning. He explained what he was doing and let her know in no uncertain terms that he was not interested in her. She seemed agreeable and even thanked him. *Okay*, he thought, *maybe this won't be so bad*. He liked being a good Samaritan and she'd obviously had trouble on the dating scene, so he would help her out with a smile on his face.

Until they began to drive to his place. He hoped she would just pass out, but instead she perked up. *Oh shit.* Then she got frisky. When he realized that perking up was coupled with going down, he began to panic. She leaned over and began undoing his pants, claiming to give the best blow jobs on Earth. While he was driving.

I know—a man's dream come true—but Doug was way past horny and not nearly drunk enough. He had to fight her off most of the trip to his place. He had visions of having to tie her up, which on a normal Friday night would have gotten him excited. But not tonight. He managed to get her to his couch and literally locked his bedroom door.

He woke up the next morning thankful that the worst had passed. She would be sober and, if she were lucky, would not remember how she acted the night before. He could get dressed, buy her a cup of coffee, and wish her a good life. But not Lori. He walked out of the bedroom and there she was waiting for him. And making breakfast. She lost no time trying one more time to "have" him.

Fuck. Under other circumstances, he might have been willing, but he was still reeling from the night before. He made her breakfast, took her to her car, and won the award for the nicest guy in the history of internet dating.

Moral of the story: Call a taxi. Buy a Chinese junk. Fire Scotty and get your own transporter machine. But don't let her in your car.

DRIVE BY

Jim and Angela agreed to meet. She did not want to give him her address so they settled on meeting on a street corner near where she lived. He would come by and pick her up. They could then go get a drink at a neighborhood establishment. They had exchanged pictures, of course, and he had described his car to her. This way she could look for his car as he looked for her. Easy. Might even become the rage of how to meet on a first internet date.

As Jim drove down the street where they were to meet, he spotted someone waving to him. He didn't recognize her, but she seemed to know him. He slowed down and then realized he did recognize her…75 pounds ago. He sped up and took off, never to be heard from again.

Moral of the story: We seem to be getting a thread of stories here. Don't fuck with your pic. And get tinted windows.

PRICELESS

I had a former girlfriend tell me this one. I will use her words without much poetic interference as she tells it very well.

> "I had a funny thing happen to me last week and thought of you and your book! So there was this guy that I went out on a Match.com date a while ago. First we had coffee to meet and then did dinner the next date. He was the Chief Financial Officer of a very small advertising agency. I had a nice dinner, but knew pretty quickly that he was going to be too clingy for me (he sent me way too many texts, was

practically asking me to marry him over dinner). So I told him I wouldn't see him again, gave him the old, "I just got out of a relationship, too soon, blah, blah blah" speech!

He texted me a few days later to ask me that if I wasn't interested in a relationship, would I consider just having sex with him. LOL, of course I said no and best of luck. He waited a month and asked again. I decided not to even respond and thought I would never see him again!

So I was at a huge conference (600 people) starting last Sunday in Scottsdale and who do I see staring at me across the bar—this guy! Couldn't believe it. I was a nice person and went over to say hi—had a good laugh. On my way out of the conference yesterday, I bump into him again and he says goodbye, hugs me, and whispers in my ear, 'Think about It.' Priceless!"

I have never tried the "I know you don't want to date me but what about a fuck" line.

Moral of the story: If you are an old dog, try to learn some new tricks.

It's a Mad Mad Mad Mad World Out There.

ON YOUR WAY UP THE RABBIT HOLE

- Don't lie in your profile! Do unto others….
- Go into a date with a smile and make the most of it. Laugh about the bad ones.
- Don't try to do anything too funky on the first date. Always look your best.
- Beware of too eager and don't be too eager yourself.
- If you have enough bad dates, write a book.

CHAPTER 16:
IT'S AN UPHILL BATTLE

(BUT IT'S GOOD EXERCISE AND THERE'S LIGHT AT THE TOP OF THE RABBIT HOLE)

When I got divorced the first time, I was a mess. Outwardly, I seemed normal, even fun, but felt that inside there was something wrong. I was innately smart and able to function well in the business world, but from a personal standpoint, felt I had major psychological issues. I had no idea, however, what they were. As it turned out from my shrink sessions, I was completely intimidated by authority, my self-esteem was so low that I thought the only way people would like me was if I was nicer to them than anyone else, and I was quintessentially passive aggressive. The middle part was how I survived.

I always wondered why I was nice to people as a kid. I felt guilty that I was nice to them only because I wanted them to like me. That's how desperate I was for acceptance. Why couldn't I be nice to them because I am a nice person—no ulterior motive? It was not until well into adulthood that I said, "Who cares *why* I am nice, someone is getting the benefit of my niceness and that is a good thing."

By the time I got divorced the second time, I had some of this figured out but was still in serious need of self-esteem. You have already read many of the realities and hallucinations I went through on this new journey and I want to end this endeavor by connecting the dots.

Let's start with a timeline to emotional health. The chronology begins from the end of my second marriage and takes you through my relationships, break-ups and breaks from relationships.

FIRST 2 MONTHS

I was hurt by the loss of a long-term relationship.

Regardless of the cause, it will hurt simply because of its dissolution. You will feel a range of emotions. I did. Anger, despair, loneliness. For some, it may be tempered by new found freedom and a sudden mid-life crisis solved—dating young women. That euphoria will be an illusion. Even if you are happy you are now single, there will come times when you look around and go, "How the fuck did I get here?" If you don't, you should not have been in that long-term relationship to begin with. You are now asking yourself, why were you in it for so long. A different set of questions and a different set of emotions, but all things lead to the same place. You are alone and starting over.

In the beginning, you will think you feel one way but it is really a reaction to your true yet hidden feelings. During times of emotional stress, it may be difficult to figure out why you feel a certain way and you may easily blame the wrong reason. This will lead to missteps in how you treat and react to others as you search for the right reasons. The first and overwhelming reaction is to soothe the hurt. You may try to do this by fantasizing about serial dating (guilty here), trying to get laid to "show" her (guilty), and reveling in anything that does her emotional harm (guilty). Unfortunately, it is only a fantasy at this point. And that sucked. You may find your own ways to soothe the hurt, but soothe you will seek.

I was intimidated by having to date again. I didn't want to do it and had to force myself. It was easy to get on line and flirt and have fun writing shit, but that first phone call—I was completely incoherent.

I was still angry and had to let the hurt run its course, but was not in control of that process. I tried to circumvent it with emotional bandages (it's called dating anything that breathes), but in the end, the hurt had to run its course and it did. It was a process. I did some stupid things along the way and treated people unlike I normally would. I forgave myself.

MONTH 3

I had my first relationship and fell in "love" way too fast. When I was sane, I knew it was infatuation. Unfortunately, that was only 1% of the time.

MONTH 5

She dumped my sorry ass because I did everything in this book I am telling guys not to do. I was needy and clingy. I wondered what she was doing every second she wasn't with me. And I did not communicate with her—at least not like someone in a healthy relationship does. If I hadn't been married twice, I might have been considered a Mama's boy.

MONTH 8

I took a little time to take stock of who I was. Very little. I started serial dating for the first time, but did begin to realize what the issue was. I talked to my sister and mother who both had great words of advice. I encourage you to be willing to listen to others. Talk to those who care about you and know you. Encourage honest feedback. Don't talk to someone who will feed your self-pity. Talk to someone who will kick you in the ass. It doesn't feel good, but necessary if you are serious about figuring it out.

Be honest with yourself. Accept responsibility for where you are. Figure out why you are where you are. There was plenty of shrink time when this first relationship failed. I felt like I was starting over *again*.

None of this was easy, but I never lost sight of who I was at the core.

During my serial dating phase, I had my first legitimate obsession. She was completely my type and we had an incredible first date. I told sis, "I just had my first date with my next wife." I felt that I was making emotional progress and was better. I was. I didn't want to see her every night, just Tuesday, Thursday, Friday and Saturday. She was not ready for anything close to a steady relationship.

This is part of the rub—she was just as screwed up as I was, but from the completely opposite view. She had just gotten rid of the husband and was now relishing her freedom and looking to prove she could do it without some asshole male. I just got in the way.

But I was making progress.

MONTH 10

Bingo. The jackpot. Even more perfect for me. And I was getting better, very slowly. Still needy, but recognizing it and trying not to act that way. I was still obsessing and frequently had a pit in my stomach. What is that pit? It is bred from insecurity and fueled by anyone you like. The pit is the fear that she doesn't like you, is playing with your feelings, has a date every night she is not with you, is fucking the entire fifth battalion. The pit meant I had not yet figured out that just because she didn't want to see me four nights a week, didn't mean she wanted to see anyone else. She just needed more space than I did. I had too much and needed the void filled. My void was still too big to go at her pace.

If I knew what I know today, we might very well still be together. It was an on again, off again relationship for 18 months. It was mostly on, but my neediness made her back off. During the times when it was off, I immediately went back to serial dating. Was it anger still, a void, neediness? All of the above. I was not cured. We seemed to be making progress when I did some stupid things that ended it for good.

MONTH 28

I decided to take a break from dating and had this great idea. Since I was such a success at marriage and dating, why not write a book about it. If you, as they say, do as I say, not as I do, then maybe you can be better at this than I was. This was actually the best thing for me at the time. Maybe when things feel like the sky is falling and you may never find someone, it's time to take a break. Regroup. Feel what it's like not only to not have a woman, but also, what it's like to focus on something other than women. For those of you who have hobbies, you are well on your way. My hobby was dating—I was in trouble. I managed by focusing on other things to occupy my time, energy, and emotion. And it worked. I came out from my cave....

MONTH 30

I found a new relationship; actually it was a woman I had two dates with when the 18-monther and I were "off." I seemed to be much less needy. Wow, where did this come from? It came from obtaining some balance in my life and learning that my happiness was not wholly dependent on a woman liking me. Though I became somewhat controlling, trying to change this woman's life to fit better into mine—where the fuck did that come from? I was never the controlling type; I was the one looking to be controlled.

MONTH 35

Well, that blew up in my face as she was not one to let her life be changed by a man. So we parted ways. Actually, she departed, and it threw me for a loop. Instead of feeling sorry for myself, I got angry and decided I was going to bang everything that walked for the next few months. No prisoners. My only goal was going to be sex. The Three Date Rule went out the window. I was going to take serial dating to a whole other level.

I guess I was pretty angry and not nearly as cured as I thought. I started serial dating again, but met someone quickly that I liked. This always screwed up my serial dating addiction. She actually wanted to spend more time with me than I wanted to spend with her. First real feeling of getting my emotional shit together. I knew she wasn't for me long term, but was perfect for a summer of fun.

But wait, where did the anger go? Where was the desire to bang the entire Jersey Shore? Guess what, the hurt I felt when Miss I-am-

Not-Going-to-Let-a-Man-Control-Me broke up with me was *normal* getting broken up with hurt. It hurts, but you get over it with time. I thought my reaction was because I was still a needy mess. No, I was just angry that someone hurt me, but it was normal and I got over it quickly. Real progress.

MONTH 38

The summer was over. We had a lot of fun and it developed into a potentially long-term relationship, but we just couldn't get there. It was the first time someone wanted to see me more than I wanted to see her. I wanted to be with her but also wanted my own time. What a revelation that was. I knew I was on my way back. It was three years later, but I was getting there.

MONTH 40

I didn't feel the need to date that much. I was not particularly excited about getting online. Actually, I was at the point where I had had enough and just wanted to settle down. I met someone who was fun but not the real thing. Interestingly, even though I knew it wasn't long term, I wasn't out there like in my former days, pounding the internet to keep the dating high going.

Then I hit the real jackpot. I didn't know it was the jackpot at the time, but something about her made me want to cut off Miss-Not-the-Real-Thing and shut down all my dating desires after two dates. The Three Date Rule was broken to an embarrassingly high number, but I didn't care anymore. Not about sex, but about needing sex to feel good. I was feeling pretty good about myself, which made it easy to engage in the first truly emotionally mature relationship in my life. I played no games, held nothing back, and communicated everything. How emancipating.

This relationship is currently two years and counting.

I went from debilitatingly needy to being equipped to handle the complete spectrum of emotional relationships in five "short" years.

I am in the best place emotionally I have ever been. My current relationship is the best one I have ever had, and based on all the right things. But it took five years. Yours may not take as long, or it may take longer. And you may not be as lucky as I was in identifying my issues and working to fix them. Just don't ignore how you feel or bury emotions. Explore how you feel and why. You may not know why for a long time, if not forever, so use whatever tools you have and never give up the search for happiness. Therapy was a Godsend for me.

ON YOUR WAY UP THE RABBIT HOLE

- As you climb the final rung there will be missteps and times you do things and don't know why.
- You will take two steps forward and then one step back, but that is called progress.
- Be honest with yourself and ask others to help. Listen to them.
- You will get there, just be patient.
- Have fun and find happiness.

I hope you enjoyed *Oh Shit! I'm Over 50 and Single* as much as I enjoyed most of the experiences that led me to write it for you. I'm thrilled you are still reading. If you would like to write a review, I would love to hear from you. I won't take it personally either way.

Yes, I will. ☺

MEET THE AUTHOR

PA Brook, Author, Dater and Know-It-All

Making Boring Fun

Trying to put an interesting spin on any topic has always been an interest. I have written dozens of articles for professional and trade publications, and made innumerable presentations in front of dozens, sometimes hundreds, of avid listeners. From writing a Star Trek themed article on investment regulations to using baseball analogies to wake up 700 people at an industry conference, I have always been able to interest an audience and yet get across the technical, sometimes boring, point I needed to make. Perhaps not on the NY Times bestseller list, my titles may sound more interesting than the content, but at least no one snoozes when they read them. Titles include: "WHERE NO (Hedge Fund) MAN (ager) HAS GONE BEFORE" with appropriate references to "Beam me up Scotty" to avoid being photon torpedoed by some nasty Klingon regulator, and "On an Island With the SEC, (Aka Diary of an SEC Exam)," a Survivor based primer on why those Government dudes win every immunity challenge.

My non-writing career has spanned decades but my thirst for finding an interesting and entertaining outlet for my views has spanned a lifetime. Now I can go from writing about how to save your association by going "Back to the Future" at 1.21 jigawatts an hour to helping single guys in their 50s figure out there is life after divorce.

And what makes me an expert? Not reading psych books, not getting medical degrees, not interviewing thousands of women. How about two divorces, a retirement savings spent on therapy, and dating a thousand women. Okay, not a thousand, but enough to know what works at this age, at this time. There is no substitute for experience.

WHO WILL PLAY ME IN THE MOVIE VERSION?

George Clooney is now married, otherwise he would be at the top of my list. Now, since he married a women 16 years his junior, I hope he reads my chapter on dating 30 somethings. It can be pretty awkward when you are the same age as your girlfriend's parents (or your daughter is the same age as your girlfriend), and when you want to go home on Saturday night, her friends are getting ready to go out.

Other choices include:

- William Seymour Hoffman, if he were alive
- Robert Downey Jr., if he were older
- Jeff Probst, because I love Survivor

www.ingramcontent.com/pod-product-compliance
Lightning Source LLC
Chambersburg PA
CBHW070558300426
44113CB00010B/1311